ADDITION

SWEE

by De\. ... ------.,

In fine, beautifully wrought prose, Henry takes us from his troubled childhood to his early adult years as a struggling writer and co-founder of one of America's most respected literary magazines. Son of an abusive, alcoholic father, and a long-suffering mother, Henry's remarkable memoir is fraught with struggle, of love lost and dreams unrealized. But it is also a story of hope and survival—a testament to the strength of one very brave and eloquent writer.

—James Brown, author of *The Los Angeles Diaries*

This is a moving, sepia-toned, and powerful look at the bonds of a family, but it also tracks the development of a deeply gifted writer and his dedication to American letters. This resonant memoir is by turns poignant and harrowing, and with each new page, I felt the exhilarating rush of recognition. In writing about his family, DeWitt Henry ushers his readers to better understandings of their own histories.

—Bret Anthony Johnston, author of *Corpus Christi: Stories*

Ranging from early childhood to the death of his parents, DeWitt Henry's *Sweet Dreams* is among the more unselfish memoirs you'll encounter. What's so engaging about this book is Henry's kaleidoscope of family mishaps and cultural adventures that involve him in someone else's becoming, which, in turn, come to be his own. This memoir portrays with warmth and grace how we mature in the crowded many more so than we do in the isolated self.

—Thomas Larson, author of *The Memoir and the Memoirist*

DeWitt Henry's *Sweet Dreams* is the inspiring true story of a life based on a deep and selfless commitment to literature, and faith in its lasting value— qualities that are all the more treasured for being so increasingly rare.

—Dan Wakefield, author of *New York in the Fifties*

Sweet Dreams: A Family History is a sharp, astonishingly detailed and vivid account of the first half-century of a writer's life. DeWitt Henry didn't go into his family's candy business, but his memoir is its own sweet treat: a delicious account of his childhood, family, sexual adventures, professional ambitions, and personal choices. I gobbled it up.

—Debra Spark, author of *Good for the Jews*

SWEET DREAMS

a family history

Also by DeWitt Henry

Fiction
The Marriage of Anna Maye Potts: a novel

Non-fiction
Safe Suicide: Narratives, Essays, and Meditations

Anthologies
Sorrow's Company: Writers on Loss and Grief
Fathering Daughters: Reflections by Men
    (with James Alan McPherson)
Breaking Into Print: Early Stories and Insights into Getting Published:
    A Ploughshares Anthology
Other Sides of Silence: New Fiction from Ploughshares
The Ploughshares Reader: New Fiction for the Eighties

SWEET DREAMS
a family history

DeWitt Henry

HIDDEN RIVER PRESS
Philadelphia   2011

Portions of this book have appeared in slightly different form in the following periodicals and anthologies: "Distant Thunder" (as "Witness" in *Boulevard* and *Pushcart Prize XIV*), a portion of "Differences" (as "First Love" in *Agni*), a portion of "In the World" (as "My Own Private Cambridge" in *Nebraska Review*), "Promises to Keep" (*Ploughshares*), and a portion of "Departures" (as "Departures" in *Colorado Review*). My thanks to these publications and their editors. Special thanks to Lew McCreary for editorial suggestions; and to David Lahm and Jennifer Rose for proof-reading. Please note that where real names are used, my information and judgments are rooted within the time of the story. I mean to portray such perceptions as limited and biased, true to me then rather than objectively "true"— then, or now, lifetimes later.

Copyright © 2011 by DeWitt Henry

All rights reserved

No part of this book may be used or reproduced in any manner whatsoever without written permission, except in the case of brief quotations embodied in critical articles and reviews.

Library of Congress Control Number: 2010940797
ISBN 978-0-9844727-2-7

Published by Hidden River Press
an imprint of Hidden River Publishing
Philadelphia, Pennsylvania

In memory of my parents and brothers;
and for my sister, my wife, my children,
and my grandchildren

Contents

SWEET DREAMS

a family history

Keep Candy Handy

I STOPPED CRAVING SWEETS in my teens, and haven't craved them since. My daughter at age eight was incredulous to hear such a thing, and I told her that I must have reached a point of overdose. There I was, youngest of four children in a family that owned a candy factory, no less. As I grew up, my friends all wanted to know: what was it like to own a whole candy factory?

The factory, founded by my grandfather, actually bore my name: the DeWitt P. Henry Company, Confectioners. My grandfather, himself named for the country doctor who had delivered him, insisted that a grandson carry on his name. My parents had put him off, naming my older brothers John (Jack) and Charles (Chuck), but given that I was the last chance, they conceded. Our father, John Henry, was the President. Each day Dad, dressed in a tailored suit, with a felt hat, and with his briefcase, left for his commute from St. Davids to Germantown in the "company car" (a Plymouth station wagon with push-button fluid drive). Occasionally on weekends, we would make a family expedition to the factory with him. I don't remember my oldest brother Jack going. I do remember my next oldest, Chuck, who worked for Dad for a while in the bookkeeping department, a poorly-lit, dingy area up some rickety stairs, to an area over the refrigerated compartments. Chuck's weakness was for peanuts and chocolate-covered cherries. My sister Judy, older than me, younger than Chuck, was my partner on these forays. My father would be seeing to some papers in the front office, where he had a big oak desk and a leather desk chair. A large, framed photograph of my grandfather hung behind him, smirking as if he had a chocolate in his cheek.

Judy would lead me to explore. We would enter the refrigerated packaging department through a heavy, vault-like door, a good twelve inches thick, turn on the lights, and all the conveyor belts full of various chocolates would be spread out as fair game. We would take paper bags from the sample room and start working the belts and bins. A bag filled with chocolates would last me for a week. Imagine the smells, chilled chocolate and ammonia. The temperature, winter or summer, was maybe 40 degrees. The lights were banks of fluorescents. Nothing moved. We prowled as freely as Goldilocks. We bit into round, oblong, and square chocolates to find out what they were: nut chews, creams, marshmallows, mints (green, pink, orange inside), coconut, nougat, caramel, and syrupy cherries. Judy favored mints. I loved some of the chocolate covered jellies and the chocolate marshmallows. The packaging room had boxes ready to fill, scales to weigh them, and the conveyer belts, motionless now, brought candy in from another department, where enrobers coated the different centers with melted chocolate and then passed them through a cooling tunnel. Depending on the season, there were specialized boxes for different varieties, such as the jellies, to be sold in supermarkets. Then there were gift assorteds, fancy boxes with waxed paper cups to be filled according to a fixed design. I must have visited during the actual work day with Mom when I was younger (I remember being introduced to some of the regulars and being treated like royalty, fussed over by a grinning woman dressed in a uniform like a nurse), but it wasn't until I was nineteen and I had my own turn working here in the summer as a helper pulling stacks of boards, and repairing them in the shop, that I really saw the factory alive at work, with some one hundred and fifty employees.

All the workers in the packing department were women and girls, wearing blue and white uniforms and hairnets. Then, there were the men in the chocolate department, cooking the chocolate and the centers in huge steaming kettles; there were also men in the enrober department. Part of my job as a general helper was to pull stacks of interlocking trays with starch molds (stacked some six feet high on dollies with wheels) to the machines where various centers would be deposited in the moulds; and then to pull stacks of the centers to the enrobing machines. My brother Jack had worked with the mechanics, keeping these machines in good repair, and sometimes making modifications. But then he'd had an accident and lost the first joint of his left little finger to the sprockets of an enrober; he quit on the factory soon after, and moved to Colorado for a second try at college.

Mom, Chuck, and Judy, all talented artists (Jack was a draftsman), helped Dad by designing cardboard boxes with cellophane windows for Easter items. They created the trademark logos, an oval outline of "Henry's" in distinctive script, which served as our trademark on stationery as well, along with the motto, "Keep Candy Handy." Dad even had Jack and Chuck take wrappers from "Henry's Mint Patty" and scatter them as litter around town, so people would think they were in demand. With great care, Mom constructed the boxes and drew cartoon rabbits, ducks, and chickens, designs that were later printed and put into production for Chicky Doodle (a yellow marshmallow chicken), Perky Rabbit (hollow inside), and for Henry's Easter Egg (filled with coconut cream). The latter came in several sizes, but the one I recall was five pounds and the size of a meatloaf. You sliced it like a meatloaf as well, dark chocolate coating a quarter inch thick, with a flat bottom and decorative swirl on top, and inside, the coconut cream, with little shreds of coconut. Finishing off such an egg took weeks, with tin foil covering the open part, so it wouldn't turn hard and stale. Chuck and Jack always finished theirs. I never did. Once it hardened, I threw mine out.

The first supermarket in our suburb, the Acme, was built just after World War II. It competed with the local grocery store, Espenshades, where Mom used to shop, and still did for meat, and the Farmers' Market, where she went for vegetables. We regarded the Acme with a degree of disdain for its impersonality and also for its architecture: just down from the florist's on the Lancaster Pike, it had a tile tower that said Acme sticking up from a modern box and plate glass window design. As we wandered its bright aisles with our cart, I remember a display of Easter candy, and that Mom remarked that the Henry eggs and Chicky Doodles weren't selling well.

I loved our national, more famous brand competitors, and Dad, as President of the National Confectioner's Association, knew many of the executives who made them: Clark Bars, with the peanut butter center; Milky Ways with nougat filling, though I didn't like the gooey caramel. I liked nut chews, but not Almond Joys. I loved Hershey kisses. I loved dark chocolate buds. I binged on M&Ms. On special occasions, Mom bought chocolate marshmallows, and other candies, of course: jelly beans, gumdrops, mints, mint patties. Occasionally, we had Whitman's Samplers (I avoided nuts, went for jellies, mints, cherries), which Dad must have brought home for comparison and research.

We went with Dad to candy conventions in the Pocono mountains, Judy, Mom and I, and stayed at a hotel. I remember the formal dining room, and a drawing, where I won a golf bag. The former quarterback of the Chicago Bears, Sid Luckman, was a friend of Dad's. I had never heard of him, but when he visited our house (having retired from football and joined some major chocolate firm), he gave me his signed book—an autobiography—as well as an autographed football. As I played with the football, of course, the autograph faded, and when I kicked the ball high in our side yard, it came down and was skewered on an iron spike on our fence. Such visits by businessmen to our home were rare. But another was by a tall, imposing man from Chattanooga, Tennessee, named Bill Brock. His company made mint puff balls, which sold in large quantities down South and Dad was working out an exchange for distribution and sales. The Henry Company would distribute Brock in the Northeast, and Brock would distribute Henry candies in the South. Brock had stepped on a piece of candy while visiting the factory and now had his foot up on the edge of our kitchen sink, cleaning his expensive shoe.

Dad had different distribution deals, all relatively small time. Uncle John, back from World War II, was his salesman. Also Jack Dreyfus (whose son later started the Dreyfus Fund) sold Henry products out of New York. Candy bars, patties, and cheap chocolates were sold through a Canteen Distributor, who placed them in vending machines. From grade school on, whenever kids heard that my family made chocolates, they always asked, "What, 'O'Henry' bars?" I never met anyone, ever, who had bought a Henry product. There were no ads or commercials. For all Dad's efforts, we never attained brand recognition in our region, let alone the world.

For a while, age nine or ten, I was impressed by Dad's role as a businessman, gave up my earlier fantasies of being a fireman or a G-man, and saw myself as one day running the factory. Without understanding a word, I looked through ornately bound volumes of something called the *Encyclopedia of Business* that we kept in our sun-porch bookshelves, and which (I learned later) Mom had given Dad, when he had worked for the Walter Baker Company in Boston, and had aspired to a corporate career. I kept his cast-off, leather briefcases, both the attaché and accordion style, filled them with company stationery, and with trade journals that he had thrown away, which I pretended to peruse. During visits to the factory itself, I played with adding machines and typewriters in the outer office.

Perhaps I stopped eating sweets because of cavities; perhaps trying to control weight; perhaps because of adolescent acne (Clearasil years). Perhaps it was because of my increasing ambivalence towards Dad, his remoteness, his weight problem and diabetes, and revelations first from Mom and then from him about his years of severe alcoholism, which began shortly after I was born in 1941 and reached its worst after my grandfather's death, when he submitted to treatment. And as for running the factory, as my brothers and sister had done before me, I soon chose other dreams.

The gift of a toy printing press when I was ten had led to my serious play in putting out a four-page newspaper, which I sold to classmates; and which, in turn, led to my writing articles and stories. In school I was praised for my writing. I loved books, beginning with YA science fiction, with paperback westerns that were Jack's passion, and with mysteries with sexy covers that Dad brought home from business trips; then, with my mother's and sister's encouragement, I tried out book club classics in our home library, such as John Steinbeck's novellas; and still later, at my sister's urging, Dostoyevski, Kafka, and Poe. That one and only summer I worked in the factory (I still have the Withholding Tax Statement for $32.50), with my freshman year at Amherst under my belt, I'd started writing a novel. I spent my lunch breaks reading Faulkner on the shipping dock. Everybody working there knew me as the third and last Henry son. The head shipper, a florid, red-faced old-timer named Bill Cassidy, took me aside for an earnest, private talk. What did I want to be? What were my plans? He'd known Jack (who by then had started a construction business in Colorado), and Chuck (an intern at Bryn Mawr Hospital); worked with them both. Dad kept him up on our lives. Did I realize the opportunity that I had here? You don't want to walk away from something like this, he said.

Distant Thunder

I HAVE NO DIRECT MEMORY of my father before I am eight, when we moved from Bloomingdale to the St. Davids house; while otherwise, my memories of Bloomingdale, dating from when I am five, or even earlier, are rich. I search for him, for where he must have been (someone is on the roof playing Santa Claus, calling to me down the chimney), but nothing is there. My sister claims a similar blank.

Our home movies predate my memory and perplex me with images that have since become confused with memory and with family legend. My earliest, or at least most easily dated memory, is of my fifth birthday, when I was digging in our backyard with a gardening fork and struck downward and into the middle of my right shoe, leaving a neat, square hole right through the shoe, top and sole. I bled, but felt no pain. I wandered into the kitchen, leaving bloody footprints, and told my mother I'd hurt my foot. Alarmed and fussing over me, she worked off my shoe and sock, but found only a bad cut between my first and second toes. Luckily, I'd missed the foot. As she cleaned and bandaged the wound, she told me I was fine, although I would need to get a tetanus shot later. That same afternoon we are at the dinner table and my oldest brother, Jack, whose sixteenth birthday is the following week, gives me my first bubblegum ever (an adult privilege); he has been hunting and brought back rabbit, which is supposed to taste "racy," and we eat as an event. Other memories, dimly: I pretend to read *Time* magazine at dinner and my mother pretends that the words I invent are what it really says, and marvels. My Grandpop Henry, a warm and friendly man, whom I love, rides me on his shoe, one leg crossed over the other; he died, I realize now, of a heart attack at his summer home in Ocean City, just nine days after I turned five.

But then we have the movies, which document this time and earlier.

There is Jack as a baby, six months old; then Chuck as a baby (Jack as a toddler), then Judy as a baby; then, finally, at the Bloomingdale Avenue house, my mother pregnant with me and turning from the camera, me as a newborn wriggling in my carriage, which my mother rocks, me as a baby being held by Jack, Chuck, and Judy, in turn, me being prodded to crawl by Judy, me as a toddler in a snowsuit being pulled on a sled by Judy at age eight, me at Christmas in a sailor suit, and Mom still dark haired, slender and bright eyed (she's always resembled Katharine Hepburn, to my mind). Another film, in color, shows Easter at Ithan, my grandparents' house and backyard, surrounded by woods; the time must be 1945, since Aunt Kitty is there with my cousin Bunny as a toddler, but without Uncle John, who is still in the Army, and since Grandpop is there, and Aunt Peggy, too, with my cousin Dale as a baby. The shock for me, viewing again shortly before or after I married in 1973, was the image of me at four apparently carefree, happy, running towards the camera in shorts and t-shirt; even more recently, as I viewed these reels with my mother, the shock has been the image of my father (he is missing from most of our films, since he was the one taking them). He is clowning for the camera, lifting me up and swinging me and finally setting me on his shoulders with obvious pride and delight—feelings I never thought he felt for me or showed. "He did love his children," my mother commented this time. At an earlier viewing years before, when I was home from college and Dad asleep upstairs, we ran the film on the basement wall at St. Davids, and she had said, "I was furious then; that was the bad time."

Our Bloomingdale house dated from 1885. There were eight rooms downstairs, the living room, onto which the front door opened, side porch, Saturday room, sun porch, dining room, pantry, stairs, kitchen and back porch; on the second floor, there was the boys' room (over the living room), my room (over the Saturday room), connected by a bathroom to the master bedroom (over the dining room), then another bathroom off the central staircase and landing, Judy's room in back, then the backstairs down to the kitchen. On the third floor there was a mattress room (where all our old mattresses were laid out wall to wall for rough-housing), the maid's room and bathroom, and a large L-shaped attic, where among two generations of family paraphernalia, was the banded, treasure chest shaped trunk that my great grandfather had brought from Ireland. Also in the third floor hallway was an old wind up Victrola, with stacks of wax records in its cabinet (the teenage acquistions of Aunt Peggy, I realize now), which on rainy days we would play, and which included such songs as "Reefer Man," "Button Up Your Overcoat," and "Red Sails in the Sunset." Then in the basement there was a coal bin, back under the dining room, which would be filled down a chute through a basement window; and in the center of the basement, there was the furnace, which my brothers had to fill, rope handled coal bucket after coal bucket, down a hopper on top; the furnace also had a metal plate in the floor off to one side. This the boys would lift up, reaching with a hooked pike down a concrete ramp underneath and dragging up and out cans of warm ash. One whole wall was filled with shelves of preserved vegetables from the victory garden out back, mostly stewed tomatoes in Mason jars. Out front was a wide plank porch running the house's length and shaded by striped, fringed awnings in the summer; here, between support columns on the Lenoir Avenue end, hung a canvas hammock, in which Judy or the boys would enclose me, turn me over and over, then let me spin back. Here also, during thunderstorms, with rain drumming on the roof and pouring off the awnings, with chill gusts, and with the lights from inside casting from behind us, Mom or Judy would bring me to watch the lightning flash: now count, each second measuring another mile, four, five; until the crack of near, or rumbles of more distant thunder. The yard was one acre. A three foot high iron fence with horizontal rods ran along the Bloomingdale and Lenoir borders, broken midway out front by a swinging gate where our front walk joined the sidewalk (I would ride the gate open and shut to grinding hinges). On the wooden steps down from the porch, there was our address, a "114" in metal numerals. Tall matching pines stood on either side out front, along with smaller bushes and trees. On the Lenoir side were two magnolias, which perfumed the air when they bloomed and afterwards littered the ground with leaf sized fleshy petals that turned brown and spotted with rot. The smaller of these, the red, standing off the sun porch, was the only tree I could climb; the light pink, which stood off the dining room and kitchen and whose blossoms could be seen from the master bedroom (a view my mother painted in oils), I somehow did climb once, only to get stuck and cry in panic until Chuck climbed up to rescue me.

Out back, along Lenoir, was the gravel driveway and the carriage barn, with hinged double doors, used by us to house two cars. Upstairs, in the earliest years, there were fifty chickens (a victory effort and Jack's first "business") and the boys would go to collect eggs each day. I was impressed by the porcelain eggs planted to make the chickens lay. Later, all the chickens were slaughtered, hung upside down, by Jack's account, killed by a single cut up the beak and into the brain, bled, soaked in a steaming tub and plucked, then sold or eaten, a sheer labor of killing that my mother would refer to ever after with revulsion. By war's end, the chicken roost was turned into a playroom, where the boys had parties, where they built a mammoth "O" gauge model train layout, and where an intercom—a little box affair, with a hook on which hung the ear piece, and a button to buzz the other end—was strung to connect them with the house, so Mom could call them to dinner.

Midway along the back property line, which joined Mr. Smith's yard (Mr. Smith taught science at Radnor High), grew a venerable oak, five feet across at the trunk and highest in the yard. A good twenty feet up, level with the top of the barn, the boys had built a tree house in the central crotch: walls, windows, roof, and a trapdoor underneath, through which they disappeared by means of a rope ladder that swung and swayed and which I was forbidden, ever, to climb. When I did test its lower rungs, its unanchored twisting and give left me hanging in fright. Later, after one of the neighborhood kids wandered into the yard, climbed without permission, and fell from the ladder and broke his arm, the tree house was pronounced too dangerous and torn down. I never got to see inside of it.

The boys dug an underground clubhouse next. Somewhere between the tree and the garden, they started with a six foot long trench for the entrance tunnel (carrying and spreading dirt along the back fence), then a pit for the main room, and covered the whole thing over with boards, tarpaper, dirt and sod, so no one could tell it was there. Even the trapdoor entrance was covered over with grass, and they would be there underground and hear Dad walking overhead (who if he'd known, had forgotten the clubhouse existed) or Louie's—the gardener's—lawn mower passing over, and exult. They did let me down once, and offered Judy too, but she refused. First, Jack, then I, then Chuck, slipped down into the tunnel, crawled forward over pine needles (laid down to keep clothes clean) into darkness to the cavernous main chamber. Jack carefully helped me down a ladder until I could stand upright. Then he turned on an electric lantern, which was hooked overhead like a regular light, showing as Chuck backed down to join us a room maybe five feet across. There were chairs, a table, a bench all around cut out of the wall, niches for comic books, coke bottles with candles, a vent for air. After investigating, Mom, at some point, despite Jack's assurance, worried that it might cave in, and she and Dad had it torn up and filled in before I was old enough to go down on my own. Dad had Louie do it, and both were shocked to discover the extent and depth of the holes: Louie had to bring in a truckload of topsoil to do the job.

Down Smith's fence to our back corner, where I loved to play in the shade and dirt, ran a long grape arbor, over the lattice of which the boys would climb, and from which, later, they had hung the chickens for killing. Police Chief Captain Bones's yard began at the corner and bordered ours back out to Bloomingdale. In front, Bones's yard and house stood level with ours, but his back yard rose steeply to a terrace, where a reservoir from the town's earliest days had been filled in. In the back corner, the slope up from our yard was only three or four feet high, but it grew to as much as six feet farther down. The entire slope had been planted by Nana Henry as a rock garden, with boulders I could jump from, one to another, without crushing the flowers between. Up on the terrace, Bones's yard was left wild and overgrown and exotic as a woods. We were forbidden to climb into it, though the boys sometimes did anyway to retrieve a baseball or to dig BB's out of the rotten tree they used for target practice out their bedroom window. The tree had been struck by lightning and burned, and crows, which Captain Bones himself would shoot at from his back porch, would flock to its leafless branches. The first time Jack let me shoot his BB gun, a pump model, he had me sight the tree from the windowsill in his room.

The victory garden was in that quadrant of our back yard, too, enclosed by a picket fence with an arbor and gate, and with plank walks between the beds of vegetables. Because the boys used to lock me in here, teasingly, it was my first thought when I heard

"Don't Fence Me In," a popular song then. Between the garden and the back porch stoop with its overhang, was Mom's clothesline, strung like telephone wires between poles and propped up with notched clothes props, which the boys later used for stilts. Where the kitchen and pantry wall abutted part of the living room and the side of the sun porch, with its door and wide steps, Mom had put in a flagstone patio, perhaps ten or twelve feet square and also enclosed by a picket fence with arbored gate. Here, in shade, my sandbox had been kept, and in one movie I am sitting at age four, sailor suited and bare kneed, beside my younger, blond cousin, Priscilla, whom I seldom saw, and who belonged to Uncle Marvin and Aunt Fronca on Mom's side, far off in New York. Off this patio, down from the rock garden and rhododendron bushes and up against Bones's shed, was a weeping willow that had grown from a twig that Grandpop had stuck in the ground twenty years before. A wooden swing hung from one branch, where Judy would push me; also we would tear off willow strands, strip the leaves, and try to snap the strands like whips, stinging, sometimes, at each other. Sometimes, I walked and turned through the fronds, which felt like hair. Patio, willow, and the area off the back stoop formed our favorite family spot, for its privacy and shade. In another film, Nana Henry sits on a bench under the willow, sprinkling us with a hose as we dart around, skinny in our bathing suits, and jump in and out of a zinc laundry tub. Fat, complacent, bemused, a little devilish: she waters us like animated flowers. Sparky is there too, a wire haired terrier, whose dog house stood by the garden, and who was later put to sleep for turning and biting me; taking "wire haired" literally, I had tried to pull his hair out with pliers. Still other films show family picnics in the willow's shade, at a table: Grandpop, Nana, Dad, Kitty. The boys and even Judy cavort around, playing on the name and riding saw "horses" for the camera; Jack marches with a flintlock rifle. Judy sits on the back porch steps, sewing, hair in braids.

On August 17, 1945, shortly after I turned four, Wayne celebrated VJ day. "Oh, Frabjous Day!" said *The Suburban*. With car horns blaring, fire sirens wailing, church bells ringing, fire engines driving around giving free rides, the biggest parade in the town's history passed down Lancaster Pike. As it approached our corner, everyone, neighbors and family, kids all ages, ran down to cheer, waving flags and banging garbage can lids. Somehow I'd been left behind, and having found two pot lids for cymbals, I ran to join them, feeling giddy to cross Lenoir and stray this far alone.

There are the Bloomingdale legends of Jack's, Chuck's and Judy's lives, before or without me. They would sneak past the doorman in the apartments down the street, ride the elevator up and down, and then get chased out. At age seven or eight, Chuck put matches in the teeth of a comb, then lit and dropped the whole thing, setting the back closet, where he'd been hiding, on fire. The boys sneaked out at night, after they'd been sent to their room, by means of the barred window (like a jailhouse window) on the backstairs landing before Judy's room. They had sawed through the middle bar at top and bottom with a hacksaw, then fit it back and camouflaged the cracks with shoe polish, so they could take it out at will, squeeze out onto the roof of the back porch, replace the bar and climb down a nearby tree. Once, when Jack climbed down, he was surprised by Dad, who was equally surprised, sitting in the dark on the back stoop, smoking: "What are you doing? Get back up there!" Then for weeks later, as Jack tells it, Dad would be puzzling over the ledges outside and the window itself: "How did you get out there?"

Both boys had been cut and seriously burned, again, before my time, when an alcohol lamp from their chemistry set (they'd put in kerosene) had exploded in their room. There was Jack's bad back, which often had him in agony until Chuck kneeled on it, knee to the spine, and somehow snapped it straight. Chuck was nearly blinded in a duel with umbrella spikes, when one jabbed near his eye. Chuck put his arm through a glass door at school. There were legends of illnesses, hives, chickenpox, measles. There were older legends of the times before Bloomingdale, up in Boston, where there had been snowstorms so deep you could build tunnels (which Judy and I tried unsuccessfully here), where there had been a hurricane that knocked down trees, where Chuck had thrown a rock across the street and hit the windshield of a passing car. He then ran into the house and begged to take a bath, to Mom's astonishment, as if nothing had happened, and was in the bathroom when the doorbell rang. Chuck had hit Jack over the head with a milk bottle. Chuck licked a frozen railing and tore off part of his tongue.

Though Mom has told me the story, I have no memory of our customary drive one Sunday, Dad at the wheel, Judy and me in back, Mom in front. "Daddy's sick," I supposedly said. "He's a sick man. Anyone can see that. Anyone can see that man is sick." And he kept driving, stiffened, staring straight ahead, saying nothing.

Or of another time, at night, when I ran to Mom: "I heard Daddy, he's not really going to cut you up in pieces and throw you out the window, is he?"

Nothing's there.

Jack and Chuck attended Haverford School (where they went not only for family tradition, but because of the poor quality of so called progressive education in the Radnor schools, which caused a number of their Wayne friends to transfer to Haverford too). Their experiences there augmented their league as brothers. They talked of Severinghast, the principal, who hit them with a yardstick for demerits, practice for the wrestling, football, baseball, and swimming teams, played jokes on the conductors on the Paoli local, wore school jerseys and caps; and then, come summers, left together for eight week sessions of Camp Allagash, in Northern Maine. They were away the summer of 1945 on a canoe trip far into the Maine and Canadian wilderness, so they didn't hear that the war was over until two weeks later, when they came out of the woods. Mom sewed their names on everything from underwear to sleeping bags; each had his own barracks trunk, and we drove them and their trunks to the 30th Street station in town and put them on the train, then greeted and picked them up there at summer's end.

At Allagash they learned to tie their own flies and to fish for pike and trout, whipping their fly rods overhead with line curling back, snapping forward, and lying gently on the water sixty or seventy feet out, so the fly would touch the water like a falling bug. Whatever the geographical, social and professional divergence of their adult lives, Allagash and their passion for fly fishing proved a sure key to kinship. Both had known those special woods (unlike any others, by their telling), the canoeing, the rivers, lakes, the rapids, the portages, the camping out, the moose, bear, the Canuck guides. Allagash, too, was where Jack contracted his love of flying, which otherwise had been bred with balsa gliders, then motor powered models through his early teens. His first year up, having won a ping pong match, he broke his toe while jumping for joy and so was left behind when Chuck and the others set out on their canoe trips. For several weeks, cast on his foot, he flew with a fish and game ranger, helping him stock lakes with fishery bred trout. The plane was a small, single wing over, with pontoons. Perched by the open door, as they swooped suddenly over treetops and down over some small lake, Jack would have a can ready, from a store of cans behind their seats. He emptied it, like a shower of silver, as the hundreds of tiny fish rippled the surface and shimmered. Then the plane would climb, engine roaring, bank, and clear the rushing trees, and they'd be off. The same pilot, who could land and take off on bodies of water smaller than a football field, later flew Jack upriver, toe healed and cast off, to find and rejoin the advanced canoe group for his last week of the trip.

Judy had longed so much for a sister that, from the moment I was born, she refused even to look at me for several weeks. But then she took over, little-mothering me as her special charge. In the movies, she is prodding me to crawl, cradling me, making angels with me in the snow, pulling me on the sled. I loved her room in back, with its alcove and window seat, where she had arranged all her dolls and stuffed animals, and where she would read to me. Her friends were the Hartsorns, down Lenoir, a family of all girls with one St. Bernard, which followed Judy home one day. We were sitting at the dinner table; I was in my high chair (I can remember) and Mom beside me, when Mom called for Viola, the maid, to bring in dinner. In came this monstrous dog instead, tall enough to rest its shaggy head on the table between Mom and me. Viola had been terrified and refused to serve anything until we got that dog out of there. At some point, the boys had learned to stand and walk on their hands across the living room. Judy practiced and practiced, Chuck even helping by holding her feet, until she could do it readily too, but then her wrist collapsed and broke. None of us were allowed to try after that. She lived in the fantasy world of her reading a good deal of the time and would play "secret garden" under the rhododendrons by the rock garden; her drawings were of elves, pixies, fairies, and fairy castles, and she encouraged me to draw too, my first crude cartoons. She took dancing lessons, ballet and tap; then music lessons. Her practicing on our upright proved maddening to all of us, but especially so to Chuck, who would pile pillows over his head. She quit because her lady piano teacher's breath was so bad. When she was in fifth grade, in Mr. Shock's class (he would be my teacher, too, at Radnor), Mom wanted to transfer her to The Baldwin School, the equivalent of

Haverford for girls, but the Radnor schools were so poor that Baldwin refused her until she had had a year of catch up work at The Haverford Friends. She was attending Baldwin, wearing a blue tunic uniform, knee high stockings, and carrying her canvas book bag for our last years at Bloomingdale. I felt jealous then, too, that my cousin, Bunny, a girl, had supplanted me in her attentions. I resented that Aunt Kitty and Uncle John invited her to the shore with them to baby sit.

My big brothers coached me to fight when I was six, and the Lenoir Avenue kids, especially Katy Boles, started picking on me. Katy was two or three years older than me and her sister Nancy was in my class at school. Most of the houses on Lenoir were smaller, cramped, and we felt, without saying so, the families poorer, different from us. The Boles lived two houses up from our barn, across the street, and they had a driveway into an old garage, which was a hangout for the girls and their friends on the block. I had set up a hose and pump around the back corner of our barn, where I played gas station with my bike, and Katy would come by and jeer at me; one day she called me out on the sidewalk, and in front of the younger kids, started slapping my face. She was bigger than me and I didn't know how to fight back. When I told Jack and Chuck, they took me into the garage and carefully showed me the three button punch: count three buttons down from the top and punch, one good punch, and that's the breadbasket. They had me practice on them—that's it, kid—told me I had it perfect, and sent me out hunting, absolutely confident, for Katy and her gang. I asked for them, western style, up and down Lenoir, and finally heard that they were in the Boles's garage. I walked right up and banged on the garage door. "Yeah, what is it?" One of them opened the door, and Katy was inside with them: "Whata you want? I told you . . ." And she was coming at me: "You want some more, huh?" I waited, counted her buttons, and without saying anything, blindly punched; then walked away, never looking back. Some time later, I was back in the house, and Jack and Chuck came in and reported that Katy Boles was crying, that her mother was all up in arms, and that I had given her a black eye. This made me feel like someone, satisfied. None of the kids teased or bothered me after that.

Unfortunately, I later tried a similar act of cool retribution on Judy. She and I had been squabbling in the back yard, and in a tantrum, I had thrown my cap gun, nicking her ankle and sending her running in tears to tell Mom, who came out, lectured, hauled me in and sent me to my room for the rest of the afternoon, all of which I blamed on Judy for telling. After dinner, Mom asked whether I'd thought it over now, was I ready to come down and apologize to Judy? I said yes. Judy was in the Saturday room with Chuck, reading or watching our first TV (an eight inch model pointing upward with a mirror reflector, which we got in 1947, first among any families I knew), and I walked right up, and without warning, as she looked up expectantly, I punched her for telling on me. The result was a spanking by Mom in the third floor bathroom, with Chuck, Jack, and Judy listening on the stairs, outside the door. Mom said, "This is going to hurt me more than it hurts you," and I didn't cry at first, but then in anger and humiliation at their listening and at the noise, and with the actual pain of her slaps, I cried helplessly.

I had never been spanked before, nor would be later, though I probably deserved to be, and I would remain threatened by the history of spankings in the family. Dad had been the boys' punisher, using a fearsome razor strop. Chuck had padded his pants once with comic books, the story went, but forgot to cry, so Dad had discovered and removed them, then hit him even harder. Mom, too, had earned her reputation with a hairbrush, and the gathering of non-victims on the stairs to listen was a family ritual. But I would be disciplined differently; and that was one of the changes between my brothers' and sister's world and mine.

Grandpop's death in 1946 was remote to me, though I tried to picture him going about his ordinary morning life, in their house, which I had never seen, at the shore, showering and shaving, when suddenly he collapsed and Nana found him later. I wasn't allowed to go to the funeral, but I was taken to visit the grave plot with Nana on major holidays, when we would put on flowers. The grave slab fascinated me because my name was there, chiseled in marble. I had loved Grandpop and felt robbed of his love and attention; death was as if he had moved away, forever; we would never see him again, and that neverness echoed as a new perception in my heart.

Their house in Ithan was sold and the Ithan world, which I felt as golden, was finished. We would drive by "snooping" occasionally on Sundays. The house at the shore was sold. Off and on, when living alone grew too hard, Nana would move in with Kitty and John, who had a house now in Ardmore. But before that and between there were a series of over-decorated apartments, heavy with upholstery and rugs and drapes, porcelain lamps, figurines, in a style of mass produced regency. Money was no problem for her and indeed, I surmise in hindsight, money kept her children attentive and loyal. Also it helped bond me to her, for she would, besides treating me as special because I was Grandpop's namesake, offer me "presents"—usually a five dollar bill, when I was older, which seemed exorbitant and amazing next to my twenty-five-cent allowance. Always, in any case, I felt the pathos of her loneliness. And an order of things had collapsed; givens had been—could be—suddenly reversed.

I am lying in the dark one night, wakened, or falling to sleep, when at one of my two big windows, which open over the front porch roof, and where leaf shadows from the streetlights regularly and familiarly play, there is something terrible, alive, malevolent suddenly, looking in, like a man, but not, with some kind of leering, angry, twisted face. It is there and real, and I scream and scream hysterically, and everyone comes rushing in, Jack and Chuck and Mom, and Dad, too, I think, and they open the window and look outside and Chuck gets out onto the porch to look and prove to me that nothing is there, and lets me look.

When Mom demanded of the boys, then and later, whether they'd been playing a trick, whether one of them had gotten out their window onto the roof and come around to scare me, they swore and insisted, and have for all these years, no. So the only explanation is a dream, or dream mixed with my seeing some pattern in the swaying shadows. But it wasn't a dream, I told them, knew then, feel now; and it wasn't shadows; and what it was I couldn't describe and can't to this day, but I know it was there, was real, was inexplicable.

When I was five or six, I asked Mom whether a woman looked different from a man. She responded in a way that seemed more important than my curiosity. After a moment's thought, instead answering me directly, she told me to knock at the hall bathroom when she was getting ready for her bath, and she would show me. So I did, the door opened, and she was standing by the tub. "Well," she asked, smiling and grave, "are they different?" All I took in quickly was the patch of pubic hair. "Yes," I answered, backing out and closing the door. I wasn't troubled or even deeply impressed by the difference, not then. A later time, we were at an amusement arcade. In the spirit of honesty, I asked her if I could look in a movie box that advertised a naked woman dancing. "Go ahead," she said, smiling, and even put in the dime. But feeling tested somehow, I chose not to.

Mom's big, cumbersome artist's easel (which she'd found abandoned in a garage of their rented house in Illinois, years before

I was born), was set up in the sun porch on the Lenoir side, "for the light." The same room, at different times, held our ping pong table, train layouts, and the matched black and polar bearskin rugs, in whose coarse, deep fur I liked to roll, and whose lifelike and lifeless heads, marble eyes, leather noses, ceramic tongues and gums, and actual fangs menaced each other, face to face (both had been kills of Aunt Peggy's playboy husband's, and came to us, I've learned, as legacies of Aunt Peggy's divorce; I imagine her toasting him on them, in happier times, brandy snifters clinking in the firelight). Mom would paint for several hours in the morning, wearing a "smock," and holding her messy pallet with its thumbhole. She mixed her colors by squeezing and rolling up the oils from the bottom, like so many tooth paste tubes, a dab of white, of red; then thinned the paint with turpentine and painted with different, long brushes. I grew jealous of her immersion and would whine and clamor for attention. Always, I felt, she painted in spite of me, and I dreaded her remoteness.

Among her pictures from Bloomingdale were the pink and white magnolia blossoms against the sky, covered bridges at Eaglesmere and Valley Forge, and a Maine fishing village seascape (many others, especially the still-lifes, from earlier and later, adorned our walls, and caused visitors to exclaim, "Kay, you mean you painted that?" and then they'd want to see all the paintings). I drove with her to and through the covered bridges, where she set up a portable easel at roadside or on a sandbar, with her open paint box. She was especially challenged by the problems of water, reflections, the play of light, by the textures of trees and clouds, and took trouble, dissatisfied past any reason I could see, touching, retouching, over and over, until the paint dried bumpy. Finished paintings took weeks to dry and then she would shellac them. The seascape was her largest and most ambitious. She based it on a photograph in American Artist: huts in the foreground, beach, choppy surf, then a towering offshore cliff from a severed peninsula. She worried while painting that it wasn't "convincing," and finally invented and agonized over a fisherman drying his nets over a fence up close; the painting won first prize in a local show and a picture of her and me standing beside it appeared in *The Suburban*. At sunset, on the sandbar where she was painting a covered bridge and I was playing with pebbles, she once said, "No one would believe a sky like that even if I could paint it; it doesn't matter if it's true; no one would believe it." I felt proud of her talent; but after the seascape, she stopped painting until we'd moved, I was older, and she had a back room to herself. Her decision to stop, I felt, was made in the context of my needing her, and I remember some elation and relief at hearing the announcement, despite its bitter edge, and seeing the easel dismantled and carried away.

Mom, not Dad or the boys, took me for my haircuts to Mike Pinto's, where there were three barber chairs, each with a basin in front and a mirror with shelves for bottles of witch hazel and different colored, scented tonics, and a hook for electric clippers as well as for various combs and scissors. A row of waiting chairs, with comic books and magazines, stood opposite, beneath a wall length mirror that I would see reflected in the barber chair mirror reflecting the barber chair mirror and my own reflected image, down a receding corridor of reflections, on and on, out of sight— an effect I found disturbing. Clumps of hair cluttered the floor, stirred by the breeze of overhead fans, and from time to time Mike or another barber swept them into a heap big enough to stuff a pillow. After their haircuts, some men got tilted back with the aprons on; their faces would be swathed in steaming towels drawn with tongs from a shiny container near the sinks; the barber would pull out the leather strop that hung from each chair and start sharpening a razor. Then off came the towels, on went shaving cream, and like a surgeon, the barber would swatch it off. Other men had shampoos, turned in their chairs with heads tilted backwards over the sinks. When my turn came, Mom led me to the chair and I climbed up on the metal footrest. Mike had a contraption for kids that fit over the adult chair arms and had a round seat in the middle, so my feet rested on the real seat, finally. Then he'd shake out his striped apron, swish it around like a matador's cape, and fasten it under my chin. Mom stood beside me and told him each cut, supervising, and he would say: "Hey, this a good kid. This a brava boy, doesn't cry. You know some kids, they can't standa have a haircut. Come in and cry and cry and I say, it'sa not so bad, this is Mike, huh? I'ma here make you look all pretty. I'ma not gonna hurt ya." But sometimes he would. His scissors would pinch and tear and once he even nicked my ear, so it bled; then apologized over and over, more upset than I was. Finished, my hair wet or tonicked, parted, combed, and snipped with the last perfectionist touches, neck dusted, cape off and clothes whisked, I would climb down to get my lollypop, as Mom paid, on the way out. Sometimes, while we were there, the fire siren at the station half a block away would go off, ear-splittingly, and Mike's assistant threw off his barber's coat and ran out, regardless of his patron, to pull on his fireman's coat and hat at the fire station, and pretty soon an engine or two would come roaring up the street, picking up speed, fireman hanging on, siren howling.

John Spaeth came back from the war with a German gas mask for Jack, which we took turns wearing for Halloween and other times, joking. It came in a dark green ribbed metal canister, with a special clasp and a cloth band for over the shoulder. Long after the mask itself disappeared, we used this can, with the Nazi eagle perched on a wreathed swastika stamped on its lid, to hold toys and bric-a-brac. The mask itself was rubber with bug-like oval glass eyes, and the serrated breathing tube, like an elephant's trunk, connected to a filter canister with German writing all over it. When you put the mask on, even for moments, your face would pour sweat. Uncle John also showed us a 9 mm Luger, which he once let Jack fire, and kept in a dresser drawer, later, in their house. He didn't talk about the war, and the official account was that he had not really seen action. He served as a medical corpsman in the back lines during the Battle of the Bulge, in 1944. He did tell Jack, only Jack and just one time, that he had been driving a jeep, gotten a flat tire, and had stopped to fix it, when a bullet ricocheted near him and he saw several Germans shooting at him from bushes on a hill; alone, apparently, he took a Thompson machine gun from the backseat and opened up in their direction. He didn't stay around to see if he had killed anyone, but the firing had stopped. Dad, who hired Uncle John after the war as a salesman for our family chocolate factory, said approvingly that the war had made John doubly grateful for his family and his life; but then Dad also derided him to us later for being "chicken hearted," "scared of his own shadow," and without initiative or fight.

Anna King was our "colored" maid. Before her was Viola, and before Viola, Catherine Dougherty, whom I was too young to remember, but who, by family report, would take out her false teeth and click them for me. Anna started with us at age fifty, when I was four, coming in days for a while, then moving in, wearing uniforms, and living over my room on the third floor, with that bathroom to herself. She cooked, cleaned, served meals, and looked after us (me, mainly) when Mom was busy or away. Broad beamed and plump, she had a moonish face and black hair, pulled back, and smooth complexioned upper arms as large as thighs. She complained often of aches and pains, and had Mom buy her a knee-pad for when she kneeled, scrubbing floors. There was always a faint, burnt wood fragrance to her and her things, her bedspread, her ironing, even, that I loved; and her manner with me was teasing, scandalized, admiring, and ceaselessly fond. She would marvel at my craving for Velveeta cheese and peanut butter (which I exaggerated for her benefit), "Oh, no, you can't want to eat all that!"; or something I'd say or draw would cause her to exclaim, "Oh, he's just so smart!" One chilly fall day during the war, Mom was down at the Red Cross, Anna and I were alone, and somehow we got locked out of the house. We were on the back porch, where there was a wood box and an axe. She bewailed and worried what to do, and I kept saying, gallantly, feeling manly and in charge, that I would take the axe and chop down the door, but she wouldn't let me, even though I told her it was my house and all right: "No, you can't do that. Put that axe down; don't you pick up that." We waited and waited, achingly, for someone to come, which was her solution; she took off her sweater and insisted I wrap it around me. Another time, while Mom was at the store one afternoon, I was in the bathroom between my room and the master bedroom, with both doors locked, and hadn't learned to wipe myself yet: this was something Mom always did; and when I called out for Mom, Anna answered. She stood right outside the door, pleading with me: "Your Mommy isn't home and I don't know when she's coming; let me in and I'll wipe you!" "No!" "It's okay, I've got a little boy too!" "No!" "You don't want to sit there all afternoon; unlock the door, now!" "No!" And so forth, be-mused coaxing on her part, total fear and shyness on mine: only Mom could, I would wait; and did, for god knows how long; but then Mom did come back, I unlocked the door, and everybody thought it was funny.

Later, at Bloomingdale, while Mom and Judy were shopping Anna's room caught on fire. I smelled smoke, yelled, and she came running, charged upstairs, and suffered third degree burns before Jack or the firemen, who came quickly, could pull her out. She'd been trying to get her money out of the burning mattress, which was where, from bad wiring nearby or a forgotten cigarette, the fire had begun.

That Anna had moved up from North Carolina, where she had worked all her life for the Reynolds family, even been given a brick house. That her husband had been an alcoholic, who beat her, and whom she finally divorced. That she had had no children of her own but that her sister in Philadelphia had sent down one child a year for Anna to clothe, feed, and school. That she'd grown attached to one nephew, Billy, and when unionization had changed things "for the worse" at work, she had moved North with him to live at her sister's, in the colored section behind Wayne. That she continued to live there, contributing to their home and never having one of her own. That as Billy grew up, married, and had children, he proved a pride to her, but a heartache too, since she had tried, at one point, to move in with him, but it hadn't worked out. . . .

She would confide all this to Mom, off and on, peeling potatoes, say, while I sat listening. Sometimes, too, she and Mom mentioned "race" or "her people." But I had little sense, ever, of her personal life, or of the world, apart from and foreign to ours, where she would come from and return. I did gather from her talk that at her sister's, at least, this was a world of violence, greed, squalor and want, that she was not loved or appreciated there as we loved her or felt she deserved, and those times we drove her home (mainly from our St. Davids house later, when she no longer boarded with us), I didn't like sending her back—one of us—to what other life waited behind those windows, those walls. But she would snort, smile fondly, and say, "Don't you go thinking that way. This is my house, here. This is my family, understand? Don't worry about me."

She is in none of our family pictures, movies or stills.

Day after day, I eagerly awaited the mailman, who would come in our gate and up the walk, carrying his leather pouch, and leave mail in our glassed-in, storm-doored stoop. I had sent away, from a comic book ad, for a Tom Mix ring, and now finally, in a square box addressed to me, it came. A tiny six gun stood on top, which, when I flicked the cylinder at the hammer, shot sparks. Another prize I sent for was an atomic bomb ring, which had a red and gray bomb mounted on it. When you unscrewed the red front and shaded or took it into a closet, the inside glowed phosphorescent.

An open garbage truck, green, and long, with high sides, came up Lenoir Avenue once or twice a week. We had sunken garbage pails out back; you stepped on a pedal and the inner lid rose up, like a toilet seat, and you pulled out the deep garbage pail by its handle from its concrete silo and lugged it to the sidewalk. There the garbage men took it, one lifting it to the men in back who trod down the garbage; they, in turn, would dump the contents on their pile and throw the empty pail back down. We could smell the truck, fulsome and sour, all the way back at the house; we held our noses, and waved with relief once it had pulled past.

The milkman came regularly in his rattling van, picked up empties, and left four quart-sized bottles (yellowish cream on top) and a pint of cream. An ice-man would come too, from time to time, carrying in blocks of ice with caliper tongs, and putting them in the wooden ice box, which, alongside the double door refrigerator, we still used. Then Burket's coal truck would back in the drive and up to the basement window. A coal chute slanted down from the bed, through the window, and into our bins; and when the truck bed rose slowly, steeply, coal funneled out, pouring down.

Mom and I went shopping.

For groceries, before the first supermarkets, to Espenshade's, where Howard was the butcher, Helen, his wife, the cashier, and Frank, the owner and grocer. All were friendly, admiring, and happy to see me, I felt, because I picked out things I fancied and begged Mom to buy; this was, in fact, a standing joke between Frank and me. Mom and I sat on wooden stools back at the butcher's station. Howard, with his blood-smeared apron stretched over his belly, and with his big, hairy arms, worked behind the scarred and hollow butcher blocks, talking soulfully. He sharpened his knife with a honing tool, then made deft cuts in a slab of meat. He took a cleaver to the bone, and sometimes different saws, hack-saws, ripsaws; he had an electric saw too. From the slicing machine, he always gave us samples of ham, bologna, salami, cheese. His knives and saws fit into a crevice in the butcher block. A scale was in the middle, the showcase to the left; and the deep freeze, with its heavy, insulated door, behind. The smells were of the sawdust underfoot, raw meat, bone, fat, and a cold ammonia smell from the meat-locker, where whitish quarters and ribbed carcasses hung on hooks. Overhead were ceiling fans, fly paper dangling. I bought my comic books here, too, as well as in the 5 & 10.

People loved Mom, I felt, not only for her patronage, but for her specialness as a person. The laundry lady at Ivan's told me in front of her: what a wonderful mother I have, how lucky I am, what a fine person. Mom told me later that people "cry on her shoulder," whether she likes them to or not, because she was a good listener; she didn't know how to say no.

I hated most waiting in the car, which I chose to do, rather than follow her into boring places, like the fabric shop; sometimes she told me to stay. No matter the season, the wait was agonizing: nothing to do, watch, or read; I pretended that the Buick hood ornament, a chrome circle around a jet-like teardrop (vandals were known to break off the circles for bracelets), was a gun sight, and the radio controls, triggers, and I slaughtered passersby. But then the wait dissolved as soon as there! she's coming! and she was back, bags in her arms, smiles, perfume, jangling keys, apologies.

I hated when she stopped on the sidewalk and got into adult conversations that ignored me (if there was a dog, I identified with it) and I pulled at her hand and whined until I earned a rebuke. I hated Kay's Dress Shop, where she tried on hat after hat in a mirror, asking my opinion, and settled on a velvet crescent with a veil; or where she tried on different dresses in a changing booth. I hated the beauty shoppe, where I sat numbly and swung my legs as she sat under a hairdryer's helmet forever, reading a magazine, smoking cigarettes.

The bank was better. I liked the echoing marble floor and grandeur of space. There was a reverence here too, as in a hospital or church. Mom went to a glass topped table for writing checks, then to one of the tellers' windows, with its forbidding grill (my own first transactions were savings books for pennies, nickels, dimes, and quarters, which I turned in for War Bonds). On special occasions, she took me with her to the guard, who wore a revolver, showed her passbook to be admitted with a buzz through a barred gate, like into a jail cell, and then an official opened the round, massive vault door, all burnished steel, brass and glass, with the intricacies of its dials visible, and we stepped inside, which was brightly lit and had drawers in the walls. He took her key, pulled out a drawer, a long, metal box, and escorted us out and around to one of several booths, where, the door closed, Mom unlocked the box and showed me, among other papers, my birth certificate, with baby footprints, and the silver dollars that somebody had given me each birthday; then she went over the grown up and official paper she wanted, put everything back, locked the box, opened the booth, called the guard, and we walked back to the man, who took and returned the box to the vault, then buzzed us out.

We shopped for me: for clothes, at Harrison's or The Wayne Men and Boys Shop; or for shoes, at Guitings, in Ardmore, where we knew no one, but the clerks were solicitous, and Judy and I took turns sliding our feet under the fluoroscope and peering down to see greenish pictures of our bones. My foot was measured by the clerk, length and width, several boxes of new shoes were brought to try, each foot eased in, laces threaded, pulled, and tied, and then I took trial steps, slippery on the rug. My old shoes, which looked shabby suddenly, were wrapped up in the shoebox; and proudly, I wore the new ones home.

I had no hand me downs from my brothers; my own things, however, as outgrown, were sent on regularly to Aunt Janice for my cousins Bobby and Peter, who were "less fortunate." Bobby and

I had always fought, when we were younger, and they had lived nearby; but after the war, they'd moved back to New England.

Doctor Truxel, our family doctor, whose first name was Cyrus, I knew mostly from house calls when I was sick and he would arrive wearing coarse tweeds and carrying his black bag. He had an aura of manly gentleness, tough, not unctuous. Dr. Buck, the only other G.P. in Wayne, and Dr. Truxel's stand-in for vacations and emergencies, was always the opposite, tall, balding, tense, whiny, reminding me of Uncle Lloyd, who, in fact, was his friend. Dr. Truxel reminded me of Grandpop Henry, if anyone.

From Lancaster originally, he had been a doctor in China during World War I, working in poor villages (an idea that particularly caught Chuck's imagination, as Truxel later influenced his own desire to be a doctor). Then he had married a girl from our area and settled in Wayne. He knew Chinese and collected Ming vases and other Oriental artifacts, with which he decorated his home and office nearby, around the corner from Bloomingdale. He had delivered me.

He would open his marvelous bag, which was also fearsome, with paneled sides that held as many vials as my brothers' chemistry set, in rows, take out sometimes a black flashlight, a forehead reflector, with the hole in the middle, and a wooden tongue depressor, and say, "Say, AH!" or put on the stethoscope and press its cold membrane to my chest, and places on my back, breathe in, out, and maybe have to give me a shot, filling the needle from a bottle, squirting to test, rubbing my arm or embarrassingly a cheek of my bottom with alcohol, then jab and done and rubbing again; or doing the thermometer, and afterwards pouring two cups of turpentine-tasting medicine for me to drink, and leaving a vial of sugar pills.

He seemed awkward and out of place when he officiated at my visits to the hospital—for instance, when I had my tonsils out—

though he would be there always, a friendly, reassuring face, with Mom's.

Mom left us to go alone to Bermuda for six weeks on January 1, 1947. She left on Doctor Truxel's orders, I was told then and for years later, to recuperate from a nervous breakdown. Before leaving, she told me she loved me; she didn't want to leave, but she had to. And she'd be back just as soon as she could.

She'd always said my prayers with me and tucked me in (the "Now I lay me down to sleep, / I pray the Lord my soul to keep . . ." terrified me with its message that I could and might die in my sleep, that my soul was mine only on loan, belonged to "the Lord," and could be taken back at will.) We had never been separated before, and, according to Judy (I have no memory of it), for these long days, nights, and weeks, I cried myself to sleep.

A housekeeper, Mrs. Pinkerton, whom we called "Aunty Pink," was hired; Anna stayed on as live in maid and cook; Nana Henry visited; and Jack, as man of the house, was responsible for the rest of us. Sixteen, then, he was in his junior year at Haverford; Chuck was in his freshman year; Judy at The Haverford Friends School, and me in kindergarten.

Dad was absent not only to my memory, it turns out, but in fact, having been admitted to the Pennsylvania Hospital Institute in Philadelphia two days after Christmas, where he would board until mid-March. (The dates I know from the monthly hospital bills, which Mom kept and later showed me, along with other papers from then.) In reluctant and troubled recollection, and having "thought about it a lot over the years," Jack corroborated the adult facts that Mom has told, at my adult urging and since Dad's death. That Dad's "bad times" were off and on, from 1943 onward, but that the worst came after Grandpop's death the fall I started kindergarten and climaxed on that Christmas Eve, 1946. Before this incident, says Jack, the drinking had been private and secret, even within the family; but this night, downstairs, Dad was drunk and sitting surly during dinner; then after dinner as we trimmed the tree, kids from the neighborhood, Jack's, Chuck's and Judy's friends, came up the front walk, caroling, and Jack was too ashamed to let them in. But Dad jumped up, roaring, and came out on the porch yelling for them to go away. I remember none of this. According to Mom, Dad had asked her for a divorce the night after his father was buried, July 14, 1946, and she had told him: All right, but not until he'd gotten himself straightened out first; that he was ill; that he needed a doctor. By then his affair with a girl at the factory had been open between them for some time. The girl had started as a clerical helper. She was a "beautiful young girl," said Mom, "not much older than Jack—she could have been Jack's date, when he was working in there." Before long, she had gotten "under [Dad's] skin"; he wanted Mom to find his fraternity pin and give it back, so he could pin the girl. He made her his private secretary, even built a private office for her after his father died. She called him openly at home: "He there?" at first pretending to be the real estate company, or on some thin pretense of business, but then with no pretense at all. He wanted to marry her, he'd repeat to Mom, and start a new family, since he'd "botched this one so badly"; other times, he was talking and thinking about suicide: "I should just go ahead and drive over a cliff. That's the only way I'll ever get over and out of this mess." The girl, meanwhile, just before he finally submitted to treatment, called up to threaten Mom, who had told her flatly she would never grant him a divorce: "Just tell him for me, the girl had said. "Tell him I said that he has compromised himself, understand?"

All along, with the drinking, once the children were in bed, or supposedly so, Mom and Dad would fight, Dad shouting, threatening, even hitting Mom. From the age of fourteen and younger, Jack would hear them and creep down the hall to listen outside their door (as would Judy, from the back room, without Jack or Mom knowing). Several times, in winter, Dad dragged, shoved and locked Mom out of the house in her nightgown, so that Jack had to help her up the porch and in through a window. Once Dad actually came at her with a kitchen knife; she knocked it out of his hand and shoved him out the door. "He could have burned you," Mom has told me, "chased you with a knife, urinated in an ashtray and up the wall, and next day, he'd have no memory; we'd all go for the Sunday drive, visit his parents . . ."

Early on, Jack began to sleep with his squirrel rifle ready under his bed (the gun that Dad had given him), but only once, during one bad fight, did he intervene, aiming the loaded rifle at Dad and telling him to quit, get out, or he'd shoot. "I would have, too," he said now, evenly; "I came that close to being a fourteen year old parricide." But Dad, speechless, wide eyed, had sobered at once, taking in the boy and gun; then turned and left. Otherwise, Mom had handled most of the trouble herself.

But then that fall, 1946, the whole family had caught measles and Mom was run down from lack of sleep. She was taking B12 shots, sleeping pills, wake-up medicines; her teeth, hair, skin, everything had begun to go. She weighed ninety-six pounds. Dr. Truxel sent her to the hospital for a heart test, which showed ar-rhythmia. He told her she was "terminal"; she had a bad heart and couldn't live another three months this way. She had to get away, say, to Bermuda. She couldn't take care of four children, and she'd be away permanently if she didn't take care of herself. He asked her what was doing this to her, and then had guessed; so she had told him about Dad. At first he told her to get out of the marriage, but when she wouldn't, put her in touch with his friend, Kenneth E. Appel, a psychiatrist connected with the Pennsylvania Hospital. Appel refused to treat Dad while he was still drinking, and called in a Mr. Chambers, who wasn't a doc-tor, but was with A.A. Chambers talked and met with Dad; and Chambers was the one they called for help on Christmas Day and who took Dad into the Institute, where after drying out, he would spend nights, while continuing to work at the factory.

Here, also, he would admit to alcoholism, see Chambers regularly, meet other alcoholics, and read such books as "Alcohol: One Man's Meat" (for which he was billed January 7) and "It's How You Take It" (February 18).

Mom, meanwhile, went ahead with her Bermuda trip as planned. She had made it clear, even before the Christmas trouble, that Dad could not stay with us while he was drinking. She had hired a housekeeper. He could go for treatment or he could stay at a hotel. Her plane left on December 29, and influential friends of her father's sent letters of introduction to influential Bermudians ("Mrs. Henry is the daughter of Mr. Jerome Thralls, a long-time friend of mine who holds a very responsible position in one of our important Government agencies the RFC. If Mrs. Henry is in need of any guidance during her visit I can think of no one who could be of more help to her than you"), though her father himself, guessing nothing about Dad, assumed that she was leaving the marriage for another man, and sent a Pinkerton detective after her. Years later, as executrix of her father's estate, she would be shocked to learn this, coming upon the detective's report in his files.

Aunty Pink I recall resenting as an interloper, who slept in Mom and Dad's room and who consumed all the chocolates that Jack could bring from the factory. We called her our "mickey mickey" after a demon in a children's book, who sneaked any candy in sight. Besides that, she was self-important, strict and humorless, so we banded together, Anna as well, to tease and manipulate her, at least in little things. Says Jack, she learned not to tell us to go to bed, but to ask. I got an ear infection, then, which confined me to bed and grew serious enough that they wired Mom to come home. (The family legend has it that I got sick to make her come back.) Dr. Truxel came and went. He told Jack and Chuck to punch a hole in the end of a grapefruit can and mount a 60-watt lightbulb inside; I was then to hold this can, with the bulb on, constantly to my ear, to keep the ear hot, which solemnly and scrupulously, I did. If this didn't work, I overheard him tell Jack, I would need an operation.

My wallpaper, day after day, became oppressive: a repeating pattern of apple trees, ladders, men picking, and overflowing baskets, which I myself had chosen (come repapering time, I'd also been allowed to scribble and draw with abandon on my walls before the new paper was put on). Anna or Judy brought me food on trays; Judy sat with me, read to me, drew; Jack and Chuck stopped in regularly to cheer me. At the worst of my fever, they had brought me Mom's special picture, in color—a tiny oval, mounted in gold, covered with glass, and hooked in a wooden case that opened and had red velvet inside. I would take out the medallion, which felt smooth and cool, gaze at my beautiful mother with the brown hair, the dark eyes, then kiss and close it in my hand.

Mom, then, foreign in her suit, and tan, and groomed for the outside world, was suddenly, actually filling my door, coming in, taking me up in the bed and holding me—all in one delirious rush.

The Radnor Primary School, where I went for kindergarten, first, and second grades, was two-and-a-half blocks away, a distance I walked by second grade: down Bloomingdale over Wayne Avenue (past Henefer's, the dentist's) to Runnymede, and down Runnymede to Audubon, across the street. The building had steep concrete steps and white columns in front (it had been the high school in Dad's time), and was flanked on the left by the block-long new high school building, and on the right, as the street curved and changed into Windemere Avenue, by the grammar school, both of which seemed distant and forbidding. On the playground black top, the older kids' swings were too big, their play too rough, and we never ventured into their territory, except as a class, with our teacher.

My kindergarten teacher, Miss Katherine Langley, was second in beauty only to Mom, or to Cherry, Mark Trail's girlfriend in the comic strip. *The Suburban* reports that she had been hired the year before, along with Wayne Miller, who had just been released from a Japanese prison camp. John Barnett and Kit Wilkes became my friends, and I had a crush on Jean Clark, whose father was fire chief and had a scarred and deformed ear, where he'd been burned. We marched and danced in circles and files; lay down for naps all over the classroom, each on a blanket (I'd fight for a place near Jean's); had storytelling and singing; played triangles and tambourines; went on nature walks; played Red Rover; observed the ant farm and aquariums on the window sills, which John Barnett supplied with turtles, frogs, and other flora and fauna, since he lived on a farm; and for our class project, dug a birdbath outside and poured in concrete. For first grade, I had Mrs. Sweazy, a stricter, older, and stockier woman than Miss Langley; we had desks, learned to write, and began to read and do sums. We climbed and slid down some kind of in classroom structure and were never supposed to slide with pencils or anything sharp in our pockets, but one day John and I went down together and he had a lead pencil that gouged into the flesh between my left thumb and forefinger: I carry part of the point there still. Miss Langley married and became my second grade teacher, too. She praised me for my writing and handwriting and singled me out to help first graders, who followed me to an anteroom and earnestly told stories that I tried to structure for them and write down.

I had my sense of nobility too. When Kit Wilkes insulted Jean Clark (we were rivals for her by then), I defended her honor by hitting him with a looping uppercut that knocked him back over two desks onto the floor—to my sheer pride and astonishment. He wasn't hurt, of course. Another time, Mimi, one of the two or three black kids in our class, who frequently lost her temper and scratched kids with her nails, picked a fight and scratched me on the arm. Mrs. Langley separated us and lectured her: "Look, look what you've done to him; how'd you like to have that done to you?" Then, holding Mimi, she turned to me: "Go ahead, you can scratch her now." I refused: "No, I don't want to scratch her. I don't want to hurt her." Mimi seemed puzzled and perplexed by my reaction, then broke into tears; and we were friends, pretty much, after that.

Kit Wilkes was a commercial model, and had to leave school sometimes for shooting sessions in town. His father worked for Sealtest milk and ice-cream, and Kit's picture mainly appeared in ads for those products. Mom was vaguely critical of the Wilkeses using their children this way (later they would use his little sister, Susie, too), but it gave Kit an aura of celebrity. They lived on Lansdowne Avenue, off Runnymede, near the school, in a house and yard about half the size of ours, but similar in style; the parents, as a couple, were handsome, young, affectionate, and, I was aware then, socially ambitious. Susie was four or five. I was attracted to their "normality," the cheerful mothering of Mrs. Wilkes, who resembled Donna Reed; the hearty presence of Mr. Wilkes, who did such things as take us to the Shriners' circus in their boxy station wagon. We read and traded comic books, stacks and bundles of them.

John Barnett, on the other hand, had the glamour of the farm and the outdoor interests I associated with Jack. A head taller than I, he would later become class strongman, but in these years, we usually wrestled to a draw and sometimes I would win. Before our class ever took field trips to the farm, he invited me over to play. Mom would drive me in the Buick, out Conestoga to Church Road, beyond Wayne's residential outskirts, to only woods and fields along the road, to stone gate posts, up a rutted, pot-holed driveway that rocked the car, past a frame house with its own drive, then steeply down to the Barnett's stone cottage on the left, with a silo ahead, a long dairy barn to the right, a creek running through, and the meadows rising in the distance. We'd be greeted by barking, leaping dogs, a few cats (there were 26, more or less), perhaps some ducks and geese scattering, and John would come running from the cottage door, followed by Mrs. Barnett, a short, plump woman, all round and soft, with straight black hair hacked to her neck, and missing teeth; who always wore sneakers and loose, smock like dresses; and whose frank and gentle spirit shone not merely in her eyes, but in her whole face. She would talk to Mom at the car window, as I got out, and John and I ran off. At first, before Cub Scouts, and before we graduated from cap to BB guns, mostly we played cowboys. With Mrs. Barnett's permission, we'd cross the creek and carefully open and close the front pasture gate; then chase up the hill, with me squeamishly wary of stepping in cow pies. The cows were usually elsewhere, being milked, or in another pasture, but sometimes if there were any, we'd charge them, hooting, and they'd scatter, surprisingly timorous for their size. Near the top of the hill was a group of large boulders, our fortress, from which we commanded the entire farmyard. We imagined outlaws or Indians attacking. Pow! Pow! Phewee (a ricochet)! John had no other playmates, no kids nearby, except some girls up the hill; his younger brother, George, was still a toddler, and the third, Barry, wasn't born yet. He'd show me proudly through the dairy barn, where we weren't allowed normally. His father and the hired man would be shirtless, washing down the concrete aisles and gutters with a hose, tending the cows, or pouring milk from big cans into a steel sink. The walls and ceilings were spotlessly whitewashed; two rows of cows faced a center aisle, with heads locked in metal collars, while they were milked by machine behind, mechanical fingers jerking. Their big-eyed heads turned as we passed, one or two loudly mooing and setting off other moos, which echoed. Past the milking room were hay-lined stalls, with wooden gates, and in the back of one was a litter of kittens and their languid, watchful mother, which were the object of our visit. The kittens were still blind, mewing like birds, prick-clawed, coarse-tongued, and so fragile, John warned, that if you petted them too much they would die. You had to pick them up the way the mother did, by the scruff of the neck. Another time he had a calf to show, just struggling to its feet and coming to wet-nuzzle us. He also raised Angora rabbits, which were kept in cages by the chicken coop, on the far side of the cottage; and which he'd let me pet. Still later, they kept beagle pups in another wire enclosure, with a dog house inside; we'd shut ourselves in and the dogs would fawn all over us. I begged Mom to buy me one, but she couldn't; they were being raised as fox hounds for "the big owner," whose horse farm was over the hill.

Inside the cottage, on the other hand, where we went only for lunch, or for shelter if it rained, the dirt and squalor of John's life embarrassed me; and both John and Mrs. Barnett seemed guarded and shy about having me see it. I never saw his room upstairs. We'd stay in the front room, which had tile worn to floorboards, several bloated arm chairs with worn and ruptured upholstery, tables piled high with family junk, and along the back wall, away from the windows, a long, sway backed sofa. George would be crawling on the floor. Mr. Barnett might come in, having to stoop at the door, with great, muck covered boots. He was a silent, powerful man, affectionate and kind with me always, yet frightening too. He'd sink down heavily on the couch, take off his boots, then stretch out full-length for his noontime nap. Originally he'd come from Wales, and his first name, Vivian, struck me as feminine and strange. He'd met Mrs. Barnett as a girl, while he'd worked on another farm, where her father had worked also. They'd married; and now he had charge of this barn, herd, and section of fields, called farm #5, one of eight, which all together made up the Ardrossan Dairy Farms.

For my part, I can't recall John's ever visiting Bloomingdale in return, though he came regularly later to our St. Davids house. Instead, Mom would take us to Valley Forge State Park, which we came to explore and know as well as we did the farm. Our favorite site was Fort Washington, an earthworks fort on Mt. Joy, with batteries of cannon, overlooking a valley where British armies had once threatened.

It was a friendship that would grow, even deepen to love, despite and because of our social differences; because of our love of nature; and because of the encouragement of our mothers. Mom felt special regard for Mrs. Barnett because of her devotion to her children; her warm heart; her personal cleanliness ("she was clean, clean with a fresh damp look about her face as though she had just scrubbed it"); her "simple horse sense" in handling her problems with her boys within their family relationships; and her forthrightness in the face of "the fancy Main Line Station Wagon set," which she encountered not only through school and the P.T.A., but later through den mothering for the Cub Scouts.

"To her the most important thing in life," Mom wrote in reply to my questioning some years ago, "was for her boys to make the right friends. This she told me many times. She was out of her element with the stylish young mothers, but she was determined to give her children every advantage, and cared nothing about 'being accepted' for herself. Both parents appeared at most school functions and scouting events. She would take the floor anytime in any meeting when she felt she had something to contribute—the eyes on her would make her blush, but she invariably offered an opinion. The mothers ridiculed her, 'Wouldn't you think she'd learn how to dress? Wouldn't you think she'd clean up the place, and fix herself up? They live like squatters, ugh.' But these women, who would drive their Cubs out to the farm, dump them at the gate, then run off to bridge parties and cocktails, did not realize how poor the Barnetts were, and that everything was done to keep the boys fixed up, looking like the other boys when they attended school."

Come Easter, 1947, Mom told Jack that Dad wanted to come home for dinner, that he missed everybody, had dried out, and wanted to start over. Jack replied that if Dad asked him a direct question he would have to answer yes or no, but otherwise wanted nothing to do with him. But he really is better, Mom had insisted; he wants another chance; he's ready to start seeing Dr. Appel now. Then Dad, when he appeared, was all bluff front, as if nothing had happened; everything was back as always. And Jack, resenting this self congratulation, at dinner sat sullen and tense, passing the salt, yes, he'd fixed the Buick's brakes, no, he didn't like math, yes, he was thinking of college. Dad, finally, from the head of the table, asked, what is this? I don't get anything out of you but yes and no. And Jack had said: Yes, and that's all you're ever going to get out of me until you straighten out! Then had gotten up and left.

Jack kept up this silent treatment until the following spring, though he worried whether he was doing something wrong and even asked Dr. Appel; but Appel had said, no, it was important; he was giving Dad something to work for and Dad needed goals now. Meanwhile, Appel was telling Mom that Dad's chances of ever coming back to the marriage were 80 to 20 against, "because he had so many hang ups."

The summer of 1947, we vacationed at Eaglesmere, a mountain resort in upstate Pennsylvania, where we had been once before, when I was two. Dad stayed at home to work and drove up weekends. Jack worked as an instructor in the riding stables and met his "first love," a wealthy socialite, Lou Kirk. We have color footage of first him, then Chuck, then Jack and Judy riding double, posting up and down the street in front of our cottage on a large roan. That fall, Judy started at Baldwin School for Girls; Chuck his junior, and Jack his senior year; I was in first grade, and friends with John Barnett. We bought our new Buick, with the "bracelet" hood ornament. Except for his hating Dad, Jack recalls, these were good times; and that Christmas was good, with Dad home. Mom was organizing her "toy shop" project for the Neighborhood League. A call went out and people donated old toys from all over Wayne, which ended up in the playroom of our barn, where they were repaired, cleaned, and repainted (Jack and Chuck helping to make one good bike out of three broken ones). I would run my finger over them in envy, because they were only for "the children."

Then came the big day, when the poor people, white and black, filed up our garage stairs (sometimes people were turned away for obviously not being needy enough), then shuffled politely along the tables and shelves where fire engines, dolls, dollhouses, sleds, wagons, musical instruments, wind-up and electric trains, erector sets, clothes, shoes, even eye-glasses were offered. The shock and embarrassment for me, as I stood there with Mom and brimmed with good will and pride, was to recognize my friend, John, from school, and Mrs. Barnett, coming up the stairs. By five the place was stripped, all my favorites gone, and only a few hopeless things remaining on the otherwise empty shelves.

Judy was involved with her new friends at Baldwin; Chuck, with sports, dating, and his train models; while Jack was preoccupied by airplanes, motorcycles and old cars, along with his "grease monkey" gang from Haverford (one of whom was Pete Conrad, the moon-mission-astronaut-to-be). He was also writing to Lou Kirk, whom he expected to see again that summer and was thinking of marrying. Later, in spring, 1948, he was working on his model A out by the barn, when Dad wandered out, watched, and absently asked him about the cylinder head or distributor, trying to show interest, and Jack had answered just as casually. From then on the silence was over.

Jack graduated from Haverford in June, having been accepted by Cornell, despite his uneven grades (he planned to take engineering). Then we all, excepting Dad, headed back for Eaglesmere. We again had our cottage, near the hotel and lake. Jack would work as a boatman on the docks. He and Chuck drove up alone in the Model A, while Mom drove Judy and me in the Buick.

Summer vacations were part of the rhythm of our lives. Aside from Eaglesmere, in my earlier years, while the boys were in camp, we had been to Ocean City in 1944 and Minnewaska in 1945. Minnewaska, in the Catskills west of Poughkeepsie, was

Mom's family's traditional resort. A snapshot shows her at four-teen, flat-chested, saucy in a sailor hat, arm around the shoulder of another girl, both in knit bathing suits, posing on the Cliff House boat dock. This dock was, in fact, where on our trip I had nearly drowned. I had gained false confidence that I could swim with-out my life preserver by Mom's holding me over the edge with a towel slung under my chest. Then when her back was turned, I had jumped off the dock by myself into water over my head, and was flailing and sinking when she jumped in to rescue me.

Turned over and hot-hulled in the sun, canoes were stacked in wooden racks at the opposite end of the dock. Mom or Judy would rent one and paddle me out to "thread the needle," which was a narrow passage around a sausage-shaped rock, above which rose the steep cliff where our hotel was. Once Judy and I saw a snake sunning itself on the needle rock, with a swelling in its middle, which Judy said was its lunch. Mom painted a view of one of the pagoda-like open huts with cedar railings and shingled roofs that perched on cliff edge along the trails and looked out over the lake and distant mountains; Dad, too, took family films: flowering bushes, cobalt lake, a tiny canoe below on sparkling water.

But no place compares with Eaglesmere, where we returned, were all together, older, and felt the need, maybe, to put the "bad times" behind. This was our family place.

The trip took five or six hours, which seemed all day. Out Lan-caster Pike, Route 30 (before there were turnpikes anywhere), through gentle, rolling Amish country, there were cities and towns all the way. At Harrisburg, we'd turn north up two-lane roads, no towns hardly at all now, only fields. We passed some-where one long graveyard, miles long, too long for me to hold my breath at one gulp, and I tried to cheat, quietly breathing in or let-ting out breath without showing. We carried a milk bottle for me to pee in. We'd watch out for Burma Shave signs with their stag-gered messages. And I'd get cranky and restless, the seat hard; and they'd keep promising, I'd see the mountains soon. And then we'd come to a place called La Porte, where wooded banks rose from the road, and I'd crane to look out for the tops; and these were "mountains." They told me to yawn, so my ears would pop; and Judy, who always got carsick traveling, would start chewing gum, though the highest Pennsylvania mountain is 3000 feet, if that. But we'd be going up, the road narrowing, winding and climbing until we came out someplace where you could look out over the mountains and see the lake itself; and then, still longer, and we'd arrive at the far end of the lake and pass a motel called "Snow White and the Seven Dwarfs," where each cottage was named after a dwarf, then cross a bridge over an inlet choked with lily pads; then back into trees, around curves, and finally we were in downtown Eaglesmere, with its general store, sweetshop, movie theater and board sidewalks, like in cowboy movies. We turned right gently uphill on a potted macadam road, and to our right would be the lake and waterfront, beach, rafts, boat dock, changing huts, and a wide expanse of tree-shadowed lawn, like a park. Farther back in the trees, was the little theater building, and up from that, the bowling alley, and then dominating, at the end of the lawn, the long hotel, with its open, awninged porch. Here guests sat in deck chairs, gliders, or slatted rocking chairs, and looked out over the lake. To our left would be the cottages and yards and dirt side streets, and that was where our cottage was, down one block, right, and up a short way, on its own corner.

A shingle over the door read "Buzz Fuzz" in rustic lettering. A parlor, dining room, and kitchen were downstairs. Upstairs, I had a room to myself, next to Judy's, and we signaled and talked through the wall; Jack and Chuck were across the hall and Mom at the end, past Judy's door. Again, though Dad came up on weekends, I am told, I recall no joy of greeting, nothing we did together, no scene in which he figures.

Occasionally Mom cooked on the cast iron stove, which we fueled from a box of chopped logs and kindling out back, where there was also a trash box (bears, raccoons and skunks were said to forage there at night). But usually we took our meals in the big formal dining room at the hotel, where we had our table assigned, and Jack and Chuck tried to teach me to wet my finger and rub it around the rim of my water glass, making a high pitched ringing sound. Chuck was best, as always. For the various courses we had a complex array of knives, forks, and spoons, and I was told to use the outside ones first and work in. For breakfast, I'd get tomato juice, set in the same silver bowl-like things that Mom's or Chuck's grapefruit came in; then eggs and bacon or pancakes, either of which would arrive covered by a silver dome, which you'd lift up and they'd be steaming. For lunch were salads, fruits, and sandwiches, with soup. We had to dress for dinner, and the tables throughout the room would be busier and fuller than for any other meal. Our waiter, one of Chuck's friends, who was interested in Judy, took our order and disappeared through the swinging doors, then emerged with someone else's round tray on high, and we stared enviously as their plates were uncovered and set out. At last, then, came ours: roast beef au jus, mashed potatoes, and different vegetables; then ice cream for dessert, vanilla for Chuck, chocolate for the rest of us. There may have been finger bowls. Excused, we'd gather dinner mints at the door and head into the lobby, where groups of sofas and easy chairs were arranged like islands, and where, for evening entertainment, in the far corner would be the violin, piano and viola concert. Three white-haired musicians played music that was whiny and interminable. When, two or three nights each week, the hotel would run a BINGO game, we'd buy cards for 25 cents each and settle back in the chairs and sofas together. We held the cards in our laps or worked them on a coffee table. The girl who was the caller would crank her shuffling basket, take out a ping pong ball, and call out "N6!" or whatever, and if I was lucky (I was sometimes, to my delight and astonishment), and got five combinations across a card before anyone else and shouted BINGO!, the game would stop. They'd check my card, and the pot for that game was mine. I won as much as five dollars in quarters from time to time, which I later spent at the bowling alley or concession stand at the beach; but the rule was frustration over bad cards with no chance, or worse, over cards that had nearly made it, when someone else had called BINGO and ruined the chance.

Behind the hotel, alongside tennis courts and a deserted saw-mill, were the riding stables, where Chuck took me for my first horseback ride. Wearing my Roy Rogers chaps, vest, bandana, hat with chin cord, and cap gun, I was granted a Western saddle (they only had two or three; the rest were English), which the stable master slung over the back of a "gentle" paint. He boosted me up, adjusted the sheathed stirrups, and told me that only green-horns grasped the saddle horn. Chuck, meanwhile, boasting that he was as good a rider as Jack (who had worked in the stable), asked for Flash, a palomino, and the fastest and most spirited of the string, which only the stable master himself and a few oth-ers could take out. As soon as Chuck was up, the horse pranced, ducked, and wheeled. "Sure, sure, I can handle him," Chuck in-sisted, hauling on the reins. "Yeah, well, go easy," the stable mas-ter warned. "Don't get him worked up, okay?" Then Chuck took my reins and led me out at a walk, just us two, to the dirt and hoof-mulched trails through the woods and around the lake and back. I was shocked by the casual way his horse lifted its tail and dropped a stream of fresh, round turds, but otherwise, I was intoxicated by the realness of riding, the creaking leather, the sway and plod of living flesh, the shake of head, blow, twitch of hide and ears. I turned and propped myself, arm stiff, hand on the horse's rump, which was as broad and solid as a table. Then, half-way around the lake, Chuck handed me the reins and told me to wait; he was going to find out just how much his horse could do. With that he took off down the trail, crouched, kicking with his heels and slashing with the reins and disappeared around a bend; a minute, two, then they were coming back, breakneck, both horse and rider set, intense; then Chuck pulled back, and, standing in his stirrups, posted past me, the horse panting and shiny with sweat. "Jesus, he can run," Chuck announced, sweaty himself and red faced, as he came up to take my reins.

When we got back to the stable, the stable master was furious. "What've you been doing with him? Look at him! He's all lathered up!" Unsaddling Flash, he threw a blanket over him; later he would have to curry him down. He swore at Chuck, over Chuck's protests that he hadn't galloped much. "I told you not to gallop. Wise ass little rich kids. Listen, don't you come round again; you're not riding here again! You want to give him pneumonia?"

Chuck, my primary mentor now, with Jack working or off with Lou Kirk, also took me exploring down the more difficult hiking trails. There were three, all starting behind the hotel, marked with signs and periodic swatches of colored paint, as they led off into the woods. The red trail I could do alone, but the blue and yellow trails, steeper, longer, and leading through rougher terrain, were taxing even for grown ups. We had to pack a lunch and carry a canteen. We found a blue marker, a stripe on a tree or arrow on a rock, then searched ahead for the next. On the blue trail we found a cave under a hanging rock, which was supposed to be where a "hermit" once lived (I'd never heard that word and the idea scared and fascinated me). At some point on the yellow trail, we had to scale a cliff.

Another time, we explored the sawmill, around which logs were piled, with rusty grapplers lying in the weeds, and mounds of sawdust were heaped, and where, inside, once we climbed a chute-like ramp, the huge, rip-tooth circular saw stood frozen—I reached out and touched the teeth. Operating levers, the big motors and drive belts were nearby, and uncut logs were still on the conveyer. The mill predated the resort, which all had been a logging area once; narrow gauge tracks led from the mill back into the woods, where a small steam engine lay on its side. Even the horse paths originally had been logging roads.

The bowling casino, adjoining the hotel, was primarily a teenage hangout, as were the sweetshop in town and the barn-like movie theater. "Nature Boy" and "The Woody Woodpecker Song," that summer's favorites, played constantly on the jukebox, and there was a deep ice cooler, into which you plunged your arm to fish out Hi-C or some other soda. The six alleys gleamed, echoing with the rumble of balls and crash of pins; and the bowlers would grimace, leap and posture as their turns came to perform. Lane 3 was best according to Chuck. Games cost fifty cents, you rented shoes, chose a ball to fit your fingers (we each had numbered favorites, which we sought) and hired or supplied a pin boy, whom you tipped. Occasionally Chuck worked as a pin boy, and once or twice, later, I tried, while he, Jack, Mom and Judy bowled. It was hard work. The balls were heavy; you had to clear the fallen pins and stick them into the overhead rack, then lift and send the ball down the return track with enough force to carry it up the alley and make it climb into the bowlers' rack, clunk against the other balls. Then you scrambled up the padded pit back, out of the way. Chuck's dream was to bowl a perfect 300, and one afternoon he claimed a 290. He would swing the ball back high in the air, until his arm went straight up, then come looping down with his approach steps, a powerful swoop, glide and release, and the ball would hook or slice as he wished and smash into the pins, sometimes for explosive strikes, sometimes for splits, sometimes sending pins leaping and spinning into adjacent alleys. He and Jack always scored over 200, while I rarely made 100 and was usually beaten by Judy and Mom.

The more Chuck and Judy grew involved with teenage friends, the more they dismissed me as Tag Along and left me on my own, or with Mom, or with my "friend," Chip, the only boy my age nearby, whom I never really liked but with whom I rode bikes, swam, explored, and hiked the easy trails, especially the mile around the lake.

Most sunny days, the family went swimming or boating, or both. The beach was small, but sandy, with the swimming area divided from the boating by a floating walkway, which joined a diving dock twenty-five yards out. The diving dock had high and low diving boards and a life guard stand. To the left were the boat sheds and docks, where Jack worked, connected to a series of changing rooms, like a triple row of outhouses, each with a bench, coat hooks and a mirror inside the door. We'd take turns changing, Mom and Judy emerging in their bathing suits and caps, and each door locked with a padlock, to which you kept the key. We were a family of good swimmers, reputably. At that summer's waterfront festival, Chuck won the men's butterfly, Judy the junior freestyle, and I came in third in the small-fry race. Jack and Chuck took part in the canoe jousts too, with Chuck jabbing a padded pole at the rival canoes, while Jack maneuvered with his paddle; but soon they were overturned.

With tackle boxes full of special lures, Jack and Chuck would row out to fish the lake for bass and pike. One memory of my going with them is of being offered one oar, which, when it dug into water, seemed to be pulling through sand; another is of growing restlessness, as we drifted and they fished. They warned me to sit still or my lightest movement would scare away the fish. More often, I went canoeing with Mom. The boatman (Jack, usually) would slide out a canoe, swing it off the dock into the water, put in paddles and a back rest, then help us in, as the canoe gave and rocked. If Judy came, she'd paddle on one side in front, I'd ride in the middle, and Mom paddled and steered on the other side in back. With Mom alone, I rode in the bow, trailing my hand, as she paddled first one side, then the other, and we glided away from the beachfront, out into the deep center of the lake. There would be just us, the water lapping, sky, breeze, distance, and the sun, and now and then the hotel launch might pass, leaving us rocking in its wash, or far off we'd see another canoe or sailboat passing. When the day grew hot, we'd head for a "cove" (another new word for me) along the shore, where pine boughs dipped over the water. The rocky bottom grew visible, then shallows, Mom shipped her paddle, and, holding or parting the branches, we slipped underneath, to eat our lunch, stretch out in the canoe and nap, eyes closed, canoe gently bobbing, swaying, and overhead the branches closing us from view.

In keeping with our family tradition of "creativity," when the hotel sponsored a little kids' costume party, I decided to go dressed as a television set, an idea as novel then as television itself. Judy helped me cut and paint a box, with a cellophane window, knobs that turned, and a wire hanger for an aerial, all of which I wore over my head and shoulders. At the party, I won first prize (did you make that? where'd you get the idea? what is it?), and had my picture taken for the Eaglesmere paper, face beaming from the screen.

Torrential rain kept us all in Buzz Fuzz one full day, reading, fly tying, playing card games, listening to the radio, or working on jigsaw puzzles. I'd heard the boys and Judy talk about other storms, other summers, when they had seen lightning "run down the street," something I could neither believe nor imagine, so as thunderclaps intensified and came instantaneously with lightning flashes, I kept my face to the window, holding aside a tasseled, crocheted curtain, and staring out into rain-slashed air. The gutters were pouring, hail pellets bouncing, when there came a flash and crash and I saw: the incandescent, dancing, jagged branch, like a neon scribble down the water-filled ruts out front; an instant, gone, leaving my eyes ringing from the flash as much as my ears and body from the noise.

That same afternoon, or one like it, perhaps after she had argued with Mom, Judy sat curled on the chaise in the parlor, beneath a reading lamp, and, staring off moodily, insisted that she had been an adopted child; she could never have been born into this family; but that I didn't have to worry, I wasn't adopted.

We crashed in heavy rain on the trip home, somewhere between La Porte and Harrisburg. The boys were an hour ahead in the Model A. I was riding in front and Judy in back, painting her nails, when Mom lost control on a curve, the car ran up an embankment into rose bushes, rolled over, and landed back on its wheels, facing forward. I remember the jolt, noise, and tumbling, then finding myself under the dashboard; a choir was singing (we joked later about thinking it was angels, before realizing that the radio had come on) and rain was drumming on the roof. Shaken and dazed herself, Mom demanded how we were, feeling us all over. She had hit her head and cut her arm, and Judy had sprained her wrist against the roof, but I was unhurt. Then Mom got out in the rain, climbed the embankment and disappeared to telephone from a nearby house. We were towed to a crossroads gas station, where after Mom called Dad and Dad had spoken to the mechanic, we waited all afternoon while they worked and banged on the car, up on a lift. We were back underway by nightfall. Jack and Chuck told us that they had skidded on the same curve, which was called "dead man's curve": and we agreed, repeating the words of the mechanic and policeman, that we'd been "very lucky."

During our time away ("the most enjoyable summer I can remember," Judy calls it in a Baldwin theme), Dad had a relapse. On into that fall, apparently, he was drinking again, involved with the girl still, and asking Mom a second time for a divorce, which she refused, all of which peaked by Thanksgiving. By then Jack had "flunked out" of Cornell too, and come back home, worried about Mom and the family. Dad told Mom that he was through with her, with Dr. Appel, everything; he was leaving, and had Jack drive him in town to the Warwick Hotel. Then a few hours later he called home and simply said, "Come get me."

The hospital bills show a second stay from Thanksgiving, 1948, through January, 1949, when Mom left for her second Bermuda trip. From Bermuda Mom wrote to Judy, "this time you must feel better having no Aunty Pink and Dad back in his own room again." Dried out, reconciled, he was staying with us, which I myself cannot remember. There is also a letter from Dad to Mom

"The one and only time he ever apologized to me," she said. It is on Judy's blue stationery with the Bloomingdale address. He writes:

Dearest:

I am sitting on the edge of Judy's bed and it is 5 a.m. I haven't been asleep. I don't know where you will be when this letter is handed to you. Maybe I will hand it to you myself, because I will be in Bermuda where you are. I hope you will forgive my barging in on you like this, but I couldn't wait until you returned to Wayne.

Kay, it has been a long, long detour, and I have been badly lost on the way, but I now feel that I have both feet on the main road for the rest of my life. I believe that I am finally the man you expected when you married me.

I hope I am not too late, because I love you with all of my heart, soul, and body. I want the chance to prove it to you "until death do us part."

John

P.S. I think maybe it was meant to happen this way to make a man out of me.

He had been in full analysis with Appel and shaken by an EKG, which showed brain damage. Despite his initial doubts, Appel was quite satisfied with Dad's progress and wired Mom in Bermuda on January 27: "Things fine. Very pleased last visit and trip. Don't discuss past considerations. Best wishes."

They bought the St. Davids house a few months later, as if to dramatize the new beginning and cut ties to the Bloomingdale past. Dad's cousin, Mahlin Rossiter, the carpenter, was working on the house by April and Alfred Reahm, the decorator, papering, painting and sanding floors in May. We moved in the fall, 1949, when I also started third grade, moving from the Primary to the Grammar school building, and riding my bike the mile to school, each way, or walking, since we still lived too close for me to qualify for the school bus.

I am eight.

At this point my memories of my father begin.

Differences

THERE ARE NO MOVIES after we left Bloomingdale; instead, the years at St. Davids are documented by sepia Polaroid stills (the self-developing Land Camera was Dad's pride), by my own and Judy's box camera snapshots; and later, by 35 mm slides as I became a shutterbug. A succession of Judy's snapshots shows me on the boat dock at Eaglesmere, in snow outside the Bloomingdale barn, and finally, leaning on our 1948 Buick in the St. Davids driveway, dressed in my studded denim cowboy outfit and brandishing a rubber knife. Leaves at my feet show the season as fall.

I can't remember the upheaval of moving, though I can visiting the house and being shown my room to be, which was in back, up spiraling stairs from the kitchen; and which once had been a two-room nursery for twins, but then had had the dividing wall removed, so only a plastered-over ridge remained in the ceiling. Together Mom and I chose a mostly green, scotch plaid pattern for the wallpaper; the trim paint would be mint green. Over and over, I heard, the house had cost thirty thousand dollars, but then we had to put in a lot of work not only on the interior, but in roofing, painting, landscaping and yard work. Mom had a wall knocked out in the kitchen, to include what had been a butler's pantry in the larger room as a "breakfast nook." A sun porch off the living room had been uncovered, and we had windowed walls put in permanently and radiators connected, so that it became part of the inside of the house. The same size, roughly, as Bloomingdale, the house was mostly brick; including the sun porch, there were seven rooms, a lavatory, a maid's bathroom, and a central hallway downstairs; four bedrooms, a hallway, and three baths on the second; and two bedrooms, a bath, and the attic on the third. A two-car garage was in back. And down a steep, enclosed stairway from the hall, there was a tiled "playroom" in the basement, with dark, massive beams overhead, a stone fireplace, and wooden bar, like a sales counter, complete with four bar stools in front, shutters that closed across the bar, and a sink, spigot and wine cupboards in back. Then, from the bottom of the stairs, through another door, was the unfinished basement—with hot water heaters, the oil burner, oil tanks, and huge boiler—and then the "laundry room," where a cage-like, slatted cabinet collected laundry from a chute that originated with a little door in the second-floor closet (playing hide and seek, I would climb into this cabinet, which was sturdy enough to support my weight, and sometimes I even squirmed out of sight into the square duct of the chute itself). Here also was Mom's big Bendix washer and dryer, an old stone double sink, with a washboard, and a sump pump, buried in a well in the floor and covered over with a wooden box. And here, the cellar door and rickety steps up the stone well outside, to wooden bulk-head doors that locked from inside with a wooden bar. In heavy storms, we soon learned, the basement filled with as much as a foot of muddy water, so we had irrigation gutters put in along the playroom walls, graded so that a golf ball would start at the fireplace, roll around, then disappear into a pipe, which joined another pipe from a different direction in the furnace room floor. Here you had to lift a drain grate to save the ball before it continued into the laundry room and dropped into the sump pump well.

A row of bells, from sleigh-type to hammer-on-dome, had to be disconnected over the kitchen doorway because we kids would tease Mom, Dad, and Anna by pushing buzzers in the dining room, living room and master bedroom upstairs, causing one to ring and be mistaken for the doorbell. There was also a speaking tube in the master bedroom wall, as on a ship, which had once connected to the kitchen, but now was defunct.

Our driveway, dividing around a large, islanded maple at the corner of Chamounix Road and St. Davids Avenue, curved down, sloping, like a private street (it was sometimes mistaken for one) past the front door, with a branching spur back to the kitchen door and garage, then up and out at the eastern corner of our property on St. Davids Avenue. Both entrances were flanked by brick gateposts with lanterns on top, which looked like kerosene lanterns, but were electric really, controlled from a switch in our foyer, and the glass panes of which proved easy targets for vandals. Ten or so additional brick posts bordered the street sides of our yard at intervals, with a five-foot-high spiked fence (each iron bar a spear) running between them. The planting along the fence included high shade trees, evergreens, and a dense cover of tree-like rhododendrons that closed our house and yard from view. On the upper terrace of the front yard, the rhododendrons had been extended to form a thicket, with a tunnel-like stepping stone path winding from one side of the yard to the other, and then, midway, on either side, with branching paths that emerged in a grassy plateau bordered by flower beds and azalea bushes. Below this, a patch of front lawn was bordered by a crescent-shaped stone wall, with an elaborate fountain and fish pond built up in the middle and matching steps on either side leading to the raised garden. Viewed from our front door, this all was symmetrical. The fountain itself was a crescent-shaped stone enclosure. Its back formed a low wall on the upper tier, while in front water poured from a basin and spilled into a turquoise hemisphere. Originally, this pond drained by underground pipe to a second pond in the rear of the side yard, which once had formed the centerpiece of a rose arbor, with benches, and again, with walks; all of which we had cleared out, and the pond filled in, leaving an expanse of lawn for play.

In front, the house had a small brick porch, ten by fifteen feet, with two white columns supporting the corners of a triangular overhang at the third floor. At its base each column was a yard or so in diameter, like a tree; and on either side were southern magnolia trees—a breed different from our magnolias at Bloomingdale, skinny, with sticky blossoms and no good for climbing. On a heavy chain from the porch overhang, a porch light lantern hung. We'd have to crawl out Dad's bathroom window to a false balcony, right over the front door, to reach for the porch light and change its bulb.

Overall, house and yard suggested, scaled down for a single acre, a little Monticello; it even had its own name "Bonalton," chiseled on the gateposts, which we covered over with wooden plaques reading "Henry." In fact, the house had been built as an outpost of "Walmarthon," the Walton estate, the entrance to which was half a mile or so down Chamounix and to the right.

Our first Christmas at St. Davids, we set up the tree in the living room. Chuck took charge of stringing the lights and decorating it with tinsel, allowing Judy and me to hang the other decorations under his supervision. Jack was too busy to take part. On Christmas Eve, I was sent to bed early, and woken after midnight, "when Santa had come." I still believed in Santa Claus, whose jolly-faced picture we had cut from magazines and pasted up at Bloomingdale, who had called me on the phone or down the chimney, and on whose lap I had sat at Strawbridge's.

A Polaroid snapshot, possibly our first, shows us posing as the happy family in front of the tree, but with me in a pout, Mom, Jack, and Judy glancing at me sidewise, and Dad, seated next to and over me on the piano seat, glowering. I had just been told off, with Dad's raised voice, for arguing with Judy; if I couldn't be nicer, he was going to take away all my presents for good. No one was on my side.

By the time of St. Davids, both Mom and Dad's hair had grayed, which gave the colored portrait of Mom in the medallion special meaningfor me. At St. Davids, it was kept open, hanging in its velvet case, on the living room desk. It haunted me to see her with dark brown hair, as dark as Judy's, and more beautiful and younger than I had ever known her.

At eight, I had no grasp of the uneasy compact between Mom and Dad, and between my brothers and sister and Dad, in accordance with Mom's counseling.

She granted him his dignity. My own sense of Dad involved respect for his power and fear of his disapproval. But I also sensed that he was demoted somehow at home; that he had surrendered to rules and wisdoms beyond him; and that he seemed distant and withdrawn, and different from other, normal fathers, such as my best friend John's farm-laboring father or my other friend Kit Wilkes' younger executive dad.

He was a business man. He worked in the world. He wore starched shirts, formal suits, silk ties, socks with garters, and wing-tipped shoes, all of which had to be kept in ready by Mom: shirts from the cleaners folded in his bureau drawers, boxer underwear likewise, socks matched and rolled, ties and suits neatly hung in his mirrored closet, shoes neatly arranged in a rack. Mom's job and ours was to support him with domestic order and to launch him each day, if not like Achilles in armor, then like an actor going on stage. When he returned home, he carried a briefcase bulging with mail.

We held dinner for him. We ate together around a formal table, starting with grace (though Jack mockingly reduced this to, "We thank you, Lord, for what we eat and us that eats it"). After dinner, Dad went to his sagging chair in the living room and read his mail, scattering papers on the floor for us to pick up, even though a wastebasket stood beside him. Later, he went upstairs to change into pajamas and watch TV in the master bedroom. Weekends, he played golf with his regular foursome and, when he returned, slept on the living room couch snoring in deep crescendos. He had his set patterns and habits, to which we deferred.

He was overweight. He was a chain smoker and suffered from emphysema, so that each cigarette led inevitably to an eye-bulging, red-faced coughing fit, which would last a full minute, and which we were supposed to ignore. If we looked concerned or said anything, he would wave us away. A carton of Luckies was the most reliable birthday or father's day gift. We also gave him gifts related to golf, and mildly mocking gifts related to weight, such as a yard-long shoe horn.

I feared him as the ultimate punisher, and when I'd been bad, I would plead with Mom not to tell him. Even though he never touched me, he would shout; and my brothers told stories of his whipping them with a razor strop at my age. In fact, the strop itself still hung in our upstairs closet for no other use than whipping, since he and the boys shaved with electric razors.

Mom intended (I realize now) to shelter me from the conflicts and the shame of his alcoholic years. Jack, Chuck and Judy had each been hurt in different ways by those years, but I had been spared because of my age, and she actively solicited their help in raising me. While I grew up surrounded by their love, the gap in our ages also made them more like older cousins sometimes, from a different family, and with experiences and memories that I could never share.

When I was nine or ten, Mom did try to explain Dad's illness to me. Thereafter I understood "Alcoholism" as something shameful and frightening, like leprosy. For Dad, one taste of anything with alcohol and he would get sick and turn into a different person. Shortly afterwards, I was alone watching TV in the basement when Lon Chaney Jr.'s *The Wolf Man* came on. I ran from the room when the good and kindly Lon Chaney Jr. character couldn't help changing, growing hair and fangs; then I bravely went back for another look, another.

For a while, after we had moved, I was scared alone in my room, remote from everyone else; awakened by nightmares or by violent thunderclaps, I would find my way down the hall and slip into bed with Dad, whose bed was closet to the master bedroom door. The first few times were okay, but then he and Mom told me to stop; that I was too old for this.

I don't remember doing much with Dad until we had golf to share, or washing the cars (he'd supervise, perched on a kitchen stool out of hose range, while Judy and I soaped, rinsed and chamoised). As a family, of course, we did some things regularly together, including the Sunday drive, trips to the factory, visits to Aunt Kitty and Uncle John, or to Nana Henry, dinners at the golf club, church (for a while early on, then hardly ever), and our nightly dinner, six around the table.

He came to the rescue when a bird, once, then a bat, once, got into Judy's room through the unscreened top half of her window, which she sometimes left open. She was hysterical, as hysterical as the stock female at the sight of a mouse, and scared of the bat getting into her hair. Dad put on an old felt hat to protect his own balding hair and sallied into her room in pajamas and wielding a broom. The bird escaped back out the window finally. But the bat he managed to hit, daze, and then kill.

We had one rare outing together after I'd become tenderfoot scout. I was 11 or 12. The scouts had a father-and-son baseball game and, since Dad had been a catcher in his Haverford and Cornell days, he was playing catcher on our side and seeming to enjoy himself. I was too, so much so that I was surprised later to look up and miss him. Someone else, Mr. Dawson, was catching and Dad had disappeared. Mom told me later at home (he himself never explained this to me), that he had split his pants when he crouched down to catch, and, mortified in the face of the mothers, had fled home. But the point, she insisted then, was that he'd tried. He hadn't wanted to leave and had felt awful that he'd had to, but he'd had no choice.

Mom sent Dr. Appel a picture of our Henry Christmas, 1950. A Polaroid taken by Chuck, it shows us gathered happily in front of a tree on the sun porch (I wear a rubber tulip on my lapel, which had a hidden squeeze bulb that made a worm pop out). Dr. Appel wrote back: "It certainly is a different kind of picture than we would have had a couple of years ago. You certainly should be proud of all you have done. I don't know anyone who has shown the patience and tolerance and wisdom that you have shown."

He asked to see her, and she began to research and draft speeches for him, an avocation that grew into the consuming, full-scale effort of helping to ghostwrite a book with him, entitled *Adam to Atom: What Next? It's Up To You.* An impossible cross between bastardized Toynbee and Appel's own home-spun, Freudian psychology, it attempted no less than to psychoanalyze the species "man," as a personality revealed through all human history. This began with man's primal drives in his struggle for survival ("primitive man: 1,000,000 years of savagery"), went on to describe man's revolt from and control of primitive impulses and feelings ("civilized man's controls: 7,000 years"), man's creation of family, community, science, art, history, industry, and then the threat of "Breaks-through of the Primitive in Daily Life." Hope for the species in the Atomic Age lay in self-analysis, -recognition, and -understanding—just as it had for Dad as an individual alcoholic— and in the sublimation of primitive emotions.

In retrospect now, as I turn through the unpublished manuscript, it seems to me more therapy for her than a project that Appel himself intended seriously for publication, but for years the collaboration offered Mom some longed-for connection with the public world and a way to serve, commensurate with her intelligence and ambition. She borrowed articles and books from Appel, got her own card to the Haverford College Library, took endless files of notes. Though the back room, off the kitchen, was her "den," where she also kept her canvases and paints, she worked mostly on the sun porch, using Jack's portable typewriter until, one Christmas, Dad bought her a large office model of her own, along with a typing table.

Jack, as oldest brother, was a hero to each of us, especially to Judy and me, for whom he filled in as father. Nineteen when we moved, he had established his identity as a woodsman, hunter, and mechanic—these were his passions (and subversive to the decorum of our social class and to the pretense of Main Line propriety)—and "mechanic," given our family's expectations, translated into the loftier goal of being an engineer, especially an aircraft designer or an architect. He had tried Cornell with that idea (mixed with the prospect, always, of working with and succeeding Dad at the factory), but then had quit and come home, to Bloomingdale, after a month or two, to be there for Mom.

When we moved, he was working as a mechanic for Hale's Buick, where we bought our cars; he had also gone into business for himself, renting a shop behind the Buick garage and next to a bicycle repair shop, on Lancaster Avenue, and restoring old cars. Girls had gone out of his life, apparently, with Lou Kirk. He and Chuck lived on the third floor at St. Davids, in garret bedrooms with slanting ceilings and dormers, and with the third floor landing and a bathroom between them. I could see all the way down to the first floor hallway as I peered over their banister.

His first car had been a '33 Chevy coupe, which he'd bought when he was fifteen from a man in North Wayne; it had a cracked cylinder and couldn't run, so he'd talked the man down to forty dollars and bought it with his egg and birthday money (we annually got one dollar for each year we were old). Dad towed the car home, where Jack took it apart, guided by a Chilton's manual and equipped with a five-dollar set of wrenches. Then Dad took the cylinder head into the factory to see if Phil Shore, the main mechanic, could weld it, but Shore had found a good one in a junkyard for five dollars instead. Jack put it on, and the car was running. Then Dad gave him two new tires for his sixteenth birthday, he got his driver's license, plates, and drove the car to school for a while, then sold it for two hundred dollars. Judy and I loved riding together in the rumble seat, out in the wind. Also it was under the rumble seat cushions one day, when Jack was cleaning, that he found a dress saber. Since the hilt had an anchor design, we guessed that it was from Annapolis, where the car's first owner had graduated. This sword, in any case, would join our family exotica. I patrolled the yard at St. Davids with it against vandals on mischief night, and later took it to college, where it grew blackened from shishkabob cookouts.

The Chevy's successor was a 1919 Cadillac touring car, which he'd found through Ted Brooks, an old car buff, who was friends with Jack's "grease monkey crowd" from Haverford. It had been listed for auction at an estate in eastern Maryland as "up on blocks, only 7,000 miles, but needs work." Jack could only offer his two hundred dollars, but Brooks went down and got it for one hundred and ninety six and brought it back to Wayne, where they took it apart first at Brooks' place, then towed it to Bloomingdale. Soon it was joined by a 1918 Cadillac hearse that another man, a car restorer, who was connected with the Antique Automobile Club, had heard of in a New Jersey junkyard. Jack bought the hearse for twenty-five dollars and towed it home in the wee hours through Philadelphia, no lights, no brakes. Our family joke was that now Jack owned two Cadillacs, while someday "owning a Cadillac" remained one of Dad's obsessions and definitions of success. After cannibalizing the hearse, Jack had the touring car running reliably, passed inspection, drove it to Haverford, then to Eaglesmere, entered it in shows, and kept it at St. Davids, along with an Indian motorcycle and a model A pickup.

The Caddy, as we called it, restored to "better than new," sat high on oversized, spoke wheels; you climbed on a running board, some eighteen inches wide, to open one of two crescent-shaped doors (two for each side) with suitcase-like handles, and stepped up again to settle in ribbed leather seats, front and back, that sat four across. Also in back were two jump seats, which lay flat on the carpeted floor and when you lifted them, like trapdoors, unfolded and snapped into place. He gave rides in the driveway, the leather top folded back, with its metal struts, and all the car gleaming—from the dark green body, which he had sanded and honed, primed, and then laid on layer after layer of paint (I had watched and smelled the paint from his spray at the shop), to lantern-like sidelights, to the oversize headlamps and big hood, with the louvered windshield that opened out, and the temperature gauge on the top of the radiator. The Caddy started with a crank too heavy for me to budge, but after a turn or two by Jack, the motor would catch and the car would shake with a throaty chugging. He taught Chuck to drive it: adjusting the spark on the steering wheel first; then working the clutch and brake, which, along with the gearshift, were upright levers; then backing up lurchingly or going forward.

The shop as a venture followed from owning the Caddy, from meeting a collector named Bob Laurens at an Antique Automobile Club meet in 1948, and from needing an answer to the question: "what next after Cornell?" His work at Hale was for a wage; the shop was a passion. Laurens, a Main Line travel agent who lived near Bloomingdale, wanted to buy the Caddy, but Jack had said no, and instead helped him to find and restore a 1911 Model T Ford. Both Laurens and Dotty, his wife, who were a childless couple roughly Mom's and Dad's age, were particularly taken by Jack, while also sharing his interest in cars. Dotty was heiress to the Fleer Double Bubble Gum fortune, so money was no object, and having sold the Model T, they went on to locate and buy a 1910 Matheson, the only one left in existence. This became Jack's first project in the shop and took seven months to finish, with Laurens searching for parts everywhere and watching over Jack's shoulder each step. The result was a masterpiece that went on to take first place in every national show that Laurens entered, while Laurens himself became an important figure in the Antique Automobile Club, known for researching old cars and bringing together the pioneer manufacturers for the first time in forty or fifty years.

As Jack saw Laurens (writing about him for a night school composition class and doubtless projecting his own feelings), the man had never finished college or become known as expert in anything, but having married a wealthy woman, had felt that he must excel in something, that "he mustn't remain a parasite." Restoring the Matheson and then becoming a leading authority on the history of the automobile had become that something.

Dotty Laurens, meanwhile, was "a teaser, typically Main Line"; Jack went into their house one day for a coke and she was walking around in her lingerie, making him uncomfortable, so he'd jumped up and run out, sorry, sorry, and avoided her from then on.

Business grew as word of Jack's skill got around. He began full-time and hired his friend, Livy Morris, as a helper. They restored a Stanley Steamer for a museum; a collector's 1909 Stanley Roadster ("a real mess"); then the original Pike's Peak Mountain Wagon, a ten-seater bus made by Stanley; then a 1915 Franklin. As for the Caddy, he sold that for eighteen hundred dollars finally and bought a 1931 Model A coupe that he restored in order to drive. He closed the shop in 1950, however, because it had, in fact, grown too much—he would have to hire more help, get more space— and that was not what he wanted for a future. In addition, the bicycle repairman in the shop next door, who commanded a tank company in the Norristown National Guard, had talked him into joining, and now the Korean conflict was heating up and they expected the Guard to be called soon to active duty.

Meanwhile, he worked for Dad in the factory, as each son would, with the open question whether he wanted to learn the business and take the factory on as a future. He worked as a mechanic, keeping the enrobers, moguls, packaging and other machines going and looking for ways to improve on them, but the long-time factory manager, Spencer, who had helped Dad through his worst times, proved to be an obstacle, objecting over and over again, at each suggestion, you can't do this or that. Also Jack had an accident. At home, we got the emergency phone call and only saw him later; somehow his hand had gotten into the gears on an enrober and he had lost part of his little finger, though they had tried to save it. I felt the shock that this could happen to one of us, to Jack, the outraged why, and then something like grief, that he would be mutilated now forever. He came home with his right hand in a bandage and sling, and when that came off a few weeks later, what he had was a nailess stump. He'd lost one third of the finger, from the first joint. He gave up on the factory shortly after, though not because of the accident, but because of the National Guard camp upstate in the summer of 1951, where he was overcome by dust in cleaning an old POW barracks and hospitalized with a severe asthma attack. He had suffered from asthma for most of his life, coughing as violently as Dad, a long, dry, whooping cough, and wheezing for breath. But in recent years hadn't been bothered much; perhaps, the doctors thought, because paint from the shop had been coating his lungs. But now the paint had worn off. X-rays showed lung spots, and the Army doctors told him he was close to getting tuberculosis. He was given an honorable discharge, and told that the only place he could live would be in the dry Rockies, anywhere between Albuquerque and Cheyenne. So, thinking of colleges, he borrowed Dad's car and drove out to explore, starting with Albuquerque and working north. He decided, finally, on Colorado A&M (later Colorado State University) in Ft. Collins, where he would study engineering starting with spring semester. He made arrangements, packed his Ford coupe, and left home on Christmas Day, 1951.

Jack's passion for guns, Mom thought, began with Gail Borden, Aunt Peggy's first husband, who had been a big game hunter, and who, when Jack had visited their house at age eight, had shown Jack a whole room with glass-covered cabinets filled with rifles, drawers with handguns, and walls hung with trophies. He had let Jack handle and help clean the guns. Beyond that was the glamour of guns in the westerns, G-men stories, and later, the war.

About the same time, Jack found Dad's boyhood rifle, a single-shot .22, in the back of a closet in the house in Boston, and as he says "adopted it," though one day he dropped it and a piece of the stock split off, which Dad nailed back on, telling him to keep hands off. When Mom and Dad moved to Wayne, Nana and Grandpop had the Malvern farm; and in addition to the .22, Grandpop gave him a 410 shotgun, both of which Uncle John taught him to shoot. He and Chuck had their BB guns. By fourteen, after Grandpop moved to Ithan, Jack target shot and hunted rabbit there; while at home, since this was during Dad's bad times, he slept with the .22 ready under his bed. At sixteen, he and his friends, Ned Lodge, Livy, Bill Koeller, drove up to Eaglesmere deer hunting, and he shot a six-point buck, which they brought home bloody on the fender of Lodge's Pontiac. Jack mounted the antlers on a plaque; the meat went into Howard's locker at Espenshades.

Always Jack conveyed a sense of gravity, honor, and respect for the rules of hunting, from getting the license, to wearing red, to never pointing a gun at another person, loaded or unloaded, unless you meant to use it, to carrying your shotgun broken as you walked, and propping your gun against the fence as you climbed over. Opposed to the proper way, was the way of hackers and dilettantes, who lacked any true passion or feel not only for guns and hunting, but for cars, motorcycles, boats, horses, fishing, or planes. Guns were for hunting; hunting was for eating and the contest with the animals; target practice was for knowing how to use your gun and hit what you aimed for, for clean, humane kills. And guns were to be cared for as machinery, oiled, taken apart, and cleaned.

The only local gunsmith was Hans Roeder, who ran a car repair garage, with the gun shop in back. During the war, Dad took Jack there when the .22 had a bolt broken and the 410 a broken firing pin. Roeder fixed both guns, Jack got to know him, and later he'd let Jack mould bullets and reload ammo for customers. Roeder and his wife belonged to a vaudeville shooting team that included the world's fastest pistol shot. Roeder would tell Jack to put an unlit match in the shop's bullet trap and then he'd light it from twenty-five feet with one shot. In return for the apprentice work, he gave Jack two old guns, a muzzle-loading musket and a breech-loading Calvary rifle, the first to load with a shell. Jack had them both shooting at St. Davids. I came with him to Roeder's when I was ten and Roeder himself in his seventies, hunched over and gnomish, in a cluttered basement shop, like a cobbler, except instead of shoes, guns were everywhere hanging from nails: revolvers, automatics, Lugers. Besides the guns, which had me wide-eyed, I was impressed that Jack sought him out and spoke to him as a craftsman, a master, regardless of the man's age, class, education, or the dinginess of the place. This was a point with Jack, in contrast to Dad; talent was what made people special to Jack.

I felt privileged to go shooting with Jack, or to watch him shoot. We went to Buddy Huggler's farm once—Buddy was more a shooting than a grease monkey buddy—where Jack let me shoot his new .22, modeled after a Garand carbine, with a clip; indeed, to shoot for my first time ever, except with BB guns. We were back in the woods, aiming for tin cans, and I fell in love with the smell of the gun, the oil, its weight, the noise and kick, the acrid gunpowder smell afterwards, and the kicking out of empty, shiny shells. Another place Jack shot was a quarry back off Route 202, near Valley Forge, which supplied gravel for the construction of the Pennsylvania Turnpike. We drove there one Saturday, when I was in fifth grade, to shoot his .44 Civil War ball-and-cap revolver, which was in mint condition and he'd bought somewhere for twenty-five dollars. He'd had to mould ball-shaped bullets for it and buy caps;

would have to tamp powder, a ball, and a wad into each of six chambers, then fit a percussion cap for each on the back of the cylinder; and when he'd shot it experimentally at home with just the powder and wad, it had gone off like a parade-ground cannon. At the quarry, we had just started down the edge and were getting ready to shoot, when Jack heard shots and saw some guys ("kids," he called them later) jumping around on the rocks in the distance. "What are they, shooting at each other?" he said, and told me stay down and in back of one boulder, and when one of the guys saw us and came over, Jack met with him out in the open, then came back. "They must be on something," he said. "They're hopheads, shooting at each other for kicks. Kid asked me, did I want to join in? So I showed him the Colt and told him, when I shoot, I shoot to hit something. He took one look at this cannon, and said, 'okay, okay,' and took off. But we don't want to stay around." And back in the pickup: "They're crazies," he repeated. "One guy had a .22 pistol; the other had a .32 automatic or something."

John Barnett was trading visits with me two or three times a week at the farm and St. Davids (where our TV was an attraction); and, at ten, we had moved up from cap pistols to BB guns. Mr. Barnett supervised John's shooting a .22 at groundhogs in the pasture sometimes, and had drilled him in a code of responsibility, sportsmanship, and safety around the farm that was similar to Jack's. Nevertheless, for sheer temptation, John and I managed to break the code, shooting at each other with BB's, as the crazies had at the quarry, for a kind of elevated cowboy play. We kept 300 feet apart and wore leather jackets, so the BB's, if they hit, wouldn't hurt. John decided to quit, however, because my new plastic rifle, with a peep sight, carried farther and truer than his old Red Ryder, and he kept getting hit and badly stung.

At home one day, alone, tired of target shooting, and with some meanness and thrill of the forbidden, wanting to kill something, I decided to shoot a robin. I lay prone and waited, just outside the rho-dodendron bushes, where one had fluttered and was hopping in the leaves; took careful aim, not six feet away, fired, and had killed it. Immediately, I felt the shock and shame of killing, for the first time. The bird had dropped right over, like that, no fluttering or strug-gle. I hid it under leaves. No one would know. And yet for all my wishing I hadn't done it, it was unalterably done, a shameful, un-sporting, pointless kill, which haunted me that night and long after.

Our first year at St. Davids was Chuck's last at Haverford; he grad-uated in 1950 and left for his turn at Cornell that fall.

All along, he had wanted to be a doctor; ever since, years be-fore, he also had shot a bird, a catbird, with Jack's .22, and broken its wing, then captured it, set the wing with popsicle splints, fed the bird with an eyedropper and finally set it free, healed. Mom had encouraged his ambition, and Dr. Truxel had let him follow around on house calls.

His junior year at Haverford, he had been playing baseball, as a catcher—his sumptuous leather mask, with its face cage and green visor, and his round, lovingly oiled glove with its deep pocket would linger on as relics—when he had reached up with his bare right hand to catch a fast ball and smashed his middle finger. They took him to the emergency room at Bryn Mawr Hospital, where a Dr. Bill Parker was on call; and, while Parker despaired of trying to straighten the finger and said they'd have to amputate, Mom, who had come down, insisted: "No, this boy wants to be a doc-tor; this is a surgeon's hand; you have to save it!" Parker went ahead and had reassembled the finger and put it in a cast, with which Chuck, I remember, would rap me on the head at Bloom-ingdale. At best they thought the bones would fuse, and Parker was ecstatic, when, six weeks later, Chuck proved able to slip off the cast, his fingers having shrunk, and to wiggle and close the fin-ger normally (he had, in fact, been using and exercising it for some weeks). From this point on, Parker and Chuck became friends; Parker helped him get a job in the cast room at Bryn Mawr; let him wash up, stand in, and observe operations, then help with them. So at sixteen, Chuck had his first try on a patient: Okay, your turn. And Chuck: I think I have to cut more here. Parker: No. And then Parker had shown him how to reach in, around, and pull out an appendix. Parker had been a drinker, like Dad; and at night would come into surgery half-drunk, then call Chuck to come help, and in fact, says Chuck, to operate for him.

This was not discussed or advertised at home, to my memory, as Chuck's exploits in medical school would be later. There were no dinner table accounts; no debates I overheard with Mom, no mocking from Judy. No shocked: How could he let you do that? Or concern, in the wake of Dad's treatment, about the surgeon as alcoholic; no legal concerns. No visible study on Chuck's part from borrowed medical books.

What was discussed were Chuck's sports (wrestling, swimming, and golf, all at Haverford), crafts elevated to an art (fly-tying, model trains, woodworking, drawing with a continuous line), and social life (music, dancing, parties, girls—including a crush on Doris Day, whose records he listened to over and over). In contrast to Jack, he drank, dated, was a stylish dresser, with buck-white or two-toned shoes, and taught and practiced jitter-bug steps with Judy and with Mom, and had entered on his prodigal, rakehell phase.

Once at Cornell, he pledged Pi Kappa Alpha and second semester moved from the dorms into the fraternity house, where he built a new room for himself and a roommate in the attic. We drove to visit him there, either for Homecoming, or to pick him up in June, and he showed us up a ladder, through a trapdoor, into his room. He also introduced us to some frat brothers downstairs, playing cards. That Christmas he had been home working on his pledge paddle, using my wood burning kit, model airplane "dope," and various carving tools and gouges. The result, exceeding its occasion, was an elaborately carved fraternity seal, along with his name and his pledging brother's, painted in color, varnished, finely sanded, and re-varnished. He told me that the paddles were for initiation, where the brothers hit the pledges with them as hard as they could. I hefted the thick paddle, thought of myself grown up, and remembered Mom's and Dad's stories of hazing at Cornell in their day—the pledge who had been tied on the tracks of a deserted railroad spur, and then a train had come and killed him. Chuck said not to worry; it was tough, but he'd get through it; and I'd get through it too, when I had to. Everybody did.

Actually, fraternity life proved Chuck's downfall; at least, by family verdict. He floundered in a chemistry class, for which he wasn't prepared, and meanwhile gambled, played bridge, and socialized. By his third semester, he flunked out. He returned home in some degree of disgrace and chagrin. Chuck, the genius, who had seen his own I.Q. scores and who haughtily claimed they were over 160 and he could do anything, had failed. No Henrys would carry on the tradition at Cornell.

That spring, he began work in the factory, mainly in bookkeeping and sales (thereby taking his first real look at the business as a personal prospect); he kept on at the factory as he took summer school at Haverford College; then he transferred to Franklin and Marshall in Lancaster in the fall of 1952, where he would graduate as a History major in June, 1954, just as the Korean War ended.

With Jack gone, Chuck was resident big brother for Judy and me for most of 1952; then during his F&M days he was home some weekends, but Mom grew critical of his socializing there too. She wrote to Jack (these and other letters Jack must have given back to her, for they are among those she saved):

> Am furious at Chuck . . . He did not come home this past weekend, nor did he call to say he was going elsewhere. We called there but they did not know where he was or when he would return. Last night, Monday, called again: no answer even late at night. Sent him his weekly food money and wrote him to call

when he received it, so we MAY find out something tonight. Some irresponsibility that he must overcome if he ever is to become a medical man. I have a notion that he cut classes Saturday and went up to Cornell for the Dartmouth game weekend . . . Anyway I'm mad with him . . .

He lived off campus in an apartment. He'd also bought a 1946 Ford sedan in Lancaster, black, "with a lousy engine" (recalls Jack, until Jack, back one vacation, had set Chuck up with a mechanic in Wayne, who had put in a rebuilt engine, and from then on it was fine). Chuck used to drive me to school or to the golf club in it. He took great pride in the car, in the upholstery and the radio, and lovingly simonized the exterior.

For a while, Mom slept in the master bedroom with Dad. They had twin beds and shared its bathroom. But then she moved across the hall into the guest room—"Temporarily," she said, "because of Dad's snoring." Soon the move proved permanent. The guest room dresser and closet held all her clothes, and the bathroom grew cluttered with her toiletries. She has denied my perception since, but at the time I had no sense of physical affection between my parents. A memory from when I was eleven even suggests my discomfort with her loneliness. She had a backache and asked me to rub on Ben-Gay. She lay facedown on her guest room bed. As she told me to rub harder, up under her brassiere strap and down her back to the top of her buttocks, where she had loosened her skirt, I felt queasy and told her I wanted to stop. "Please," she said, "just rub it in. That feels so good." But then she realized my aversion. "Thank you. Go on, I'm sorry I had to ask you. But there's no one else home to help."

Judy moving through these years would make her mark at Baldwin—academically, in English; creatively in writing and in art; and athletically, after a try at lacrosse, in swimming, and in water ballet. Her social life involved some crushes, few dates, and centered mainly on her Baldwin schoolmates, who shared in these activities, and in the summers, on the Martin's Dam swim team, where she became a star, working tirelessly with an older coach, Jules Provost, who would later teach me Science at Radnor, and who served, according to Mom, as one of several "surrogate fathers" for her.

She wrote to Jack, shortly after he left in 1952, about Dad (she was in 11th grade): "I just picked up this letter again. It is now morning and I am determined to say everything I can possibly think of NOW and get it mailed. . . . This past weekend Mother and Daddy entertained some week-end guests, the Goodlaws. It is the first time that Daddy has let himself or Mother entertain since Dee was born. The experience was good for him and a welcome break in routine for Mother. . . . Poor daddy. I have gotten to the point where I have no feelings but pity and disgust for him. He must live the most unsatisfying empty life with no real interest beyond his own welfare. I used to think I really hated him, but he is so pathetically like a little child, weak, and helpless, that I couldn't hate him. It would be horrible to be a man physically, and practically a baby mentally. It sounds silly, but if you could see how he craves pampering, and nearly has a tantrum when things cross him, or how he frets and worries over every little thing— . . . I really shouldn't be writing stuff like this. Quite unchristian and very childish. Nevertheless, I do feel this way about the old monster. . . . I've often wondered if you really hated him. I think you did for he nearly ruined you. I, fortunately, missed almost all the sordidness. . . . Good lord, what a depressing subject to waste time writing about—Please excuse me—."

Like Jack, Judy hated debutantes and coming out parties (wanted none for herself, mocked the girl next door, who did have one), and Main Line society in general.

Judy's classmates, some ten of them from Baldwin, invaded our privacy that summer in order to paint our spiked iron fence. They were raising money for their class, the fence was flaking and rusting, and Dad would have to pay somebody to do the job, so he took them on as a good cause. The painting was no small task. First each section had to be scraped and cleaned with sandpaper and steel wool; then an orange lead primer was put on; and after that had dried, two coats of black paint. We had gallons and gallons of both the orange and black paint. We had spotted tarpaulins and newspapers; we had dozens of brushes soaking in turpentine. The girls would arrive on humid summer days, hazy days, troop in for lunch, for the bathroom, and be out there nine to five, their cars parked in the driveway. And Judy, of course, worried whether we impressed them all as normal, sociable and relaxed; likewise, she worried whether the girls, with their loud portable radios playing, their cigarettes and their chatter, might raise our neighbors' eyebrows or prove offensive to Mom.

One friend, a tom-boy, Kathleen McLellan, had a jeep. Judy herself never did manage to learn to drive, though Jack had tried teaching her in his old pick-up, back and forth, in our driveway.

At Baldwin, they told Judy to work on her posture. She slouched, had curvature of the spine, and needed to improve her walk. She was to balance a book on top of her head, and of course, we all joined in to imitate her, as she practiced walking, sitting, and rising, all with a volume of the *Britannica* on her head.

Judy's favorite thinking place was the Walton Estate, where she would go alone or sometimes take me, out through a path in the dense woods behind our back neighbors' houses. By this path, which I retraced with John, often, when he visited, Walton's was ten minutes or so away—you waded and pushed through overgrown bushes, ferns, and low hanging branches, with dankness, cobwebs, and with shade from the branches interlocking and arching above, while woodpeckers hammered, echoing, and cicadas whirred. You'd come out, then, following a creek, above the smaller of two ponds, set in the estate's open expanse of lawn, gardens, driveways and walks. A big white house, lived in, was to the left, far off were the gatehouse and wall, and far to your right, the castle-like main mansion, deserted now. Judy's spot was at the spillway from the upper, main pond where a picturesque waterwheel was attached to a stone cottage, a mill, actually, with a wooden door and tilting tile roof, and inside, through a mesh of antique gears, a mill stone crunching round and round on a pedestal. Though miniature, the waterwheel and mill were "out of a story book," an illustration brought to life, say, from the Brothers Grimm, and all the more appealing for being deserted and in disrepair. There were flat boulders to sit on, where water poured and splattered over the wheel, the wheel creaked, turning, and a channel began that fed into the lower, smaller pond, across the road. When we couldn't find Judy at home, usually she'd be here, writing in her notebooks or diary or drawing sketch after sketch. Mom would sometimes drive to Walton's searching for her.

Judy and I shared a bathroom, with one door opening in from the backstairs landing where the door to my room was, and the other door, with a full-length mirror on her side, opening in from her room. The main door to her room opened in from the second floor hall. The connection of our rooms, and their isolation, in a way, from the front of the house, separated us both from Mom and Dad and from the boys (when they were home) on the third floor. Judy had put toilet paper in the keyhole of her hallway door, to discourage peeping, of which, she told me later, both Jack and Chuck were guilty.

Our bathroom was yellow; Dad's was blue, Mom's pink. Judy left hairpins all over, and had a habit, too, of cutting her hair over the toilet, so there would be strands and snips of hair everywhere. She took bubble baths. Once she left her diary on a shelf by the tub and I looked through it, but when I teased her about Tom Eglin, or someone she had written about, she was deeply hurt that I had invaded her privacy and made me swear never to look in it again. We would play on her bed, rocking cat's cradle, back and forth; or scratch each other's backs. She had her wisdom teeth out and swelled up horribly, and was bedridden for a week with ice packs on her head. Her mouth was bruised where they had clamped it open.

She dieted perpetually, worried that she was fat, especially in the caboose; and she sunbathed for hours, too, out on the patio, which I found mindless and boring. She would baste herself with lotion and just lie there, sleep, sometimes read.

She had a reputation for eating leftovers off our plates, so a legendary joke has me walking into the kitchen, stamping on her foot, as if it were the lever for a garbage can, and when she opened her mouth to yell, shoving in a leftover piece of chicken.

She was shaken by reading Poe's stories, especially "Pit and the Pendulum," and then later, Kafka's. Where I was an avid reader of young adult science fiction, of some of Dad's Perry Mason mysteries with lurid covers, and of Jack's westerns: she introduced me to adult reading, meaning to challenge me. She gave me Dostoyevki's *Crime and Punishment*, Steinbeck's *The Red Pony*, and Bronte's *Wuthering Heights*.

In addition to her racing on the team at Martin's Dam over the summers, she devoted herself to water ballet for her last years at Baldwin, practicing and practicing in their chlorinated, indoor pool, with music playing over loud speakers. A group of six or eight girls were choreographed to swim in perfect time to the music. Together they would make flower patterns, gathering together, then spreading out. Judy and one other, Irene McKenna, were the best, and senior year they worked out a routine to the instrumental, "The Blue Tango," the strains to which still beat in memory, dada-DA-da-da. They swam at each other from opposite directions, fluidly; they made a ring, each holding the other's feet, and slowly revolved under water; they stuck one leg up in the air, toes pointing, then slowly sank, without a ripple.

Jack's homecomings were momentous. For Christmas, he would drive some thirty hours straight through from Colorado—which seemed a determined and slightly heroic feat. We wouldn't know he was coming, or when, and then he'd appear late at night, three or four in the morning, and collapse in bed. Waking the next morning, I'd hear that "Jack is home," see his pick-up truck outside, and be told I shouldn't wake him, he needed his sleep. Noon would come and then afternoon, and I'd have to see him, and creep up the third floor steps to his room, crack open the door, and it would be dark, shades drawn inside, but there would be Jack's smell, of grease and gasoline and sweat, that would make the closed room fetid, but in a way I liked. There he'd be, out cold, looking skinny and angular, sleeping in his underwear. I'd have to shake and shake him to even get an eye open, and he'd groan and look blurry and sink back, and then I'd get a wet face cloth and try that, which usually did it. He'd get up, then, slowly, good humouredly always, but more mysterious now with the drive and his distant life behind him.

He quit Colorado A&M after two quarters, in the spring of 1952, and visited home that summer, along with a black and white collie named "Sparky," which he liked to keep along for company, and which was run over by a truck and killed soon after he returned to Colorado. It was "God's country," he'd told us, past describing, and aside from the climate's relief for his asthma, he had fallen in love with the hunting, fishing, and mountain wilderness. He went back to work in the Rockies, driving big lumber trucks and "skinning" various kinds of bulldozers, making logging roads and clearing timber. This was when he found a second dog, which he named "Lady," as a pup. Some of the loggers had tied a can on her tail, with firecrackers, and Jack had saved her; she, in turn, later saved him. She used to ride on the hood of his bulldozer, watching out for falling branches; if anything fell, she'd jump down and hide under the bulldozer. One day a tree fell on the bulldozer, and it was the signal of her jump that caused Jack to jump, just in time, where otherwise he would have been killed. In any case, the next year he fell and hurt his back, and came home to have a slipped disk fused at Bryn Mawr hospital. They didn't operate, but instead put him in a body cast with braces, and in traction for six weeks, upstairs, at home, and Lady was with him. We used to play war games with lead soldiers on top of his rumpled sheets, with the hummocks, hollows, and wrinkles serving as terrain; this was how he and Chuck used to play, he told me, when they were sick and younger. He also read stacks and stacks of paperback westerns, every Luke Short and Max Steele.

In fall, 1953, he worked for a plastics company in Wayne, designing a machine to corrugate plastic sheets; then worked in Germantown for one of the first Volkswagen dealers anywhere, who sent him to a mechanics school that certified him to work on VWs, Jaguars, and Porsches. This led to a job for Speedcraft, in Exton, and immersion in the field of foreign cars, which were looked on generally as more oddball than prestigious or desirable. It was still the postwar decade of the high-finned, buxom-bumpered, four-door family car. Jack would bring home a "sick" Porsche overnight and take me with him for a trial run with it on the turnpike, the only road where we could do up to 75 mph legally. The bucket seats, which made you stretch your legs out, so you sat close to the ground, were special, as were the seatbelts, like on a plane, and the flat, wooden dashboard and leather upholstery. Speedcraft was owned by George Carlin and his head mechanic, Otto Linton, and in addition to being a dealership, they owned and raced cars, with Otto driving.

Before long, on his own, Jack bought a small, boxy British Ford, called an Anglia, and a Fiat sedan, one of which he cut down to its frame to make a hill-climb racer, while cannibalizing the other. Later they were joined by a Javelin Jupiter, which he drove back and forth to work, and which resembled an MG, only with a Jaguar body (long before these names meant much to any but a few cognoscenti, mostly racers).

His hill-climb racer had, besides a supercharger, a modified design in the valves he had worked out. He would tool parts for it in the basement, where he had left his workbench, vises, small lathe, and a drill press from his antique auto days. He worked down there weekends and at night, and we would hear the chirp-whine of the lathe bit going against metal. He said there wasn't any metal part he couldn't make on the lathe. He'd also brought home two or three acetylene tanks, as tall as me, with gauges and valves on top, and hoses connecting to a cutting torch; these he kept in the garage, where he had painted a pattern on the left half of the floor, and where he proceeded to build this thing (that pattern stayed there, oil-stained, long after his next leave-taking, as would the lathe, silent and unused in the basement, and covered with a cloth, along with the scatter of his tools on the workbench). When the racer was finished, it had no body, only the chassis, gas-tank, bucket seat, roll-bar, steering wheel and motor and wires and radiator, all open to the world, so that it looked like an advanced soap-box racer. He took it on a trailer to several meets, where none of us ever went, and he won several hill-climbs with it, telling us later how the others with slick cars and jalopies and hot rods had jeered at him and the homely contraption he was driving, until they saw what it could do, and then they all had crowded around, wanting to know what it was, how he'd hopped it up, what the secret was.

Meanwhile he worked as a mechanic, and then as a pit mechanic at meets, for Otto Linton's racing cars, including an Osca and a Maserati. He told one anecdote of going to a race in Gettysburg. His job was to go up early and inspect and set the cars for peak performance. So Saturday morning he was out running the course, when the car overheated, so he rolled to a stop and opened the hood two miles out, and was sitting on a log waiting for it to cool, when an Irish setter dog came up, licked his arm, and petting it he saw it had on a leash and that at the end of the leash was a "familiar looking guy," who was President Eisenhower off walking around the farm. So Eisenhower sat down with my brother and chatted for fifteen minutes, with Secret Service men standing around.

Next he got his SCCA license and started driving in the races for Otto. He drove at Watkins Glen and lots of little meets, as well as at Sebring twice, where the second time he came in second behind Stirling Moss.

Eventually, however, he concluded that there was no future in working at Speedcraft and in the sports car world. Partly this was because his asthma was still bothersome, but mainly he was put off by the people, primarily by Doris, George Carlin's wife, who was cultivating George's mechanics and drivers, including his friends Buddy Huggler and Galloway Morris, as eligible bachelors, whom she'd try to fix up. In any case, the sports car world was a party world; Jack wanted nothing to do with the society part, and had told her as much, but she wouldn't leave him alone.

By the summer of 1955, he had decided to return to Fort Collins to look for business opportunities that would let him make his life there. After driving there and back for a vacation with Chuck and me, he moved in November, bought a trailer, and went into partnership in an excavating business run by a man he'd known earlier, George Devers. By that point Judy was married and off in Harrisburg, and Chuck had shipped out for Korea, so I would be alone with Mom and Dad, except for Lady, whom Jack had left behind.

For Christmas, 1950, Judy had given me a toy printing outfit, similar to one that Chuck and Jack had once owned. It was a Swiftset, with rubber type, each piece notched to anchor in a metal slot, which you managed with a pair of tweezers; the slot, then, was to be wedged with a mounting tool between rubber tracks on the press's rotating drum (you turned its crank, like a miniature mimeograph), getting ink from one roller, and printing, as a lever engaged the pressure of another from below, and you fed paper between the drum and the pressure roller.

This first press was a "Star" and printed a sheet 4" by 8". Judy helped me set and mount the first type, along with some stock pictures, which you pasted on rubber slugs with rubber cement. It read "Dee's Paper / Dee got a printing press / For Christmas / He hopes that everyone / Has a Merry Christmas." Before long, using one of the logos supplied in the kit, I was producing *The Swiftset Rotary News* for my fourth grade. By spring, I had saved enough allowance (ten dollars) to buy the "Ace," a larger press that printed paper 6" by 8" and allowed a two-column format of type. The enlightened firm in Chicago, The Superior Marking Equipment Co., from which I bought it, accepted not only mail order from kids for the presses and supplies, but also published a 16-page *Swiftset Rotary Printers' Journal*, which ran articles on design and "The Rocky Road to Journalism," as well as short reviews and reports on work by owners of toy presses. It invited kids to send in samples of printing, which if judged "outstanding," would be awarded a Swiftset Master Craftsman button, certificate, and stamp. I launched *The Grammar News* with my new Ace in April, 1951, twice applied for and was denied Master Craftsman awards in May and December and finally, proudly, won one on March, 1952. I was in Mr. Shock's fifth grade by then and had formed The Inkwell Printing Company. In May, 1952, I launched *The Eagle News*, which grew into *The Eagle* by September, which, in turn, went through at least eleven issues, before concluding in May, 1954.

All of this for me was high romance, praised and encouraged, of course, by Mom and by my teacher, Mr. Shock, and largely thanks to Mr. Shock, respected by my friends and classmates. A corner of my room I organized to resemble Dad's office. Likewise, at school, Mr. Shock let us put our desks together in any way we liked, so John Barnett, Kit Wilkes, Rudy Nottage and I joined ours to make an office against one wall, with an Inkwell Printing Co. sign behind us.

As I researched and wrote articles to print, I followed Mom's and Judy's example; as I designed my pages, I was aspiring to art, like Chuck; as I fell in love with the machinery, I followed Jack; and as I imitated business, Dad. I studied Gutenberg, Caxton, and

Benjamin Franklin with excitement, and, visiting the Franklin Institute in town, I haunted the antique corkscrew press on display. My life's ambition was to own a printing plant.

I wore a denim apron and a green plastic eyeshade, like printers and editors in the movies, and sat at my desk for demanding hours hunched over my plastic cases of different fonts of type, each case honeycombed with compartments. I picked each letter from its compartment with tweezers, then wedged it into the slot for printing. A page took twenty-five slots, each slot holding some sixty pieces of type; then after printing, all the type had to be redistributed into the type case.

In the fall, 1954, I started using a hand-operated platen press and metal type, which I bought through the mail, having saved my allowance, earnings from *The Eagle*, and money from odd jobs. I set this up in the basement, along with discarded cases of unsorted type that town paper gave me when they converted to linotype, and two big type case racks, with slanted tops, like the ones in cowboy-movie newspaper shops, which Radnor High School was throwing out. I had learned real printing, beginning in spring, 1953, when I worked on my Printing Merit Badge for scouts. The counselor for this was Mr. Harvey Rettew, who taught printing and mechanical drawing in the school print shop, and who took me on then, and through 1959, as his apprentice.

While no Kerouac-reading bohemian, intellectually and spiritually Chuck was skeptical, searching, and rebellious in other ways.

At F&M, while reading Marx and Hegels during the same season that Eisenhower delivered his famous warning against "the military industrial complex," he developed a dogmatic theory about America's war economy. He saw it as morally neither right nor wrong, but simply how the country worked; all wealth and prosperity were postulated on war. And if we didn't have a war, then we would have to start one. He went on to read all world history in a similar light: all war had economic causes. As a student, carrying on the posture he had evolved, for whatever needs, during our dinner table debates, and harboring his I.Q. like secret proof, he was hopelessly stubborn. If his professors questioned his views or disagreed, they were mediocre, to be dealt with, not listened to.

He also edited the campus humor magazine, *Hullabaloo*, where his cartoons celebrated sex. In one, a stacked woman has fainted at a circus, and worried spectators suggest "rub her wrists . . . rub her cheeks," just as a balloon vendor strolls by crying, "Rubber balloons!" Another, a cover, has a plug with hairy legs chasing a socket in high heels.

An art class there led to his experimenting with etching, scratch art, and pen-and-inks. His first etching showed an exhausted, naked, starved creature, chin in hand, sitting on a boulder, while other, similar creatures scoured a devastated and barren landscape for food or gold. A pen-and-ink had a destitute bum picking up a smoldering cigar butt from in front of a luxurious, packed, and presumably Presbyterian church. Later there were some nudes, copied from photographs, and extraordinary pen-and-inks based on photographs of the college buildings and campus sites, which were used for the inside covers of the yearbook.

Chuck had taken Judo as part of his Air Force ROTC at F&M, and told me with solemn confidence that it had taught him to kill with his hands, and that just as boxers could be arrested for manslaughter if they got into regular fights—their fists legally designated as "deadly weapons"—so could he. He decided to quit ROTC, because it would mean having to serve for sure and for a longer tour than if he were drafted; but he had gone to paratrooper school, learned to pack chutes, and taken hard practice jumps on cables, but never from the air. As things turned out, our local draft board was after him, and he was drafted into the Army upon graduation in June, 1954, entering the next big phase of his life.

The Korean War had just ended, so, after basic training at Fort Dix, N.J. (where Dad, Mom, Judy and I drove in the Buick to visit him), then an assignment to the Signal Corps in Kansas, he was shipped to join the occupation army in Korea, and was soon assigned, given his college degree, to the staff of the army newspaper, *Stars and Stripes*, and promoted to Specialist, 3rd class. His tour would last until 1957.

Shortly before his Kansas time—Christmas, 1954—we were all home together. Jack had come back, and Judy had brought her "serious" boyfriend from Swarthmore, Hans Friedericy, to visit (he was staying in the guest bedroom). A Polaroid picture, taken by Dad, shows us all on the sun-porch in front of the tree again: Chuck in uniform hugging Mom, Jack kneeling, Hans with his arm around a smiling Judy, and me standing to the side in a new suit, like Napoleon, hand in jacket—I am thirteen and in eighth grade. Later in that visit, Judy told Mom, Chuck, and Jack that she and Hans were going to be married (secretly, they had already been married), and that, in fact, she was pregnant. At that, Chuck, in a scene I have only heard about, exploded all red-faced and shouted, "We're not going to have that nigger in the family!" (Hans was half-Indonesian, half-Dutch and his father had been Dutch ambassador to Indonesia and was at that time Cultural Attache to the U.S.) But Jack told him to shut up or he'd floor him; then told Judy warmly, it was great.

Later, as he went to Kansas, then overseas, Chuck gave—or loaned—Hans and Judy his highly prized car. They had been married officially on February 22, 1955, Hans had graduated from Swarthmore in June (Judy, of course, dropped out, though she had been doing well) and taken a job designing bridges in Harrisburg, where they settled, we visited often, and their first baby, John, was born come fall. From this point, however, there would always be tension between Judy and Chuck, flaring again, briefly, when she and Hans thoughtlessly sold the car for fifty dollars, as if it was of no worth, and without asking Chuck.

While stationed in Kansas, Chuck, because of his carpentry and lettering skills, was ordered by all the non-coms and officers to make desk plaques with their names. He took the occasion to make me one, too, in elegant gothic text, that had my full name, and then the word "editor" underneath.

He visited home on leave before shipping for Korea, at which point he also made me a shellacked wooden sign, which said "The Inkwell Printing Company" (this I posted over the bulkhead entrance to our cellar); and, following on Jack's encounter with Eisenhower, as Chuck and Dad flew to the West Coast (Dad was combining a business trip with wishing Chuck bon voyage), they stopped over in Chicago and were waiting in line to use the airport urinals, when they recognized Adlai Stevenson standing right ahead of Dad. Dad would later boast of this encounter—he'd been next to use the urinal—regardless of his opposition to Stevenson's politics.

Chuck wrote us often, and at some typewritten length, from Korea. He would, actually, as a *Stars and Stripes* staffer, follow around many of the OCS celebrities, but wrote "all were bums, except for Bob Hope and Jane Russell." The best foreign cameras were cheap in the PX, so he bought a 35 mm Leica to start recording the sights, and he encouraged me to save up and send him money to buy a good camera for me too (I had by then progressed from a 120 mm box camera to a 35 mm Kodak "Pony," and was trying to be arty). He also wrote as an informed source on the Army bureaucracy and the true political situation behind the official reports. I forget the big issue of the time, but he was staunchly against the Republican line, and told Mom to tell Grandpop Thralls this and that. But what moved him most, and what proved cause to involve Mom and Dad directly in world affairs, was the sight of disabled orphans.

By the following December, he was news. A reporter and photographer from the *Philadelphia Inquirer* had come to our house, talked with Mom, and posed us together for pictures.

He had been writing home, all along, about the disabled children in Seoul; he had visited orphanages, and spent his Army salary, trying to help. "Throughout the land," he wrote, "there are thousands of destitute orphanages, attempting to care for the helpless, homeless products of war. All are overcrowded and understaffed; and there are yet more than 5,000 waifs wandering the city streets, begging, sleeping amidst the bombed-out ruins and sewer pipes. . . . Even those fortunate enough to have landed in an orphanage need help. I have seen such children partially dressed in rags playing with rocks or a splintered board, their feet obscured by hordes of black flies, and their bodies covered with open festering sores." He sent us pictures of children taken with his Leica, as well as pen-and-ink sketches of their crying, harrowed faces. Then he wrote Mom and Dad: instead of a Christmas present for him, why not spend the money on something for the children?

"Project Happiness" began with Mom mailing him a crate with toys for about 60 children, which she'd gathered from her Neighborhood League connections; Dad, also, put in boxes of candy from the factory. Chuck received and distributed these with the promise that "more presents will be coming, especially clothes, around Christmas time, from all the neighbors around my home." Dad, accordingly, had prepared an orphanage-size shipment of candy and persuaded another company to do likewise, and Mom had organized the clothes—all of which was reported on the front page of the Inquirer, December 3, with the headline, "GI Plays Santa to Crippled Orphans," along with Chuck's Army picture and his best sketches.

The Army itself was not pleased, either stateside, where a General assured Mom that all shipments to Chuck via APO in San Francisco would be expedited; or in Seoul, where, after the shipment did arrive well after Christmas, higher-ups appropriated it, and it was only Chuck's contact with a newswire reporter that forced them, finally, to let him go ahead: "Main Line Soldier Treats Youngsters in Korea," the wire photo reads. In the picture,

Mom noticed, he wore a wedding ring; he later explained that he'd had to wear a ring, in order to keep the women from soliciting him.

When he came home and was mustered out, in late 1957, he brought me the Canon camera I had saved up for and sent him one hundred dollars to buy. He also brought hundreds of color slides of Korea and Japan, the people, the buildings; a red silk kimono, with gold thread elaborately woven to depict a dragon; and a renewed determination to study medicine and to return to Asia someday, to serve humanity, like another Schweitzer.

Getting into medical school, however, was another matter. He worked at the factory again, briefly, went to the University of Pennsylvania summer school for six hours of Chemistry in 1958, and, thanks to the influence of Dr. Appel and Dr. Truxel (who vouched for his seriousness and aptitude, despite his college grades), he was admitted to Hannemahn in Philadelphia. He would live and study at home, commuting to and from town by train, until he graduated in 1962. My last year-and-a-half of Radnor—my own dating and driving years—he studied incessantly, not alone or at a desk, but on the sun-porch couch, TV going, a medical book on his lap, underlining things in the midst of family conversation and commotion, and staying up late into the night.

One visit home, during her freshman fall at Swarthmore, Judy mockingly urged Mom to dye her hair brown. "There's nothing sinful about it. You always want to make sins of everything. It's perfectly all right to dye your hair. Just to see what you look like anyway. You can wash it out again. I want to see you with brown hair—the way it was once."

Mom gave in—"All right, yes. I suppose." And Judy went out to buy the dye herself. She came home later and disappeared with Mom into Mom's bathroom, closing the mirrored door. From my seat on a bed, I heard Mom complaining, doubtful, excited, "I shouldn't, I know I shouldn't!" And Judy's arguing, always reassuring, water running, footsteps.

Finally the door opened and Judy came out: "Now, don't laugh at her—it looks just fine. But you know how bashful she is—!"

She called for Mom to come out.

"No, Judy. I don't want to—."

"Come on, Mother, it looks fine. Don't be idiotic."

Then Mom came out. Her hair was brown, a deep, unnatural brown, darker than Judy's. I tried not to show how startled I was, but I couldn't take my eyes away. Her hair was brown, her eyes bright, and her face was lined, streaked with tears.

Dad wasn't home, nor was Chuck or Jack.

"I should never have done it. I knew it was stupid. Look at me!" Mom said, turning her head and scowling in the mirror.

But it wouldn't wash out, or not entirely. For hours, they tried rinse after rinse, and Mom's penance, presumably for vanity, was to have pink hair for a week.

Despite the presence of my older brothers and sister, my first awareness of sex came from friends at school. I had heard that fucking was something dirty that older kids did, but I never connected it with having babies. In fourth grade, my friend John played an undressing game with a girl who lived up the road from his house. He told me that girls looked like a circle with a line down the center, and Kit Wilkes said his sister looked like that. John continued playing with the girl, until one day playing Mommy and Daddy, she told him to put his in hers, and he "peed" inside.

John and I had been exchanging afternoons (my place for TV, his for the farm) since Kindergarten. Now Kit Wilkes joined us, since his family had moved to a new house near the farm. As we played in John's hayloft, Kit proposed that we each drop his pants and show his rear end to the others. We did this a few times, but then lost interest. Eventually Kit stopped coming over because his parents objected to the farm and to John's poverty.

In fifth grade, another friend, Dale Jackson, insisted that fucking was how you made babies, which I doubted. I believed that having babies had to do with kissing hard and with something like osmosis, which happened if a man and woman were together for a long time. Troubled, I asked Mom. She took me aside for a private, serious talk. Dale was right. "Fucking" was a bad word for it, as opposed to the proper word "intercourse." But, yes, that was how the man's seed got inside the woman to fertilize her egg; and, yes, she and Daddy had done that to have each of us.

By the time I was thirteen, fascinated with Judy's body, with older girls in tank suits at the swimming club, with cheerleaders, and with nudes in Mom's art books and magazines, as I was studying a tiny photo in an ad for an art school, which showed a nude woman, I made a ring of thumb and forefinger and moved it over my stiffened penis, wondering if this felt like intercourse. The surprise convulsion and sticky discharge, which wasn't pee, frightened me. I had seen a human reproduction film at school, with diagrams, that explained ejaculation and menstruation as natural events, but I didn't make the connection yet. I worried that I'd hurt myself. Still, instead of telling Mom, I waited until morning and when I found out I still could pee and seemed fine otherwise, I experimented again.

Anna's room at St. Davids, "the maid's room," was in back, off the kitchen. Past the foot of the backstairs was a short hallway, with her room to the right and Mom's study ahead and opening left. There was a single bed, dresser, closet, and private bathroom, with windows overlooking the drive. Mom kept her sewing machine there too, and later would paint there because of better light (her one window in the study was overgrown with ivy and bushes). Anna, however, seldom slept at our house. She would come in two or three times each week, help with the laundry, the ironing, polish the silver, help with vacuuming, making beds, putting folded laundry into drawers, emptying waste baskets, and generally, room by room, straightening up, dusting, and cleaning the bathrooms and the house. Where my own room was concerned, I tried to beat her to it, so there was only vacuuming to do. Otherwise, I'd come home from school and find everything aimlessly rearranged; my cap guns (which I kept in special notches and holes in a small bookshelf), my books, souvenirs, toys, my printing supplies and drawings. This upset me increasingly as I grew older.

Also, in her mid-sixties, Anna did less and less real work around the house. Mom would pick her up early, 8 a.m., from a row house in Bryn Mawr now, near the hospital. She might vacuum or dust, but mostly I recall her cleaning the silver, the trays, coffee pots, creamers, candlesticks, as well as all the silverware, to take off the tarnish. She would talk with Mom, eat lunch; then at 4:30 or 5 p.m., Mom would drive her home. She was stooped and arthritic.

At my most critical and insensitive teens, I asked Mom why we kept Anna, why we paid her, since she did so little work. When Anna had been sick, on occasion, Mom had tried some other "girls," who had references, but who turned out, in their thirties or forties, to be unreliable. One talked back, refused to do silver; another sneaked drinks during the day from our liquor cabinet.

Mom answered: "She knows too much. Your father wouldn't hear of letting her go."

Where Philadelphia was essentially Democratic (its mayors, like Dilworth, Irish- or Italian-American), the Main Line suburbs, where I grew up, had been G.O.P. forever. Dad proudly belonged to the Union League, an organization dating from the Civil War. His political assumptions and loyalties seemed to have been shaped under Calvin Coolidge; he perceived the party of Coolidge, Hoover, and at long last Eisenhower, as the party of business, commerce, and free enterprise, while the Democratic interregnum of FDR and then Truman had been a nightmarish rule of Labor, the unpropertied and uneducated, and, paradoxically, the egghead liberal and/or Communistic theorists.

In all this, I doubt that my father ever had any serious political opinions, and believe, on the contrary, that his politics, like his religion, were primarily a matter of social concern. He had his sense of class, and also, given the breach of his alcoholism, an exaggerated need to conceal his "stigma" and to belong, at any cost.

Down on Catholics; down on Jews because they were different and socially "unacceptable," yet respectful of them too, because of their business acumen and belief in family betterment. Down on the "colored," except as servants and menial laborers. Down on Italians. Down on the French as decadent.

He hated Truman, a common haberdasher, despite Truman's opposition to the unions, which Dad also hated. He hated John L. Lewis, Jr., and Jimmy Hoffa; union bosses were thugs and gangsters, lining their own pockets. He hated Bishop Fulton J. Sheen, as a proselytizing TV priest, but even more so for personally converting my mother's brother, who had married a Catholic. I never heard him mention Father Coughlin, the Radio Priest of the late Thirties, whose Catholic anti-Semitism and opposition to FDR might have appealed to him, yet whose Catholicism itself would have been suspect and offensive.

Two specific hate objects were Frank Sinatra and Sammy Davis, Jr., both of whom, in Dad's view, violated the Protestant work ethic in becoming rich by simply being entertainers. Their success oddly subverted true success. The same was true of sports stars. He did, however, admire Lena Horne, perhaps because she could pass for white; whenever she appeared on TV, he would watch and listen intently, saying, "Now that woman is talented," as if her talent were in spite of, or all the more amazing, considering her race. Other entertainers he enjoyed included Lawrence Welk, Perry Como, Bing Crosby and Bob Hope.

Also held in high regard was Harry Brown, a Vice President of Central Penn Bank, who along with Ed Chasney and Bill McCleer, was a member of his Saturday Foursome. Harry Brown amused Dad with his affectionate oddities; despite considerable wealth, like a comic strip tycoon, Brown was penny wise, and Dad loved to tell stories about his dressing in gardening clothes, old shoes, and gloves and cutting his own lawn or tilling his own garden. Other successful friends and acquaintances in my father's pantheon included Bob Watson, a VP and regional manager of Sears, and Sam Hinkel, President of Hershey's.

He admired Eisenhower, sharing Republican nostalgia for MacArthur, but agreeing with Truman's firing of MacArthur over use of atomic weapons in Korea. He disliked Stevenson not only as a Democrat, but also as an intellectual, and possibly a pinko. He liked Nixon. I don't recall his watching the McCarthy hearings on TV, but I did myself, and I was as contemptuous of the defendants citing the fifth amendment as I was of prizefighters who constantly resorted to clinches, rather than really fighting. Our home library certainly included blatant Cold War titles that Dad studied and swore by, such as *None Dare Call It Treason* and *What You Must Know About Communism*. These prejudices were, in general, the majority views in Wayne.

He believed that Blacks were inherently shiftless and immoral, citing the pilfering of light bulbs and other supplies at our family's candy factory and the high absenteeism of unskilled help. He spoke with as much disgust of such and such a white workman who "had gone black," as he would of a homosexual.

He believed in integrity in business dealings—that fair-dealing and honesty were more important, and more profitable in the long run, than deceitful tactics.

He believed that life insurance was the best possible investment, and stock speculation the worst. One could invest savings and be assured of stable income, or invest in blue chip stocks with a chance of appreciation. He had no doubt that the American economic system was sure of a great and inspiring growth, that business forecasters could forecast, and that business cycles followed orderly rhythms. With the exception of entertainers and the like, he also assumed that the possession of wealth was a sign of success and that success itself was universally worshipped.

He believed in the best possible education for his children, including college. The reason for education was "practical"—his key word, always—in that it promised well-favored young people jobs as a matter of course.

He believed that ambition, hard work, loyalty to the firm and a knack of salesmanship would bring personal success.

Poverty, of course, was the result of incompetence, ignorance, or of very special misfortune, and should be looked to by local charities, like the Neighborhood League, or the churches. Welfare was a mistake.

Profanity in front of women and children was unacceptable, though it was a sign of manhood and equality among men of like age and status.

You got what you paid for. Bargain-hunting was unseemly, and, in the long run, self-defeating. Wholesale items broke easily or proved inferior otherwise. Also paying in cash was a prouder, better thing than buying on time.

Given all this—that my father was dogmatically racist, sexist, classist, capitalistic, patriotic, Presbyterian and Republican—starting with my mother, and then with each of us children, I think in each of our lives, as part of love, we waged a losing battle to change, or at least widen his mind. This he defended like a citadel—indeed, the citadel of personal sanity, the self that had found its way through the "hang-ups" behind his alcoholism, to a structure of truths and values that allowed him to cope not only with the world, but with us, too. In loving us, of course, he sought to impose his truths on us for our own welfare. Then, too, respecting and testing our differences, he enjoyed provoking us.

Mom had a falling out with the Presbyterian Church after we moved, and especially with the pastor, Rev. John T. Galloway, whose son, John, was in my class at Radnor. She complained that nobody in the church was there with help when she and Dad needed it; but rather, during his alcoholic times, they all avoided our family. Consequently, though Judy and I continued Sunday School, and Mom sometimes went simultaneously to church, Dad never went except for Easter and Christmas Eve, and Jack and Chuck were always allowed to sleep late on Sundays—or at least they were at an age where their refusals to get up had to be respected, while Judy's and mine were not.

I did pray every night, through my teens. At first my prayers were personal, bless everybody, help me; but then they became a recitation of the Lord's Prayer, because in church or in Matthew, it said that if you only had one prayer, then that was the one to say to God. Pre-sexual atrocities and defiances I begged the Lord to forgive, such as playing with matches, or killing the robin. And then, later, I had sexual ones.

Mom said conscience was the voice of God inside.

She said hell was knowing what you could have done and did not. Hell was the living torment of guilt—there was no place, literally, of fire and brimstone and torture, but rather hell was all inside us, as we live. This impressed me.

Jack wasn't irreligious, the way Chuck became later (bitterly viewing the church as an institution for the self-congratulation of haves). He just wasn't interested in getting dressed up in slacks, jacket, and tie, and going through the social pomp with Mom and

Dad of being seen there, in the Henry family pew, in the church that Great Grandpop Henry had helped to found and build, and the second lectern of which Nana Henry had donated in Grandpop's memory.

Jack's sense of awe and worship came from nature, from being out in the woods, and from communion with his own natural center, where he ruminated—while working on his cars, or motorcycle, or over the lathe in the cellar—the contradictions of instincts, conscience, and experience, until his reflections yielded wisdom.

He believed in character, in individuality (trusting his own heart and nature as truer than whatever local society dictated or subscribed to), in warmth, honesty, generosity, in being readier to give than to take, and in responsibility, in caring, as a rescuer and protector, and as the man in the family. No doubt there was some adolescent exaggeration in his sense of honor, with models in the sheriff, the good guy, the frontier hero in the westerns he read. His mission was to be noble, loyal, industrious, equal to the needs of those he loved, to answer for family tragedy, for preventing or healing it—to face the adult complexity and danger itself and to mediate it for us, soften it, shelter us somewhat from its pain.

I was shocked to learn that perhaps six or ten kids in my class at Radnor were Presbyterians when I saw their faces in Sunday school. Among them were Kit Wilkes, Barby Spillman, Sue Shellenberger, Ann Palmer, Rick Skillman, Wendy Trout. Other kids, like Pete Allen, John Barnett, and Howard Hopson were Baptists, and this troubled me; and still others, Episcopalians, which was almost like being Catholic; and then the rest were Catholics, religiously beyond hope, believing in popes, cardinals, nuns, and even "graven images." With no Jewish classmates at Radnor at all, I remained largely unaware of this particular difference until coming to know my freshman roommate at Amherst, along with other Jewish classmates and teachers in college.

Actually, Aunt Kitty and Uncle John Spaeth were a mixed Presbyterian and Catholic marriage; they had agreed that my cousin Bunny would go to Presbyterian Sunday school and church with her mother, and young John, Jr., to Catholic school and church with his father. They also had Jewish neighbors in Bala Cynwyd, whose boys were daily playmates of Bunny's. All this, while never clearly discussed in my presence, contributed to a slight awkwardness and restraint when we visited there, on their turf.

At Sunday school, the elementary playroom overlapped with kindergarten, and, as in regular school, I wanted to impress the teacher. Once girls became important, towards fourth and fifth grade, then Barby Spillman became an added Sunday attraction to look forward to, in competition with Kit Wilkes.

Catechism and Bible story instruction gradually intensified, with books to read as homework and even tests. Then as preadolescents, our class moved to another building and we were being trained for true church membership.

The grown-up church was above all boring. The program read like a menu and I was always looking to see when one part would be over and how close the end was, or the next hymn. The building itself was all heavy stone, which made it cool in summer, with high arching ornate rafters, lights hanging on chains, and stained glass windows depicting various stories in the old and new testaments. The windows were beautiful, with their primary colors and lead seams, like a jigsaw puzzle, especially when direct sunlight cast through them and projected their colors inside. Then there was a stage in front, with choir boxes on either side, big organ pipes, the organ to the left, and two raised stone pulpits, one on either side. Up front and down the aisles, the carpeting was maroon and deep; the pews were a polished mahogany with cushions and racks in the back with Bibles and hymnals.

Near my twelfth birthday came my time for official joining, and I was lined up with six or seven of my peers in front of the congregation; we recited the Apostles' Creed, and were each given a new Bible with our name embossed in gold on the leather cover.

From about that point on, Sunday mornings would become a matter of contention and suspense, whether to get up, dress up, eat, and go, or whether late sleeping, apathy, or rebellion would prevail, and we would all have a luxurious morning of reading the Sunday comics and otherwise playing (including Sunday golf games—golf being singled out by Dr. Galloway in his sermons as his main competition), as if it were Saturday. Gradually, Mom's attempts to encourage church as a regular, important thing, gave way. Following Jack's defection, Judy began rebelling, not liking the content of church or its social life, given her own crowd. Then Mom would go alone, but more and more infrequently.

When we did go as a family, for the big holiday services, we paraded in, Mom and Dad smiling at the world, with maybe a hard hand squeeze or stop-fooling look for one of us, and each of us dressed in our best, Mom wearing gloves, perfumed, Dad finely groomed and in his tailored suit, and we would sit and sing together, and I would lose my voice in the surprising harmony of many flawed or mumbling voices, along with, now and again, a purity of real singing, like Mom's, which was close enough to hear, or sometimes Dad's deep base. We would each be given money for the offering, not too much or too little, as if neighbors would know as the plate was passed on. This was a silver plate with a velvet liner, an usher or deacon would start it down each row, while heads were bowed, then another would get it at the other end and empty the contents into a velvet sack on a stick, and the entire collection would end up on the altar up front, to be blessed by Dr. Galloway and celebrated by a singing of the Doxology. When the service was over at last, there would be a prayer of benediction, all heads bowed, eyes closed and down, during which the organ played gently, and Dr. Galloway scooted down the aisle to the back. A burst of joyous recessional music, we'd all stand, and Dr. Galloway would be at the door shaking hands goodbye to each family filing out. He would have some special recognition for us: "My, my, the Henrys! Good to see you back! Haven't seen you for some time! Don't see you enough!" Once I made a sarcastic comment about his sermon, like, "Too bad he couldn't make it longer" or "He's never seen a poor person," and Mom shushed me because he had overheard, but pretended not to have.

Then, at the oddest off times during the year, he would appear, awkwardly, some evening, at our front door at home. He would come in and be stiffly entertained, cup of coffee, plate of cookies or cake, sitting on the living room couch. Why had we been missing church?

After he left we'd mock and laugh at him behind his back. Of course, he did always leave with a renewed, generous pledge for the year, which Dad insisted on giving.

Meanwhile at dinner we collectively continued to discuss the hypocrisy of organized religion, the social gospel that had replaced any moral urgency, psychology, Paul Tillich, and the other new religious philosophers of the Fifties, whom Mom read in connection with her work with Dr. Appel. By no accident my term paper senior year in high school—the writing sample that helped to get me admitted to college—would be on comparative religion, with the thesis that no one religion was right, that each had its dogmas, and each, rather than embodying "truth," embodied a kind of necessary fiction.

Dad was upset, when, at fifteen or sixteen, I printed my personal Christmas card in the basement and handed them out at school: "Happy Commercial Holiday, from An Agnostic."

Life won't let you get away with that. It's all right with me, but don't think you can do that in Life.

Mom and Dad both spoke with grudging reverence about Life, warned us about it, as something beyond their control, beyond the perimeters of the Henry sanctuary. Jack had gone out into it; Chuck sallied into it; then Judy: and they were sallies, in a sense, both to test each fledgling adult, and to bring back reports from the hinterlands of chance, wrong values, anarchy—the destructive/creative element that had been so carefully excluded from our territory. No wonder Dad patrolled its borders with both pride of proprietorship and vigilance.

Life as they spoke of it was not God, or even Nature, but something realer and more immediate, involving the interplay of self (and the constituting forces, strengths and weaknesses of self) with social forces and realities, with Nature, with History. If we had household gods, and in a deep sense, I think we did really, Life was the most powerful. Harsh, sacred, precious, cruel, dangerous, tricky and inscrutable, impersonally judgmental, all at once.

This had, of course, nothing to do with the magazine, except that those grand abstractions, Life and Time, had their salience at mid-point in such a century, such lives.

"Just two things about your mother," Dad warned me. "Don't ever expect a woman to be like her, because nobody can live up to her. She's a truly remarkable woman. Whoever you marry, don't measure your wife by her."

And the second thing: "Your mother is a wonderful person, but you have to cut the apron strings. I'm telling you for your own good. She won't mean to hold on, but you can't let her either."

Dad's own mother, Nana Henry, was an obligatory and influential presence throughout our St. David's years. From 1946, the years of her widowhood were spent primarily alone, in a series of ornate apartments, sometimes with a paid companion, most often not. One apartment was in Wynnewood. Then she grew lonely, gave Kitty money to build an apartment over their garage in Ard-more, and moved in there. Then for the longest stretch, during my later teens, she lived in a new complex down from The Bald-win School on Montgomery Avenue in Bryn Mawr. For a while Aunt Peggy moved back from St. Pete in Florida (her Pete Beatty marriage having ended in separation) in order "to be near fam-ily," and took another apartment in the same building upstairs, but would drink, grow maudlin and otherwise distress Nana, and before long moved to a flashier high-rise in Radnor, leaving Nana in peace.

Ultimately, Nana would move from her apartment first to a Bryn Mawr nursing home, with a room next to Nana Thralls (Mom's mother, also widowed by then—1965—whom Mom tried to keep with her and Dad, but finally conceded to put in the home). The two Nanas could not get along, so Nana Henry then moved to an-other, posher nursing home in Devon, where she died in 1969.

That she died unperturbed, self-satisfied and proud, I found dif-ficult to accept, seeing her, through Mom's eyes, probably, as the source of many of Dad's problems. She never admitted that either Dad or Aunt Peggy had been or were alcoholics; or that she bore any responsibility for their breakdowns. Dad never blamed her, as far as I could see. If anything, he was a model of filial piety. He called her regularly. He would stop alone on the way home from work to visit with her, late enough sometimes to be late for our dinner. He would force Mom to invite her for Sunday dinners, with us going to pick her up and take her home; then once she was actually in our house, Dad would abandon Nana to Mom or to us kids, and disappear, to sleep, or watch TV. Partly his piety had to do with stock in the factory, hers, Aunt Peggy's, Aunt Kitty's, and his own need, as president, to maintain majority control; partly, too, Dad enjoyed showing us off, the house, the yard, everything "nice" for her approval, as if we were fulfilling the life and future she had lived to build.

I surprised Mom during one such visit, with her back flattened out of sight behind the kitchen door and her fists clenched. "I can't stand it anymore," she hissed.

The Anthony Wayne Theater, our single movie theater, was ornately Victorian, with an overhanging marquee outside and a castle-like facade. The three-sided ticket booth, with a circle to speak through and a loop to get your tickets, was out front under the shelter of the marquee.

Black people sat in side seats from the left aisle, down the sloping floor (each row of seats had a dim light shining at the end, and usually an usher with a flashlight would show you down where you wanted, or where there were vacancies), and whites sat in the center and to the right, as well as in the balcony upstairs. Capacity, including the balcony, was five or six hundred, and for good movies, the house each showing was regularly sold out.

Initially, I went with Judy or with Mom. There were Saturday matinees, with serials before the feature, like "The Lone Ranger," "Flash Gordon," "The Green Hornet" (I had also listened to radio versions of all these and others, including "The FBI In Peace and War," "Gunsmoke," "The Shadow," "Captain Midnight," and "Dr. Christian" with Lew Ayres, from my Bloomingdale years through the early Fifties). In addition to the serial, and more important, to my taste, would be two or three cartoons.

Overhead, in the ceiling, was an ominous, ornate oval, like a huge broach, or, I imagined, a spider, with light bulbs in and around its design. We preferred not to sit under any portion of this, and whether Judy was only joking about the danger, I seriously dreaded, well into my teens, its suddenly falling. I sat in the back rows and tried to figure precisely where it would fall, how many people would be hurt or killed. And just before the movie began, its lights would dim to a minimal glow, but still keep on enough so you could see its dark bulk and outline. Also there were light fixtures in a series of Roman alcoves down the walls, with murals of Anthony Wayne and Revolutionary War scenes, and these, too, would dim.

Up front, from speakers flanking the shallow stage, with its gaudy proscenium and folds of pink velvet curtain, the Blue Danube Waltz would be played. The main curtain would part, then a transparent curtain, mauve-colored, would stay and the picture come on, its beam spreading through the dark and picking up curling cigarette smoke or dust all the way from the projection booth, high up and behind us; it would be accompanied by its own music; and the transparent curtain would part and there would be the real screen and movie.

By age nine, I was going alone there for Saturday matinees with Kit, John, or other friends, a parent dropping us off and picking us up. Then at ten, in fifth grade, Kit and I went on double dates to the matinee with Barby Spillman and Sue Epps. We had started social dancing at Mrs. Hill's School of Dance, which met on Saturdays in the Saturday Club. This was extracurricular, but most of the kids, excluding the poor and the black kids, attended. Judy and even Chuck had done their turns with Mrs. Hill, back when. Sue Epps had a lunch party at her house another time, when as my rival for Barby, Kit Wilkes had won out, and Sue herself had decided that she liked me. They set up a fixed game of spin-the-bottle (a kind of ultimate dare then), where, with only four players, you sat across from your intended kissee, which in Barby's case was Kit, not me. When the bottle spun off center, I tried to claim a kiss from Barby, but she refused, so I was forced to kiss Sue on the cheek several times. Our sexual progress, then, was from close dancing, to cheek to cheek, to head on shoulder (which could make my heart race), or at the movies, the slow, insinuating attempt to put my arm on the back of Barby's seat, and all the degrees from there to letting it drop so I touched her shoulder, to having her actually rest her head on my shoulder. Kisses were cheek kisses, when and if. At some point we started going on double dates to the movies or to dances at night, always with Mom acting as taxi for me, or Chuck; on the trip back to the girl's home, they would wait in the idling car while I walked my date to her door.

Besides any number of Gene Autry, Roy Rogers, and Hopalong Cassidys (which had melodramatic simplicity and vividness, loud, brassy music surging on the soundtracks, guns that barked rather than went bang, and a richochet sound, something like pschewww!), the features included "Friendly Persuasion" (with a date), "The Red Shoes" (alone with Mom, who would sometimes take me to special grown-up movies), "Raintree County" (with Judy), "Wee Geordie" (with Mom), and then the Disney films: "Snow White," "Pinocchio," "Fantasia," "Song of the South." As the 3-D craze came in, I saw "King Solomon's Mines" and "Carousel," wearing special glasses. "Beloved Infidel," which I saw with Mom, impressed me, as it showed F. Scott Fitzgerald (not having read anything by him, I only saw him as a Writer), struggling to finish a novel and hanging different chapters up on the wall. I also liked the romantic part, where the Sheilah Graham character reads a chapter and says huskily, "It's us." I am shocked now and then to recognize late night on television something that I remember seeing in The Anthony Wayne, on a big screen, in the midst of three hundred faceless neighbors in the dark.

By 1957, when I got my driver's license and had the use of either Mom's Buick, or more likely, Dad's company station wagon, a lot of my movie-going was transferred to either the Main Line Drive-in, in Devon, or the Exton, farther west, summer and winter both. Prior to that, non-movie dating had been restricted to parties, though there were some I would hear of beforehand, hope wretchedly to be asked to, and then come to realize that I was pointedly not to be asked.

Ann Palmer, new to Radnor, blond, intelligent, was the first girl to really like me back, however briefly. We dated in the spring of 1955—the spring of Judy's marriage, of my 8th grade, and of

Chuck's tour in the army—and she was partly the reason for my having my own first party that June. We made out at these parties, and this time, dancing first in the dark, as other couples slouched or lay together along the benches Chuck had built, we lay down and stroked and kissed each other, until the first step of Mom, Dad or Jack on the stairs. After that summer apart we stopped dating and Ann started going steady with Rick Skillman. In mind and talk, boys were obsessed with the stages of getting to first (kiss), second (feel breasts), third (feel and finger vagina), and home (all the way), and girls seemed equally obsessed with limiting our progress. Ann was my first second.

From 9th grade on, I played the field without much success, dreaming, lusting, talking, but never really making out or getting romantic. Third and home would not come until my senior year, spring and summer 1959, with Kathie Ross, and love.

My boyhood friendship with John Barnett, to our mutual embarrassment, had started declining with the move from grammar school to junior high. We were in different home rooms, but more than that, John's father, Vivian, had been gored by bulls, had had an operation, then after the operation had had lesions, and had been bedridden for six months, never to be himself again afterwards. From the age of twelve John had to take over his father's labor, to keep the family's living, and had been working constantly with no time to visit or play. As a result he had become incontestably strong, the Samson of our class, and immediately found his place as a workhorse guard on the football 125 pound team, then junior varsity. There was also now in junior high, the social difference. He looked foolish, with hair that stood out and up; his clothes were too small and shabby; in his self-consciousness he would stammer and grin; and he smelled of the farm, of manure: all of which excluded him from the world of parties, make out or otherwise, dances, dates, girlfriends, or popularity. Later, ninth or tenth grade, after his role on the football team made him more acceptable, and after he himself had studied the situation, he became better groomed, more sociable, and started taking out one of the plainer girls in our class.

At age eleven, I had been begging Mom to buy one of the beagle puppies from John's farm, when Jack returned in the summer of 1953 with his new dog, Lady. Lady was mostly collie, and not particularly bright; Jack had had her fixed in Colorado. She was smaller than a regular collie. Her coat was tawny reddish, with a white collar, belly, front legs, and blaze from mid forehead, between her brown eyes, and full around her snout; also the tip of her tail was white.

Jack was her master. He would take her with him with when he could and she loved riding either in the bed of his pickup or standing on the passenger's seat with her head out the window, face in the wind.

The summer of 1955, between my eighth and ninth grades, after Judy was pregnant and living in Harrisburg, and during Chuck's leave before shipping out for Korea, the three Henry brothers set out to explore the open road and, at its end, Colorado.

Jack had built a tubular tent frame to fit on the bed of his Dodge pick-up, covered it with canvas, and with parental financing and blessing, we packed in clothes, guns, cameras, camping and fishing gear, and headed West on June 26, 1955, to return on July 17, since thereafter I was due to leave for Camp Pocono. The idea was for Jack to explore business opportunities in Ft. Collins, and, before Chuck left, for the three of us to have a bonding experience. Lady stayed home with Mom.

In adult hindsight, of course, I realize that the idea was also to get us out of the way so that Mom and Dad could settle their marriage again; that this was the time when Dad had asked a second time to leave and start over with the same girl as before.

We drove straight through, Pennsylvania Turnpike, Ohio Turnpike, Indiana Toll Road, then dropped down on Route 30 from Chicago to cross the Mississippi at St. Louis and pick up U.S. 40 across Missouri and Kansas, taking on each state like a new adventure, a blur of truck stops, diners, gas stations, towns, cities, villages, lives settled and stationary, while our life was pure motion, flat mid-western vistas, flatness such as I had never seen, distance and the overbearing sky, a sky with different weathers, and storms in different sectors, trailing pillars of rain. From Missouri on, the two-lane highway paralleled train tracks and would be punctuated by grain elevators, from town to town; here interstate tractor trailers sped, or toiled up grades, and you saw their lights coming from miles off, like stars, or you came up behind them, and had to wait to pass; now and then we passed big wheat combines, harvesting. We kept on driving steadily, with Jack and Chuck taking turns, one sleeping in back, the other driving. I tried sleeping regular hours at night in back, with the flap down, despite the heat, to keep out the exhaust. We drove the full 1500 miles in two-and-a-half days, with only rest stops, no motels. Perhaps 100 miles from Denver, from just within the Colorado border, Jack told us to study the horizon, west, and we would see a thin, low bank of clouds, which would be over the Rocky Mountains. Before long, where we had seen nothing, we thought and then were certain we saw a white ribbon along the horizon, which gradually widened. After another 50 miles, we plainly made out irregular snowcaps, and the ribbon, purpler than blue, of the mountains themselves.

Thanks to Jack's letters and accounts, which built for me on western movies and novels, Colorado was an exotic land, with mountains inconceivable to Easterners, the highest of which, I knew, having studied it as my project for eighth grade Core class, were over 14,000 feet. Denver itself was one mile above sea level. Dad, Mom and Judy had flown out an earlier summer—perhaps when I'd been at Boy Scout camp—and Dad, according to Mom, had pooh-poohed the Rockies; he'd seen the Alps, after all; seen one, you'd seen them all. Dad had taken Polaroid pictures of Mom and Judy, in July, in shorts and summer blouses, standing with Jack (who wore his usual checkered shirt and blue jeans) in front of a sheer wall of snow, two or three times their height, the remains on Cameron Pass of the previous winter's accumulation. Dad must, however, have been terrified to drive or to be driven there. (Some years later, on another trip, he refused to drive near the edge over the same pass, so we could see; and teasing, I pointed out that even if the car went off the highway, the slope down was gentle, but he had some fixed idea of an abyss, a brink, and more than driving in the middle of the road, he drove in the wrong lane, gripping the wheel, hugging the uphill side).

This trip was Chuck's and my first look. By the time we reached Ft. Collins and rented a tourist cabin across from an A&W root beer stand (we consumed a five-gallon jug each day we were there), the mountains were a steady presence, fifteen degrees up from the normal horizon: foothills first, which began five or ten miles away; then purple against the tawny plain and foothills, intermediate peaks, jagged; and beyond and above them, fainter, the uneven saw tooth of the snowcapped highest range, the snow itself brighter than clouds. Sunsets over that range were breathtaking, as high clouds drifted east, and as their undersides were touched with salmon, purple, pink, scarlet, yellow, against the dark blue of incoming night, which closed high overhead, like a huge hemisphere from the east. The air was thin, dry and clear. Dust from the unpaved roads surrounding town smelled like bacon frying.

Between Jack's looking up of potential business contacts, including George Devers, who ran one of three small excavating businesses in Ft. Collins, and who was looking for a partner, we went for forays trout fishing up the Poudre River in the Cache le Poudre Canyon. The road, paved for the first twenty miles, then changing to gravel and hardpan, wound along with the river, which varied from fifteen to forty yards across and was fast and turbulent except for rocky pools. Meadows and groves of willows and aspen trees spread out in the lower parts of the canyon, and here and there a cabin stood on the other side of the river, with a private bridge across, but then the canyon walls rose up to crests covered with sagebrush and scraggly pines, which closed out all but a span, overhead, of the sky. River and canyon would weave higher and higher, the road beginning to rise above the river, until, ultimately, after fifty miles, the road crossed Cameron Pass, which led into North Park. There were turnoffs along the way, so drivers could make way for logging trucks. Foothills gave way to thickly wooded mountains, gray peaks far above.

From as far as we could venture in a morning, pick-up trucks and campers would be scattered along the river, wherever the fishing looked promising, and Jack would sneer at the Denver or flatlanders' plates (Colorado licenses being coded by county). We would stop for two- and three-hour sessions at empty stretches, sometimes longer. I confess their fishing bored me. They waded off separately—they had rented or borrowed hip-waders—fly casting over and over, occasionally catching a fish. I had tried with my spinner rod and salmon eggs (squeamish about night crawlers) without success, and mainly would go off climbing or exploring, taking pictures, and enjoying the terrain. But they would be gone, lost and imperturbable in their pleasure, and I felt captive to this side of them, however I might try to share it, and however they tried to help me to.

Jack's business completed, we planned a full weekend high in the mountains, up a logging road to some hidden and hard-to-reach headwater, with beaver dams. Here the woods were all aspens and pine, and the stream by which we camped ran cold and clear, so pure I could drink right out of it without fear of germs. They caught trout there, cut and cleaned them in the stream, then cooked them over a campfire, to my dismay (I was put off by the tiny bones), urging the specialness on me, when what I really craved was Spam. Then we settled down, in moonlit dark and mountain cold, for sleep on our air-mattresses in the camper, them with heads to the tailgate, me in the middle with mine to the cab. But I had trouble sleeping and woke to the whine and hum of mosquitoes and a hot, swollen hand, which had been exposed outside my sleeping bag. I got up, climbed out, and shut myself in the cab, rolling up the windows tight, and keeping the map light on, so I could kill any mosquitoes that had followed me in, and spent the rest of the night swatting, right until dawn. My hands were so swollen from bites that I had no knuckles. Jack and Chuck, next morning, worried first that I had killed the truck battery with the heater and map light—that we were stranded in the wilderness—but Jack finally got the motor to start. Then they had me hold my hands in the stream, hoping that the icy water, which did numb my pain, would make the swelling go down; but when it didn't, even after half a day, reluctantly they decided to pack up and cut our expedition short—something I felt miserable to cause—and drive back down the mountain, to civilization, where they took me to an emergency room. The swelling, of course, proved to be nothing, no allergy, poisoning, or anything medicine could help—just a lot of bites together. I was tenderloin, apparently, for mountain mosquitoes, even if I wore repellant, while Chuck and Jack were mysteriously immune. Of course, the best fishing places always swarmed with gnats and mosquitoes.

We left Ft. Collins soon after, taking the long way home, heading South. They tricked me into drinking from a canteen filled at a roadside sulfur spring in Colorado Springs, which rotten egg taste I spewed out. Parking in the lot for the Broadmoor—a luxury hotel Jack insisted we see, where movie stars and other celebrities regularly visited—we changed into clean clothes, and went in to sit in the spacious lobby, pretending to be the children of an oil magnate staying there, loudly saying things back and forth about this oil-well and that, Daddy and Senator So-and-so, and causing eyes of nearby guests to widen and stare. I failed to see the faces, but Jack and Chuck smothered laughter as they took my arm, strolled, then hurried out, figuring that enough had been enough. We continued South, through the Texas panhandle, jackrabbits in our headlights beside the road past counting, through as many states as we could brag of having been in later, Oklahoma, Arkansas, Tennessee, Kentucky, West Virginia. On home. This had been my grandest and longest time away from home, though in the keeping of my brothers. Chuck left for Korea, then, and Jack in the fall to settle in Ft. Collins and to go into partnership with George Devers, never to come back, it would turn out, keeping all this distance now between himself, his land, his home of choice, and us.

After Jack left, I claimed Lady and she seemed to choose me as her substitute master. We played together, chased, or ran, with me on my bike, giving each other joy and companionship. She had her habits. As we came and went, Mom on errands, Chuck to Bryn Mawr, me to school or golf, we either had to lock her in the cellar or attach her to her chain, which was attached to a corner of the garage and some hundred feet long, so she could do her natural functions in the grass behind the garage, and otherwise rest, tongue lolling on hot days, under the bushes on the near side, where she had dug herself a hole. As I grew busier, she seemed to be chained forever, barking ferociously at squirrels, cats, rabbits, and delivery people or any other stranger: charging like a cartoon dog to the end of her leash and then being yanked back short by it, then leaping against its pull and sometimes straining and managing to slip her collar and take off after whatever it was, or whomever. My bedroom window, directly over the bush, overlooked the compass of her chain, so when she set up a fit of barking, I would yell for her to stop, then if she didn't, I would throw a glass of water out my window on her. She was as afraid of water as the wicked witch in Oz.

Sometimes when she got loose, she ran off across backyards towards Walton's and came back reeking of manure. She had found a compost pit she favored and would roll in it to lose her scent, I guess. So I would spank her and admonish in a stern, deep voice—her ears would go flat, and she'd whine and cringe, tail tucked between her legs—and then give her a hose bath, holding her by her collar, and using soap. When she did get wet, she shook herself starting with her nose, in a kind of peristalsis that went on down her collar to her midsection to her rump and finally her tail, and anyone or thing within ten feet would get the spray.

Jack had trained her as a pup to come at his whistle, which was in imitation of some wood bird in the Rockies that only he could do, going on for ten or fifteen whistled notes up and down the scale. He would do that over the phone from Colorado and we'd hold it to her ear and she would go crazy, tail beating, barking; her love and loyalty never diminished. She was scared of loud gun-like noises and firecrackers, thanks to her traumas as a pup in the lumber camp; a loud thunderclap would bring her whimpering and crouching, tail between her legs and ears back flat; likewise a car backfiring.

When I turned sixteen, between tenth and eleventh grades, Jack arranged a job for me during the hay harvest on a ranch in Colorado, which was owned by Gordon Turpin, a cousin of George Devers, Jack's partner. Jack and George would go fishing there, and Jack had helped Gordon to clear some willows once with a bulldozer and to grade a road. The ranch was in North Park, one of three high parks in the Rockies, each ringed by the peaks of the Continental Divide. In addition to some coal mining in the past, and logging in the surrounding mountains, it was primarily cattle country with twenty ranches, ranging from 2000 to perhaps 8000 acres each, including leased government lands. All were family enterprises, dating back three generations to homestead grants.

A remote place and snowed in for nine months of the year, North Park could be reached only from the east by Cameron Pass (10,295 feet), up the Poudre Canyon from Ft. Collins, from the south by Rabbit Ears Pass (9,426 feet) from Steamboat Springs, or from the north by the highway down from Laramie, Wyoming. The largest town was Walden, in the center of the park. The Turpin ranch was twenty miles west from Walden and close to the western slope.

I flew out alone—my first flight—snapping pictures from my window of clouds, as if clouds were news, and of the tiny ground features below, pictures and pictures and pictures, 35 mm slides now with a Kodak Pony. Jack met me at the Denver airport and drove me up to Ft Collins, where he was living in a trailer in a trailer park behind where our tourist cabin had been.

For the few days I stayed with him, he showed me around Ft. Collins, starting with a visit to George Devers' back lot on the west side of town, where their excavating equipment was parked, facing the mountains, and proudly painted blue and white with "Devers / Henry Excavating" on the side. He had three backhoes, mounted on tractors; two dump trucks; a big drag-line crane; two D-9 bulldozers; and a flat-bed truck for carrying the bulldozers. That week he was digging basements for a housing development, so we'd get up early, eat breakfast in the diner nearby, go to the yard, start up the backhoe, and ride over to the job, where he met other members of the crew, including George, and start digging with the backhoe. I grew used to watching, then and on other visits in years to come, the speed, delicacy and grace with which he operated this and similar heavy equipment. There was a rhythm, accompanied by the squeaking of hydraulic hoses, to the arm reaching out, digging down, drawing towards the operator and curling under to cradle the full bucket of rock and dirt, under and up, and then swinging and extending, all in one smooth motion, to unload on the growing pile of dirt. The motion was as fluid and seemingly effortless as that of a human hand and arm, as he rapidly worked a panel of levers. This was his life, now, day to day, and I took pictures, again, to show back home.

Later he drove me up the Poudre Canyon over Cameron Pass and into North Park, to Walden, and then out the dirt highway to the ranch, where after visiting and introductions, he left me.

I would be totally on my own. My adventures here would be separate even from Jack, something I would have in common with no one in the family or in my world back home. I would report about them on my return, much as Chuck reported his discoveries of Korea and Japan.

The boss was Gordon Turpin, a balding, wiry man in his late fifties; Helen was his wife; Donna (my age) and Susan (older) his daughters; and Bill, twenty-four, his son. Bill was married to Marion, who had grown up locally, and they had a three year old, Peggy Ann. Normally, as a family, they all lived in town—Walden—where Donna was finishing school, but summers moved out to the ranch. Bill had just gotten out of the Army, where he'd been stationed in Kansas, and this was his first summer back for three years. They all slept in the main house, along with the foreman, Ben, and a city cousin of Gordon's, who would help with the haying.

The main house, a white-stuccoed "A" frame, stood exposed on a treeless, dirt-and-sage-covered bluff, from which it overlooked the half-mile of road in from the highway. On the house's downhill side was a woodshed, and on its uphill side, what I took for a garage, but which turned out to be the bunkhouse, where I was given my pick of ten or so sprung cots with mattresses, since no one else had been hired yet. I chose the least sway-backed, in an ante-room with only one other cot, and with a dirty window at my head, facing east. A creek ran below the woodshed, from the fields behind the house, with a wide expanse of marsh grass and willow bushes all along its course, winding north and east. Perhaps a hundred yards down from the house, in front—down a steep path and over a footbridge; or the long way around back down the entrance road—was the grouping of barn, corral, and tin-roofed machine shop.

Once haying started, I would be paid seven dollars per day for driving a jeep tractor with a dump rake, as "scatter raker." In contrast to the newer, larger hydraulic rake connected to an orange Allis Chalmers tractor, which was used to rake mown fields into long wind-rows, the scatter-rake's job was to gather any left-overs between wind-rows and to deposit its load onto the wind-rows, with a graceful and accurate release; also to follow behind the scoop-rake and collect its leavings as it scooped up wind-rows. The scooper was a cut-down Ford truck, with a hydraulic fork in front, on which was mounted a four-sided, slatted crib, with scooping teeth; it would follow a wind-row and gather up the hay into a mini-stack, tilt back the crib, then run over to the main stack, leaving its load in front of a wide ramp, called a slide, built of logs. Here another cut-down truck, called a pusher, with a telephone pole attached to its chassis, and a high wooden gate attached to the pole and moving on metal rollers, revved up, charged, and the gate pushed the mini-stack up the slide and over into the crib and growing haystack, where two or three men, stackers, worked with pitch forks to distribute the hay and tie each load in. Stackers had the hardest, dirtiest job on the crew and were paid fifteen dollars per day. Other drivers were paid nine or ten dollars, because of the complexity of their skills and machines. The mowers had to mow carefully to the contour of each field, had to watch the mowing path for any rocks and lift the mowing bar to keep from breaking teeth; also before and after each day's work, they had to sharpen their mowing blades in the shop. Not so many years before, I was told, all the harvesting machines, the rakes, the mowers, the pusher, and the scooper had been horse-drawn. They still were on one of the neighboring ranches, the Barrows place.

The hay harvest, progressing from field to field, would leave a haystack every ten acres; these would be some thirty feet high in permanent wooden stockades, or cribs, designed to keep elk out. The hay was winter feed for the livestock. A horse- or tractor-drawn sled would cross the deep mountain snows, load up from the top of a stack, and then scatter the hay out for snowbound cattle. Winters were polar, reaching thirty and forty below, with snowfalls accumulating usually to eight or ten feet. The Turpin ranch was 5,000 acres, supporting roughly 300 cattle. Eight hundred acres were irrigated to grow hay, resulting in roughly one ton per acre (ten tons per stack), a rich mountain yield, some of which was baled and sold outside of the park. In the distance, north, across the highway, we could see the Barrows place, where stacks were already going up. There was no south, because of foothills, or west; east was all Turpin range, as far as we could see. Before haying started we worked on the irrigation ditches, on welding and otherwise fixing up the mowers and other equipment, and one day we caught horses, saddled and rode out to move a herd from one pasture to another, opening vistas to me of new areas of the ranch, along with the thrill, at last, of real cowboy work.

Soon Gordon drove into town to hire more men for the crew, and returned with two older men, with their own car, and an acned boy about my age, whose name was Larry. Having been spoiled by several days' privacy, I was apprehensive of intruders in the bunkhouse. Larry took the other cot in my anteroom. In another day or two, three more men were hired—two to work off bail from the Walden jail. "Shit, kids," one of them complained, when they came in. The third we concluded later must have been an ex-mental patient; his name was Tom, and he was tall, thin, and gawky.

The men struck me as kindly, and on their best behavior. No booze was allowed. There was no TV, except in the house. No radio. Just work. Up at 5 a.m. Breakfast by 5:30 or 6. Out to the fields by 7 or 7:30. Work until noon, drive back in for "dinner." Out again by 1. Work until 7:00 or 7:30. Come back at dusk, wash up for supper, have supper, laze around the table joking and jawboning and talking about tomorrow, then straggle up to the bunkhouse, and no real light there, except a hanging light bulb, maybe, 9, 9:30, lights out, sleep the sleep of the exhausted. Drifters and itinerants, they bragged of travels, of broken marriages, grown kids. They'd work through this haying job, then blow all their pay on new clothes, whores and a bender, and go on for some other job, picking grapes, oranges, working oil fields maybe, pipeline.

I had learned in school, then scouts, at scout camp, and in working at Dad's factory: not to stick out; to take people on their own terms, let them think well of themselves, without challenging or confusing them; to watch for the prevailing style and customs and support them; to keep myself to myself. Otherwise, everybody came to this job as an equal, with no past, no record: just as who and what they were, proved to be. You were what you did.

Larry and I had our ages in common, but Larry was overeager to please the bosses, anticipating their needs and ever-alert for ways to be useful. Bill would be repairing the mower and Larry would pick up the right wrench and have it ready before Bill even asked. I felt lazy and stupid by comparison. "Never trust anybody was his motto," Larry confided to me, speaking as a survivor in the vagabond world. He'd run away from home in Indiana, where he'd been brought up on a farm, but then had been caught fucking a cow by his bible-mad father and thrashed and thrown out. He still carried the guilt of that. He'd never had a woman. The hired men teased him about his acne and his virginity and promised to take him to Mission Street in Denver after haying: we'll clear up your face right fast.

Tom got on everyone's nerves; though both Larry and I, perhaps because of our ages, felt obliged to feel sorry for him. He was working as a stacker, along with the two men who had their own car. He carried a notebook and wrote things down constantly, say, as we were riding in the back of one of the trucks out to the fields. He rarely spoke, and never sociably; but in a nervous, shrill way would proclaim about the majesty of the mountains, God's justice, or the purity of air, the vulgar uses of mankind—manic, rather than intelligent stuff, I thought, half-baked Swendenborgian stuff. And then he'd sink into deep, brooding silence, or pull out his notebook. He both developed and provoked a sense of persecution, and finally jumped off a stack in a rage, walking off the job and back to the bunkhouse across the fields, convinced that Bill had intentionally dumped a full load of hay on him, up the slide with the pusher, while he was still working to tie in the previous load; not only that but that the other two stackers had been confederates, standing clear. Gordon, at that point, reluctantly fired him and drove him into town.

I got tagged with the nick-name "Speedy," or "Ole Speed," because I tore around the field on my jeep tractor in third gear, bouncing and jouncing, swinging over wind-rows and dumping my scatter rake. I didn't have my license yet, so I was elated by the chance to drive and to care for the tractor, to which I grew so attached I considered buying it and driving it back, somehow, to Pennsylvania. When I wasn't driving, one or two days, they tried me as a stacker, and I struggled to keep up. Physically the work was as demanding as football practice, and as team-oriented and grimly directed. Larry and I looked forward to rain days, when we'd see a pillar of rain moving down the mountains, and work would be stopped; or days after rain, when the weather was clear, but the hay was too wet to cut or stack, and we got permission to catch and saddle ponies and explore the back range of the ranch, up into aspen-covered hills.

I had my camera with me, and took roll after roll, to show back home. While we were out riding, I gave Larry my camera and he took my picture: I am in my physical prime, hard-muscled, lean, mountain-tanned, not needing glasses yet, wearing work shirt, Levi's, a rolled straw hat, and reining in my paint pony with mountains and high clouds in the background. As a picture this came as close to how I wanted to see myself as I ever had been.

When I came back to my junior year at Radnor, I was the class cowboy. Dad joked that I had stepped off the airplane, dressed up in my new rodeo clothes, with hayseed still in my ears, as if I'd never had a bath or shower.

I had spent most of my haying money on western clothes: a brocade silver-with-roses-and-pearl-snaps shirt; striped rodeo pants; engineer boots; broad belt and silver buckle with thunderbird inlay; bandana and slide; corduroy jacket with a yoke on the back; and an expensive, broad-rimmed white felt hat. All this was ordinary dress-up out there, I explained. It's how Bill dressed up to take Marion to a dance. I had a date with Tucker Merrill shortly after my return—on my own now with a driver's license—and went to pick her up in my new outfit. Her little brother answered the door and called: "There's a cowboy here for you!" And her parents came out to see. The trouble with my shirt proved to be that it could only be dry-cleaned and when Anna put it in the regular wash by mistake, the colors ran, permanently ruining it.

I tried to tell John Barnett about the ranch at school—about the hay harvest, but besides having scouts, school, and his girl, he was busy with haying himself, which they did differently at his farm, using a baler. His was a dairy farm, not a cattle ranch, so we found little common ground. Mom and Dad, however, greatly admired the color slides, and asked me to mount a show for the Spaeths, for Nana Henry, and lastly, along with Chuck's slides of Korea (soon after he'd come back), for Grandpop Thralls in his Brooklyn apartment.

"We're not rich," Chuck insisted frequently. "You and Judy think we're rich, but we're not. We're not even close."

"What are we then?" I asked.

"We're well-off. Well-to-do. We're comfortable."

Well-to-do I still found awkwardly better off than most of my classmates, except for Billy Pew and Frank Scott, who transferred for senior year to our Radnor class from private schools, Haverford and George School. Pew's family was Sun Oil and Scott's was Scott Paper Products. Frank had his impact on Rudy Nottage, Weesy Mallinckrodt, Dave Bowman, and Pete Allen, to some extent. Weesy was one of the truly glamorous girls in the class, tall, with long blond hair. Rudy, Dave and Pete were in the Decades, along with Jim Anthony: our crooning rock quartet that actually had a recording made of "Silhouettes on the Shade" (side 1) and "Stagger Lee" (side 2), which was played by local DJ's our senior year. Frank Scott, whose older brother Chuck had labeled "bad" at Haverford, lived a mile down Chamounix from our house. Frank's parents went to Europe our senior summer and he turned their house into a non-stop party, where I stopped by, with Dave Bowman, only once. Frank fancied himself an artist. He had a motorcycle and would go roaring past our house, goggles on and Weesy, with her hair streaming, hanging on in back. He got the notion to sandblast a mural onto the long, unbroken wall of his family's living room and was working on it the time I visited, having taken down paintings, and moved and covered furniture. I heard later that his parents, horrified on their return, had to have the whole room re-plastered and painted. As a bearish, bushy-bearded, sandaled, jazz-digging bohemian, he had his following. Billy Pew, who went steady with Doerte, the German exchange student in our class, had a Christmas party and I remember feeling intensely awkward—I think we all did, his public school friends. It was in a stone mansion you approached up a long drive, where you were greeted at the door by a butler, and then were introduced to his stiffly smiling parents.

Judy Stradley's father, a lawyer and horticulturalist, owned his own nursery off Sproul Road, some thirty acres or so, with a tractor and horses, which he stabled in an ancient barn with a hayloft.

Marion Watson's family had a big house back in the Ithan woods.

The majority of the college-bound, WASP, dating, party-giving and -frequenting kids were from medium income families with fair-sized houses. The Michels (lawyer), Galloways (minister), Teels (schoolteacher), Colburns (insurance agent), Kricks (real estate), Beesons (lawyer), Kings (doctor), Yerkes (pharmacist) and some others were members at St. Davids Golf Club or Martin's Dam. In North Wayne, Howard Hopson, Ann Palmer, Rick Skillman, Barby Spillman: all lived in roomy Victorians. Others lived in smaller brick or stone bungalows, set among the larger houses on densely planted and tree-lined streets: Tucker Merrill, Fuvvie Bye; and still others in newer, modern houses, in developments, like Larry Arnold's, Liz Medica's, or Kathie Ross's.

Relatively poor included families living in two-family houses without yards, row houses, or apartments, whose parents were blue-collar, and whose expectations were for trade, service, or business careers, rather than for college. This included mainly Italian kids and kids from cultivated black families; in the first instance, Joe Iacone, Franny Angelini, Jack Capelli, Paul DeSantis, Corky Cappola; in the second, Jim Anthony, Ethel and Margie Carroll, Diana Farmer, Claudette Johnson. It also included Paul Englebert, Joy Bennett, Harold Little, Neil Pine, and Dave Bowman.

Definitely poor included John Barnett, Earl Blackwell, George Holman. John's case I knew; those of others, I assumed, belonged to areas of town off-limits to me, such as Highland Avenue, towards Devon, or the black section behind St. Davids Golf Club, which Dad referred to categorically as "Henry Avenue." I was aware, on dates, at parties, how parents looked at and placed me, where on the scale of social prospects I fit in. Mrs. Ross liked me; the Merrills liked me; the Davises liked me. The Watsons couldn't care less.

Among our own ranks, the group that determined status was initially one of girls: Marion Watson, Sue Shellenburg, Ellen Bleecker. They decided on the boys, then had parties. There was a sorting out. You had to have a party to get invited to parties.

You had to go the parties to have a girlfriend, or so it seemed to me. Of course there were equalizers. Sex and sports, as well as other intangibles, personality, say, a sense of humor, style, or a way with cars were factors as important as money, or more so. Football and other sports, besides creating heroes for the girls, established grounds among the guys for camaraderie; and the girls, seeing how the guys admitted and admired another guy, would start to look at him with favor. Joe Iacone, for instance, bashful, gentle, our starting fullback, was dating Marion Watson for a while.

Dave Bowman and Judy Stradley were a cross-class romance; likewise, hard-working Dick Curley and Peggy Krick.

Dave was a victim of divorce, living with his mother and sisters in what must have been a cramped and embarrassing apartment over the A&P. Neil Pine was the only other classmate I knew with divorced parents; but where Neil was edgy, a bully, and later transferred to another school, Dave was our class James Dean, whom he resembled in looks, as well as in his brooding, tragic manner. His father was an ad-man and playboy in New York, with an apartment in Greenwich Village, something like that, but whatever alimony he sent barely supported them. Dave's oldest sister had graduated years before, but his next, Joan, three classes older, had been head cheerleader, outshining even Holly Melcher. They all, including his mother (who, he has told me recently, was then having an affair with our married football coach, which caused a hushed scandal), were blessed and cursed by charm and good looks. In 11th grade English, our tough-minded, middle-aged teacher, Miss Rose Ferdinand, singled out Dave and me, and we became friendly rivals in our study of *Macbeth*, where we puzzled and argued about the concept of amorality, as opposed to immorality. Senior year, she had us debating whether the world owed us a living; Dave thought yes, I disagreed. I know I began writing seriously, and, for that matter, drawing and painting, which was our other talent in common, nearly as much to impress Dave as to impress Miss Ferdinand or the other kids, and I think he did likewise, both of us pushing towards some notion of the cool, a quality that was knowing, bold, and a little over our heads, and that concerned sex, love, God, and contempt for hypocrisy. But then besides art and writing, looks, a fair performance at football and track, a readiness to fight if challenged, a rapport with all kinds of kids, and a hip way of being first to catch or coin a witty expression or gesture—"Hey, g'om"—Dave also had the glamour of the Decades, where as lead singer, backed up by Pete Allen, Joe Iacone, Jim Anthony, and Rudy Nottage (also Paul Michel, sometimes, on drums), he held crowds spellbound, girls swooning. I envied him that popularity, and later his romance with Stradley, who resembled a thinner Natalie Wood.

Twelve out of 156 kids in my Radnor class were black. That included Diana Farmer, whose father was Dr. James Farmer, an official in the N.A.A.C.P, and Jim Anthony, our class president, who went steady with Claudette Johnson. It also included Earl Blackwell, slow-witted, good-natured, and sleepy, the first person brought to mind by the pop song, "Charlie Brown, he's a clown." As co-captain of the football team and center for basketball, Earl drew laughter for inevitably scratching his crotch while mumbling speeches into the pep-rally microphone. He ended up, immediately after graduation, as a sanitation worker.

Rudy Nottage was a special case. His friends were primarily white. In fifth grade, he used to walk Barby Spillman home because she lived around the corner, and partly he and I became friends because of my pursuit of her. His mother was a live-in domestic and his father the gardener for a rich family. He was one of the most popular kids in our class, respected for his humor, his generosity, and his brains. I remember the shock and outrage of everybody when Harold Little, who had been Rudy's best friend, lost his temper during a softball game in sixth grade and called him a nigger; whereupon Mr. Shock took Harold away for a long, searching talk, and afterwards Harold, who was a troubled kid, tearfully apologized, first to Rudy, then to all of us.

Rudy as a friend in sixth grade invited me to his house, which was the upstairs of the garage, a sizeable outbuilding to the Victorian main house of what once had been an estate and now was a yard of three or four acres. I saw his room, though I did not meet his mother, and we mainly played outside. Then I wanted to invite him to my home, but Mom told me it would not be a good idea. Anna knew Rudy's mother from church. Mom did not directly forbid me to invite him over, but in her way, she did warn me, and I came to understand that I was not allowed to have black kids for visiting friends; that society, which meant the neighbors, frowned on it.

In high school, Rudy was class wit. He also was a starting half-back in football, from the pound teams all the way to varsity; a winning sprinter in track; and he played alto sax in Mr. Napier's twenty-piece swing-band. Then he joined Dave and the others in the Decades. His yearbook entry says "hopes for college."

At eighteen, the summer after graduation, mixed up with Scott and company, Rudy knocked up a girl from Henry Avenue, and did the right thing by her, so the last I heard as I went to college, was that after his taste of the privilege, he had been dragged under by circumstances, back into poverty, domestic life, and low horizons. I always spoke up for Rudy to Dad, as my friend, as someone I liked and admired. So it was with some satisfaction, axioms verified, that Dad sent me a local news article later on, after I had moved from college to graduate school. Rudy had walked into Avil's, the dry-cleaners, and shot the clerk there to death with a shotgun; he had been tried and sentenced for first-degree murder and sent to prison. Drugs had been involved. I tried to imagine him, Rudy, fighting his domestic world, baby crying, married to a girl he did not love, hating his life and the menial job he needed to support it (he tried gardening I think), still in touch with the rich boys, who otherwise were no better or more gifted than he was, and thinking of their wild parties, and meanwhile the mid-sixties civil rights movement in the news, along with the protests against Viet Nam.

I try, but I can't imagine him. Not Rudy. Not murder. Not prison.

Fall, 1955, Judy, at 20, married with Hans and keeping their Harrisburg apartment, and still using Chuck's car, had her baby, John Christian Friedericy. Her pregnancy over the summer had fascinated me. Now there was a baby and Mom, Dad and I would drive the hour on the turnpike to visit.

Children to Mom were sacred, and she spoke rhapsodically of childbearing, her own role in creating and in nurturing life. Through this sentiment, as well as through my own brother love, I viewed Judy's pregnancy as a family miracle. So much was centered on it. John was born right after our brothers' trip to Colorado. Chuck was on his way to Korea. I was taking pictures. John soon replaced my dog, Lady, as my model, with Mom and Judy overly appreciative of the results. John barely sitting up with a cap on his head, big smile. John in a bouncing sling-chair. John, after they had moved from their apartment into a trailer in Harrisburg, smoking Hans's pipe upside down as he tottered in an outside crib. John in Dad's lap, held at arm's length while Dad mugged at him.

Dad was in his way as excited about John as Mom was in hers; for him, I think, this was proof of redemption, proof of life going on, with the next generation the start of a new role for him as grandfather, a role where he would bear no guilt or resentment, and where he might equal or surpass his own father with us in the past. Dad reveled in John and in the babies to come.

Another specialness for me, in a way, was to be relieved of my designation as "the baby of the family." All the others had had an experience of me as a baby and I had never had that experience myself (give or take my younger cousin, John Spaeth) until now. Also now I was an "uncle," an adult designation none of my friends or peers at the time could boast.

Lust seemed a matter separate from my loneliness, and was an agony and burden to me. There was dating, and the sweet parrying of personalities and vanities with this girl or that, leading to making out; but separate from dating entirely were sheer physical longings. At fifteen or sixteen I was masturbating nearly every day, and sometimes two or three times a day. It got to the point where I marked my calendar every time I succumbed, and prided myself if I abstained for two, even three days. Once I triumphantly abstained for a whole week. This was before I had pictures to inspire me, but once I did have a stack of photography magazines, shrewdly merged into a stack of comic books and other magazines, they would call out, and surely I could just look, but looking, I'd grow feverish and weak, and always they would overcome me. Pleasure was just that little choice away.

I discovered the magazines innocently enough, through my interest in photography, an interest that then became my cover for seeking them out and collecting them. The first were annuals, sold on the newsstand, 1956, 1957, and they would have tasteful and stylized nudes scattered among the usual landscape and other artful shots. Then I discovered the Fawcett hobby series, *Prize Winning Photography, Photography Handbook, Candid Photography, Salon Photography*. These had whole sections of nothing but nudes, and I went to shy and trembling ends to procure them. I would stalk the paperback book store near the Wayne railroad station, where I knew one was in a rack, go in, not have nerve, go back out, circle, pass again, until I finally mustered myself, bought it nervously, hot faced, with shaky hands, wrong change, along with something else respectable, say *Golf Tips*, and fled. The descriptions of ones I could not find convinced me to order them all in a bunch, direct mail, and on a day that I was sick and feverish with flu, staying in the den on a daybed for Mom's convenience in bringing me meals, in she came from the mail with the package of them. "Here are your books," she said, and stayed to watch as I opened it and tried to cover my guilt (surely I was transparent to her) by feigning great technical interest in the, say, salon photographs. One whole book in that package was on *Photographing Nudes.*

Kathie Ross came to Radnor in 11th grade, transferring from Lower Merion, where she had gone for two or three years. They had lived in Puerto Rico for a while, then someplace in the South, before her father had got a job in Philadelphia. Her transfer to Radnor was the result of his promotion on that job, a new prosperity, and their buying a ranch house in a development off Sproul Road. But hardly had they moved, and had she started Radnor, when her father died suddenly of a heart attack. I had been aware of her before his death, but had never really known or dated her, so I never got to meet him. All along, she had been going steady with someone named "Ace" Townsend from Episcopal.

We met at Sally Yerkes' party, talked, slow-danced, drank punch or beer, and kissed. She liked me, without my trying to persuade her to, though she would put me through the ordeal of yearning, pleading, and of trying to win her from Ace, until she finally broke up with him.

She was small-breasted, athletic, and wore her hair, light brown, in a page-boy. Her face was square-jawed and thin-lipped, but she was pretty in a tough way; and her tanned arms and legs were firm and beautiful. I was attracted to her combination of suburban good looks, madras shorts and all, her wit, her anger, and later, to her family pathos. She had a sister a year or so younger, Carol, and a brother four years younger, Johnnie. Mrs. Ross still had black hair, was slim, played golf, and gave and went to cocktail and bridge parties. Mr. Ross had been a Navy man at some point, and his portrait showed him in an officer's uniform. They became a family who welcomed and even seemed to need me, as a fatherly man (I felt this), away from my family.

As for Kathie's anger: she warned me she could be a bitch, and that she was a bad sport; that when she played tennis for Lower

Merion, she had thrown down her racket and walked off. That she was like that; she had no tolerance for frustration. There was a hoody bravado about her, too, looking for kicks. Everything sexy and raw about dancing, she loved. The wildness, the drunken bacchanal. I worried about her loyalty to me in the midst of that, and would get jealous when she slow-danced or flirted with Paul Michel, even while he was going steady with Marion Watson. A picture of Kathie and him, obviously bombed and hugging at a party, found its way into one of the yearbooks.

Another time, after we were going steady, after she had told me, "I love you, hon," and I would feel triumphant, superior, and normal, all at once, to be driving with her as my girl, and she would automatically sit in the middle, instead, as other girls had, edging purposely away to the passenger's door, and she would put her hand on and under my thigh, possessively. After I had that sense of belonging, which I had seen and envied others finding and enjoying, but never thought I could. After our petting had taken its progress. After we had parked. After I felt her breasts, and lower. After I had asked to feel her breasts inside, and had fumblingly unhooked my first bra. After we had kissed and kissed, especially in her driveway, so it steamed up the car, and Mrs. Ross would have to blink the garage light. After I told her about Dad's alcoholism, the first I had told anyone, girl or otherwise, as a way of sharing: then she had told me, as an equal revelation, about the family gardener in Puerto Rico.

She had been brought up there, where her father was stationed, I guess. When she was eight or so, this man, the gardener, had shown her his penis, had had her play with it, and then had taken down her pants, fondled, and lain on top of her, but she had been too small and he couldn't make it go in, so he had ejaculated outside of her. She told me this in context, partly, of talking about her bad-girl appetite for sex, and for the illicit. And shocked, I told her I wanted to kill the man, over so many years. She said her father had felt that way too. But that the experience didn't seem so bad to her, the way it did to others; that she had liked and wanted it, in a way. Musing.

I exercised to have muscles, since Kathie told me that muscles were as exciting to girls as breasts were to boys. I worked my way from twenty to fifty to seventy-five push-ups. I started wearing a tank top to school, which Mom had bought me, no less, with no sleeves, in order to show my muscles off, and which drew frowns from some of the teachers, who had marked me as college-bound and respectable. They didn't like the way Kathie and I walked, arms around each others' waists, in the halls, either. At some point, Mrs. Long took me aside and warned me not to let my reputation slip.

After sessions of heavy petting on dates, at parties and at her mother's house after school, sessions that included her letting me unhook her bra and feel her breasts and nipples, and finger her, and much dry humping, and sometimes in the steamed up car in her driveway, her masturbating me until I came into a handkerchief: we'd actually made love for the first time, albeit by mutual accident.

We had been in Dad's Ford station-wagon at the Main Line Drive-In, kissing, with me sitting under her, and her straddling my lap, facing away from the movie screen, and my pants were off and my penis free and hard and instead of just rubbing it on her panties and against her vulva, I pulled her panties down under her dress (no one outside could see) and around her buttocks as much we could, and then was rubbing my penis against her wetness and hair, and then the impulse just to work it in a little way became irresistible and her motion too, so I slipped in all the way, deep inside her, hot and wet, and unimagined by any approximations, along with the awareness and elation of what we'd done, that we were fucking, and first time for both of us, and no tearing of a hymen or anything painful or bloody for her. I was able to thrust several times, enough to be really doing it—this fearful, astonishing and irreversible act—before I felt on the verge of coming and pulled out. And for then that was enough. The threshold was crossed for us. We loved each other.

Soon after that first time, early in June and after graduation, we plotted that Kathie would come over to my house when Mom was away, a certain day. I was to call her. The day, when it came, was tense and abrasive; I was restless with Mom to be gone, then called Kathie and her mother hadn't brought back their car yet, and the afternoon was passing. On the surface, we kept things innocent, she was just to come over, nothing more than that, so we could be together and I could share my home life with her, show her the house. But there was deliberate stealth to it. Mom wasn't to know. All along there was some fear that Mom would not approve of her, on any grounds; whereas Mrs. Ross openly welcomed me. Kathie had to come before Mom came back, and the longer our plan was frustrated the more irritable, cold and impatient we became to each other on the phone. But then at last she called and was coming, though it was late. And then she arrived, parking her station-wagon right out front.

What happened then was not entirely innocent or spontaneous. I had read and been impressed by a scene in *Some Came Running* by James Jones, where the teenage writer sneaks his girlfriend home and makes love to her on his childhood's bed. Excitedly, I showed Kathie around. We went down to the cellar and I showed her my print shop, and this was important to me, to be showing her my most personal and private world, and I kissed her down there, against my type cases, and then we went up to see my bedroom, where she looked over my writing desk and stuff on the walls (it was a humid, sticky afternoon, too), and after hollow preliminaries, like nothing was intended except one friend looking over another's room and books, we started kissing and making out in some awkward, semi-stoop on the floor. Then I had her blouse off, and half-lifted, half-urged her onto my bed, and had my shoes and pants off and penis free. She didn't want to take her bra off, because she was afraid of Mom coming home, something like that.

And with no more sophisticated idea than to repeat and embellish on our drive-in experience, I was in her, on top of her, for real, three, five, six strokes, when I felt myself coming and pulled out, to catch most of my ejaculate in my palm. I got up and hurried to the bathroom, to wipe my hands and flush the evidence, then wash myself, and when I came back to Kathie, we did, in fact, hear Mom's car in the driveway. Kathie groped for and pulled on panties, then Bermudas, shrugged into and buttoned her blouse. Me too, my underpants, pants and shirt. Heart pounding, I felt fatalistic: just here it comes, and no escape. But Kathie hurried down the front stairs, out the front door, and managed to drive off, just as I clambered down the back stairs to greet Mom, who came in the kitchen door with packages. Here, I confess, memory fails, but she must have been puzzled and suspicious. "Whose car was that? Wasn't that Kathie I saw? Why couldn't she stay?" I must have lied and Mom must have let me lie. Did I say it was someone else? Judy Stradley, for instance, and that she'd just been passing and stopped to say hello, but was late getting home? Or that it was Kathie, and she'd only stopped for a minute, and was late. "Well, she should at least have stayed to say hello. Didn't you hear me coming in? I don't like that." Whatever Mom permitted me in this, she didn't like, but she didn't cross-examine me or force the issue, either.

A day or so afterwards, Kathie left with her family for eight weeks at their summer resort on Squirrel Island, off the coast of Maine. We'd talked about my coming up to visit. We'd also worried whether I had pulled out in time, whether any sperm had been inside, whether she might get pregnant. And for the next two weeks, hearing nothing, I wrote her everyday. I holed up in our basement playroom, where it was cool, and where, with Chuck's old typewriter, I had set out to write a novel over the summer. In my letters I kept asking, emphatically, how she was, assuming that she would know what I meant. I was living through the real possibility of disgrace, of not going to college. I prayed to God to help. To forgive me. To make it be all right. If such a small slip as that, such a natural, good, necessary thing could result in ruined lives, then where was justice? I thought of Mom and Dad, how they would react. I was too young to be married, too young to have a baby, to have life's responsibilities close down around me.

Kathie, meanwhile, promised not to mess around, but then went on to write about her high times messing around, and wanting to know about mine. "All the boys up here are either older or younger than I am. I miss you terribly. I just want you to know I could never do anything up here or any other time that I might be separated from you or that I would be afraid or ashamed to tell you about. Last night I had a blast. I wish I could write you letters as good as you write me, but you know I'm no writer. Be assured I feel the same things you do." Finally, in early July, I sent her a telegram: "Are you okay?" and got back a special delivery letter, she was, "You haven't done anything wrong. I love you. How's that? Everybody is kidding me about your daily letters, but I love it and they can't wait to see you. Well, just one more thing: DON'T WORRY!!"

Relief. Hosannas. She told me later, she'd been amused at how upset I'd gotten. She hadn't even thought about it.

We continued to look forward to my visit. I poured out my heart in letters with no self-consciousness about cliches: "When I get to Squirrel Island, my love, we will lie on pine needles in the shadows of the forest floor." She wrote back: "Two more weeks and you'll be here. I'm so excited. Please let me know what day, and how you're coming."

Days, I swam, played golf, or both, then closed myself in the cool of the basement and wrote away. Besides letters, I was writing my "novel." Called "Search for Stone," where "stone" meant something fixed, true, and certain, it concerned a younger boy, whose search for meaning resembled mine, and also resembled the boy's in Ray Bradbury's *Dandelion Wine*, which I'd been reading. My boy was drifting towards self-damage, if not suicide, but then I wanted him to recognize his value and to take responsibility for himself.

Mom and Dad had hedged all along about the Squirrel Island idea, and I had been embarrassed to ask, but now they flatly refused to let me go. No arguments. Why not? But I promised! Mrs. Ross thinks I'm coming! No. It's not proper, Mom said. You're too young. If you were getting married, that's the kind of thing you'd do. Mrs. Ross just isn't thinking. She's more lenient or permissive about these things than we are. Sorry.

This was their power play, as parents. I had to write Kathie, sorry, but my parents wouldn't let me.

From then on things were never the same. A choice had been made. When Kathie came back, in August, she had already turned her mind to the new life at Duke, a life without me, as I went on to Amherst College. We saw each other, and I wrote her in an unsent letter: "You have been losing hold day by day until you can't even accept me as a friend. I'm sorry about the sex we have shared since you have been back, for your part it was without love, for mine it was a last desperate attempt to keep some sign that you still liked me. I have found faith in something, and knowing how hard it is for me to do that, you must also know it is impossible for me to lose that faith now. I found faith in you. You have a lot of things influencing you right now, college, the freedom you want, but I think there is something for both of us that will eventually reach through all that, and that you will come back, we will come back."

We never did.

College Years

THE FALL OF 1958, as I had begun my senior year at Radnor, my parents had taken me for a tour of New England colleges—Yale, Wesleyan, Dartmouth, and Amherst. Cornell was omitted. Either it had proven to be bane enough to my generation of the family, or it had been ranked as inferior to these four by my placement counselor. Academically, I had done well all along at Radnor, and though I felt that I could excel at any subject, English and History were my favorites. My proudest piece of work, which I submitted with my applications, was my research paper on comparative religions.

Did I want large or small? Urban or pastoral? Yale I found formal and alien; Wesleyan, where Vic Butterfield (who had been Dad's fraternity brother at Cornell) was still president, was familiar to me from past visits, and we generally favored; but when I saw Amherst, something just clicked. I felt at home. The beauty of the campus took me. In my interview, which centered on my essay, I felt at ease. When we drove on to see Dartmouth, my heart had already been decided. Then Amherst granted me an early acceptance.

My senior grades fell off a bit, thanks to my preoccupation with Kathie, but I graduated third in my class. Of my 150 classmates, perhaps thirty were college bound; the rest sought unskilled jobs or enlisted in the Army, and two or three were pregnant. One classmate, at our all night graduation party, ran down Judy Stradley's back lawn, tore off his clothes, and took a flying dive into a pond that was only ankle deep at that point. He broke his neck, aged 17, and survived to face life paralyzed in a wheelchair.

From my parents' perspective, as the one unscarred by Dad's alcoholism, I had the best chance, seemingly, to fulfill my potential. Jack, after quitting Cornell, and after following his vocation as a mechanic, had enrolled in Colorado A&M with the idea of an engineering degree, but again had dropped out. Chuck after quitting Cornell had finished premed at Franklin and Marshall, then served his tour in the Army and only after years of soul searching had finally buckled down to four years of study at Hahnemann Medical School, followed by another four of interning. Judy, because of her pregnancy, had left Swarthmore in her sophomore year and married Hans. I was supposed to benefit from these lessons, I felt, though I had no goal beyond some vague fantasy of someday owning a printing company. I only knew my high school world and Kathie.

Jack was married in Colorado that summer—coincident with my pregnancy scare with Kathie—and Mom, Dad, Chuck and I drove out for the wedding. My parents felt relieved that Jack had married at last, that he was no longer alone, and that he had joined the world of conventional society. This relief, however, was mixed with perplexity and dismay about whom he had married.

June was two years older than Jack. They first met in 1957. She had been divorced, but her ex would come home Saturday night for ten years (I paraphrase from letters she later sent me about her life, in hopes that I would write about her); he liked to work out of town, on Sunday she would pack his clothes and he was gone again; he drank worse and worse, beat her and their three children harder, waved the shotgun, threatened to kill them, to rid him of them so he could marry "a real hot gal."

Simple fear kept June from taking away his visiting rights. They divided the horses, she sold hers, gave the jeep, kept the Ford, kept the furniture, the poor run down house, the only place the babies had lived, gave him clothes, his guns, his legal papers.

The septic tank had plugged and her brother Ralph set out to fix it and worked a deal with Jack Henry on his backhoe to dig the leach line. "When it was dug"—June wrote—"the lean man stepped off the digger and approached the skinny gal only to find that I owned the farm, Ralph's sister." According to June, her little girl Terry proved to be their go-between. When he had returned to back-fill the ditch he had let Terry ride on the tractor, and "no man had ever treated her so kindly." Terry had invited him to her birthday party. About every two weeks Jack would call and come over and watch TV with the children; he took the gang fishing. June needed an escort to PTA banquets and Jack said he'd enjoy a free dinner. So Jack became her "scared bashful escort." She washed his laundry, cleaned his trailer house (which was never locked), and regularly brought him dinner there. "He was a lonesome individual. And since he had never really asked me to marry him, only taken me for granted, I insisted he say the question out loud."

I was the wedding photographer. The newlyweds moved to June's ramshackle house on the outskirts of Ft. Collins through the winter. They visited St. Davids together for Christmas, 1959, along with the "ready-made family" of Larry, Terry and Dale, whom Jack legally adopted. I remember that Lady fought June for Jack's lap.

Mom, who talked with June at length on the phone and who received hundreds of hand-written letters from June that were more than naively crude (claiming as their excuse June's hillbilly persona and earthiness), saw June as having an Amazon complex, a would-be Belle Starr, cracking a bullwhip. She wrote to Mom: "At least your son loves his wife, but he should word his phrases more differently. In the west I learned to speak and understand very plain statements and not the fancy phrases of the Eastern Educated husband of mine, so I am teaching him some hot phrases of mine. In my days of being a truck driver, I carried with me a stiff nine foot bull whip, to snap over the top of slow moving cattle, and then into the truck and to Denver, and if some old rancher wanted to be cute, I would very politely say step two steps back please or I will let you have it with my whip."

I found June bawdy and good hearted, and a fit soul-mate for the sportsman, nature-loving side of Jack. Jack had rescued her and her children. With Dad's help, he bought out Devers and designed and built a new one-story house, south of Ft. Collins. This would also serve as the shop, shop yard, and office for Jack Henry Excavating. June insisted that she share the business problems with him, taking an accounting course and attempting to run the office, while Jack worked maniacally, from before dawn until after dusk.

At Amherst, I had been assigned a room in a freshman dorm, with a roommate from Long Island. Most of the freshmen were from private schools, and thereby were better prepared than I for the sudden crush of college courses. Among my letters home (which Mom dutifully saved), I wrote: "The work is challenging—the teachers, wonderful and frustrating. It didn't take long to figure what they were driving at. One, we are not authorities on anything; two, high school did no more than fill us with meaningless facts; three, we are here to develop and discover everything all over again. All the guys are swell, and it's nice to be proud of knowledge for a change. It is a great life, dedicated 98% to studies, which it should be, and 2% to an occasional weekend mixer." I was averaging low B's (instead of my high school A's), with trouble in Math; however, had "gotten through to my English Comp teacher. Tell Chuck that he really likes my writing and in his own cynical way has praised it. It puts the extra burden on my writing the next class assignment better than the last, or else. But I love it. Three themes a week are due and I turn in an average of five. I may major in English rather than History—it certainly is my first love. *The Amherst Literary Magazine* is coming out next month. I'm going to submit a story or so. I think it would be a good place to start."

By six weeks, I was clearly failing Calculus and barely passing Physics. At the same time, I had one of the highest grades in Composition, and had both a story and a poem accepted by the literary magazine, which led to some campus notoriety. The editors wanted me to write more and to join the staff. And come spring, I found myself being rushed by fraternities—flattered and sought after by witty upperclassmen, some of them writers or English majors.

I chose Delta Kappa Epsilon, whose stately house was on the fringes of the campus, up a hill, and within sight of Emily Dickinson's house.

I still wrote letters to Kathie at Duke. I had her picture on my desk. While other freshmen sought dates from nearby Smith and Mt. Holyoke, I felt worldly and sufficient to have had my adult romance, tantamount to marriage, and to have my girl from home. Despite her letters back, however, protesting loneliness for me, she was dating an upperclassman, a twenty-four year old junior, who had been in the Navy for two years. Neither Thanksgiving nor Christmas vacations worked out as reunions. She skipped Christmas at home and wrote me in January that "if Larry ever does leave you can pick up the pieces if you'll still be around, because there will be pieces." They were pinned by March, and married in April, though I didn't get the news until July.

As I began my sophomore year, she was separated, living home, and I had visited her there, captivated by the baby, a girl, which I helped her bathe and powder. Her mother out, baby asleep, we started to make out. This continued. Larry lived in Kingston, N.C. She saw a marriage counselor, hoping to save the marriage. I took off a special weekend in mid-October and traveled home to see her. She had just come back from Kingston. This time, baby asleep and her mother out again, we talked and drank in their living room and ended up making love on the couch. I used a condom for the first time, having learned this much from my fraternity brothers, but when we finished, the condom had slipped off inside her. A week later, she wrote to me back at Amherst, "It is my turn now to worry about being pregnant. I couldn't go back to Larry because it wouldn't be his baby (he knows that we haven't had intercourse for months). I couldn't marry you because I am not divorced. It would take me about a year to get a divorce. I couldn't go to school because I'd have another baby to take care of."

I don't recall my response. She soon wrote, however, that the pregnancy had been a false alarm. She had learned a lesson. "'Thou shalt not commit adultery,' and that is exactly what we were doing."

We didn't write after that. She and Larry were reconciled and moved on in life. I was popular suddenly at Amherst, dating a Mt. Holyoke girl, involved in fraternity life, and absorbed by my classes, the literary magazine, and my writing. Mom and Mrs. Ross would meet and talk in the supermarket or at the golf club and I heard later that Kathie had been divorced, then remarried; then, I think, divorced again.

I felt that I had found a new world of belonging at Amherst, and was happier during my college years than I had been since our family had begun breaking up with Jack, Chuck, and Judy leaving.

Amherst romanticized learning. I felt that I was learning more than was dreamt of in my parents' philosophy. That I knew beyond them. I was convinced that I was part of a new educational adventure that rendered all other educations inferior, especially the rote learning kinds.

From the arch, scowling Arnold Arons in Physics, where I failed and failed, to the toe-tapping William Pritchard, to the cranky, eccentric Ted Baird, the witty Benjamin DeMott, the quiet, attentive William Heath, and the poetically casual and bemused Rolfe Humphries, my teachers' minds seemed beyond me, wiser and keener in their own processes of thought and inquiry, yet able to spot moments of promise in my work, an idea, an argument, a kind of phrase or metaphor, and to single out such moments, to my surprise, for praise.

I was encouraged to believe that I was one of the best student writers. "You are so good sometimes, you scare me," Humphries said. From sophomore year, I was elected editor of the *Amherst Literary Magazine*, in which I published my own fiction nearly every issue. I felt singled out, and my classmates and fraternity brothers became an appreciative audience. I drew on my ranch-hand experiences in my writing, and in the guise of characters from the ranch was writing about my relationship with Kathie and aspiring towards a novel (this ended up as a novella, was my senior thesis, and the second "creative thesis" ever allowed by the college).

One of my fraternity brothers had a family friend who was managing editor of *McCall's*, Margaret Cousins; she had heard about Amherst's experimental composition courses and asked him for samples, so he had shown her my papers. She wrote to me, writer to writer; a regular correspondence and friendship began, and in my junior year, she got me a summer job as an articles assistant at *Redbook*, which proved to be my introduction to Manhattan, and my first adult, paying job.

I lived in the DKE fraternity house for three years and immersed myself as much in its world as in the world of the classroom. Barry Goldwater was running for President and had proclaimed college fraternities to be "laboratories of democracy," or words to that effect. We had our rituals, our secret goat room, our initiation ceremonies, passwords, handshakes, and our hooded robes reminiscent of the Masons, KKK, or other brotherhoods. We had collisions of backgrounds, characters, values, ambitions and ways of life as well, most obviously between the hard-partying, loud-music playing, card-playing, girl-chasing contingents, and serious students, who worked reclusively while others sought pleasure.

A slightly different collision existed between materialists, more often than not history, political science, or chemistry majors, and altruists, more often than not English majors. In their different ways Michael Naess, otherwise an actor and playboy from a wealthy shipping family in New York; Warren Stearns, an arch conservative from a Catholic business family in Chicago; Andy Blue, a Goldwater conservative from a New York Jewish family; and Tex Hudspeath, from a Texas business family: all demanded material wealth from their futures, however they could get it. Not unlike my father in college, they knew they wanted money, and were preparing for business careers.

On the other hand, Wes Franklin, an Altoona, Pennsylvania, mortician's son; Richard Wirtz, son of Willard Wirtz, who became Johnson's Secretary of Labor; Dennis Clifford, whose parents were Leftist teachers and labor activists in New Jersey; Jimmy Goldberg, son of a government lawyer in the State Department; Steve Baldwin, son of a career diplomat; David Hamilton, whose father was "Mayor of Miami" (Miami, Missouri, where he had relocated from a Chicago newspaper career to the life of yeoman farmer): these were readers, talkers, debaters, witty iconoclasts, and truth-seekers. Likewise David Lahm, who had won a national jazz piano competition his sophomore year and whose mother was the song-writer Dorothy Fields. They wanted progressive social roles, to serve society, to be teachers, lawyers, doctors, to write, to create art, and gave little thought to futures other than graduate school.

We belonged to a world that was changing. When Kennedy had been inaugurated in the January of our sophomore year, we had seen him only as an unknown, signaling instability and change for better or worse from the Republican years to whatever would come next. I lack recall of the Bay of Pigs debacle, or over that summer, the cold war face-offs leading to the Cuban missile crisis.

We did tend to be studying anti–cold war books, such as Robert Heilbroner's *The Future as History*, which emphasized the socialistic aspects of American capitalism and the capitalistic direction of the Russian Socialist system. We laughed at home bomb shelters as lunacy, though we had progressed from A to H bombs (with talk of cobalt bombs to come), and the dangers of fallout from atmospheric testing were in the news. We were oddly uninvolved in the space race—Gagarin in 1961, Alan Shepard, Virgil Grissom, then John Glenn in 1962 for the first U.S. manned orbital flight. We were only dimly aware of the civil rights marches and issues; in the spring of 1961 some Amherst students joined Smith, Mt. Holyoke and U. Mass. students for a bus expedition as Freedom Riders, but neither they nor their cause were prominent on campus. As undergraduates we snubbed the counterculture crowd, the SDS, and felt too valuable for the draft. Military service portended no Viet Nam as yet, and several of us went into the Air Force or Naval academies. Others, like myself, depended on deferments for graduate school, but more out of snobbery and a love for learning than out of political objections. No one would burn draft cards until 1965 and later. Drugs were still viewed as a degenerate, lower-class aberration. We were also a pre-pill generation, and many married early for lack of precautions.

As college life preoccupied me, dispatches from home reached me in jolts.

Lady had been left with Mom when I left for college, and in my junior year she was hit by a car—she chased—and died in Mom's arms, as Mom told me on the phone. Mom had been reading Faulkner's *As I Lay Dying*, heard the barking, horn, tires' squeal, and Lady's yelp, and then had run to her: that was a tearing, final loss for Mom, which she grieved more deeply, it seemed, than she had for the death of her father. She vowed there would be no more dogs, ever; no more vulnerability to that kind of love.

I heard that Chuck was dating, and then that he was engaged to Nancy Mervine, a nursing student my age at Bryn Mawr Hospital, where he had offered to take me for intern parties. Unlike Chuck's earlier hope—the blond and wealthy Patricia Watson (daughter of a business friend of Dad's), who had married a continental Frenchman instead of Chuck—Nancy was a Jennifer Jones brunette, whose parents from upstate had had a professional portrait painted of her, larger than life, because they were proud of her beauty. They were modest, nice enough middle-class people, who seemed to look up to Mom and Dad, and saw Chuck as a catch. The wedding was the August after I graduated. Jack couldn't make the wedding, so I was Chuck's best man. For a wedding toast, as the little brother who had grown up under Chuck's teasing and domineering, I wished Nancy well in her efforts "to love, honor, and—most of all—to obey." They had their first baby, Chuck, Jr., the following spring, and lived in a hospital apartment at Bryn Mawr. A year later, as Nancy finished her nursing degree, Chuck took a residency at Woodberry Memorial Hospital in New Jersey—a surgical practice far enough away from Mom and Dad, and from Nancy's family, to be on his own, and yet near enough to visit frequently. They moved into a starter house in Winona, where Bob was born in 1965; then Scott in 1967; then they moved into a large Victorian house, easily the size of St. Davids itself, if not of Bloomingdale, in Woodberry.

In my sophomore year at Amherst, Hans and Judy had moved back east from Illinois to Charlottesville, Virginia. Originally they had lived in Harrisburg, where we visited nearly every weekend and where John had been born in 1955. Hans worked for an engineering firm as a draftsman. Then he decided he should get out of commercial engineering and teach instead. He went for a Ph.D. at the University of Illinois, where they lived in a trailer park, and where Lucia was born in 1958. Ph.D. in hand, Hans, whose research was with particle accelerators, took a teaching and research appointment at the University of Virginia. They bought a house. A third child, Bonnie, was born, and I visited them there both with Mom and Dad and on my own. Hans's research was classified, and as he worked with Atomic Energy Commission officials, he grew so alarmed about the potential for war that just before the Cuban missile crisis he labored all summer to dig, build, and stock a nuclear bomb shelter according to AEC specifications in their basement—an obsession that both my parents and I, from my distance at Amherst, viewed as lunacy.

Otherwise he and Judy seemed happy. When I visited them, I idealized their house and life-style. I enjoyed the wanton painting of wainscot and banisters in primary reds, blues, and yellows. I felt spookily at home with the worn, relocated furniture from St. Davids and the Henry past, a couch, a rug, a chair, an ottoman, the dinner table and chairs. Hans, after work, like a curious variation on my father, would flop back in his living room chair, beer in hand, and lose himself in a science fiction novel. Or he would light his pipe, one of many, and puff away, ready for philosophical debate.

From the first, I thought, Judy's point in loving Hans was to defy our family's repression and provinciality. He loved progressive jazz. He fancied himself priapic and passionate. As part-Indonesian, he was sensitive to white racism. As a European, he had his ways. He drank openly. He farted in company. He told me, "You don't realize it, but your sister is a real bohemian." He, Judy, and the children would all bundle in bed, a physical closeness unimaginable in our family. He was comfortable with his talents as an engineer and harbored no aspiration of his own to be an artist, but he was himself the son of a prominent Dutch novelist and diplomat, and he proudly supported the creativity of his wife and children. He was not an American, and not a man in the image of John Henry, our father, though in every contact I witnessed between him and Dad, he seemed to appeal to and to contest manhood in Dad's terms—as if to boast that he, Hans, also was doing well as a businessman, a provider.

Hans's father had been important to me, and had taken an interest in my promise in high school. He had sent me a published translation of his own best story in one of the first literary magazines I ever read. Later, he visited us at St. Davids, toured my basement print shop, praised my earliest self-published writing, and still later read and wrote to me about my fiction at Amherst. I grieved to hear of his death in 1962.

In the World

CALVIN PLIMPTON, Amherst's President, congratulated me as "Poet!" when he gave me my diploma (a hard-earned magna cum laude, thanks to my grades in English and despite freshman D's in Math and Physics). Our class of 1963 graduated expecting opportunity in a society that welcomed us. Aside from graduate schools and jobs, the New Frontier cry of "ask not what your country can do for you, but what you can do for your country" seemed to credit the civic value of our talents.

Ted Baird, my Shakespeare teacher, had taken an interest in me senior year. He invited me to his house, which Frank Lloyd Wright had designed for him gratis in response to a fan letter years before. Did I want a Woodrow Wilson Fellowship? He backed me for one and wrote me a recommendation for Harvard, where I was accepted.

I had also been offered a job at *Redbook* for that summer. Maggie Cousins had recently left *McCall's* to become a Senior Editor for Doubleday, where she hoped to see me published. I sent her my thesis, not as the saga-length novel she had hoped for, but as a novella. I had been in Eudora Welty's class that spring at Smith, and Maggie wrote (they were friends): "I had lunch with Eudora when she came down to present Faulkner with his gold medal. She says you are very talented." If not book publication, since my novella was too short, I craved the windfall of publishing a short story or of winning some writing prize—magical escalation of the world's notice; however Maggie soon wrote me that my novella was unpublishable, although she did attach a reader's report that found it "haunting," and reminiscent of a one-act European play.

I was living a Manhattan summer. I found my first serious romance since high school, a career woman at *Redbook*, named Sandy. I thought I knew the city. I shared a sublet on East 89th with an Amherst classmate. I had my car, street parking on alternate sides to avoid tickets. Given that this was Yorkville, a German neighborhood, with Beerhauses, German language bookstores, and German speakers in shops and on the streets, I tried to improve on my elementary German by loitering along the river and listening to conversations between people on benches. Nights I was translating Kafka. I wrote hasty attempts at Kafkaesque stories, which I sent to *The New Yorker* and had returned with notes.

In the windows across the street were no fewer than five separate, attractive exhibitionists, one of whom I wrote about and tried to meet—an older blond with two poodles. I stopped her one weekend while she was walking the poodles, explained that I was between college and graduate school, working for the summer, and writing; that I had been watching her, thought she was truly beautiful, and was writing a story about her. She was amused and encouraging, told me her name, asked to see the story, which I gave her on the street next day, and she said she'd read it, gave me her number and said to call after work—two rings, hang up, then call again as a signal (she had a lot of nuisance calls and ordinarily didn't answer)—and come over for tea or something tomorrow to discuss it. As she pulled her blinds that night, she coyly waved to me. Next day, all anticipation at work, I went home early, waited until I saw her go into her apartment, and rang the signal. No answer. Rang again. Rang for hours, her blinds drawn and windows dark. Next afternoon, or next, I tried without the signal and she answered, nonplussed: she was sorry, busy, couldn't see me, no, it had been "a mutual misunderstanding." Later that night, as I sat in my window, reading, I heard a sash go up and a loud, bass voice ask, "Is that the guy?" I glanced over and saw a shirtless black man, as hefty and muscular as Jim Brown, leaning out of her window and pointing at me. Enough of that. She hadn't liked the story, I concluded. She must have mistaken the imitation of Kafka for proof of my own strangeness.

Meanwhile, Sandy and I had gotten to know each other at work, mocking together such bad prose in the unsolicited fiction as "she was violently ill over a small piece of sand" or "he lifted her into the saddle with a stiff erection." Her favorite writer was John O'Hara. She was my age or a little older. From Philadelphia, like me—Germantown to be exact—she hadn't finished college, but had come to New York instead, and been working and living independently for several years. Her independence, frankness, and sense of humor impressed me more than her looks, which were neither sexy nor glamorous; she had a round face, wore glasses, and was overweight. When one of the married editors, an older lech, had asked suggestively what she thought of the latest *Life* magazine cover, which showed roiling snakes, she had replied sweetly, "Well, I hate snakes, but I just adore penises," which had shut him up. She was sitting a town house for friends in the Village and invited me for dinner, a romantic, edgy dinner, that led to our stumbling embrace, and my first in-the-world sex with somebody savvier than me about it. We went on to have trysts in her Cornelia Street apartment; also, when my roommate was away, in my apartment. At work we would be overwhelmed by lust, and one day helplessly embraced in my cubicle, then broke apart, flustered, for fear that one of the art department people had seen us.

For friends in common, we went to weekend parties networked through my former fraternity brothers, four of whom shared an apartment near Columbia; two of them with their girls invited Sandy and me to join them at a lakeside family cottage in the Adirondacks. The host turned out to have parents, however, so girls bunked with girls, boys with boys. Though my friends liked Sandy's sense of humor, they made me feel that she remained an outsider, and that they disapproved (as if they implied, "You can do better, Henry"). Another weekend we drove alone to Wellfleet, on Cape Cod, to a cottage she had borrowed. There I grew sexually weary of her, and she turned ravenous, demanding, and angry. She believed in and encouraged my talent, but had no conception of the future I faced in graduate school, or how we might continue, once I left. Indeed, as I did leave for that new life without her, and she returned to the intensity of her publishing career, the romance was over.

My first day in Cambridge, I found a furnished room for eight dollars a week three blocks from Harvard Yard; the on-premises landlord, a man close to my age dressed in a white dashiki, liked my "spiritual vibes." Apparently he had chosen the other nine roomers on this side of the double-entry frame building, as well as ten on the other side, by similar means. Each side shared a half-kitchen, a pay-phone, a foyer mail-table, and two bathrooms (one with tub, one with shower), accommodations reminiscent of a co-ed fraternity house. The house owner's name was Bob Randolph and he had recently converted to the teachings of a stateside maharishi. Formerly a meat-eating, overweight degenerate (by his own account), son of a capitalist whom he hated, who had pretended to punish him as a boy and told him to yell for the mother's benefit, and who had left this house to him as an inheritance, Randolph was now on a macrobiotic diet, gaunt, and living with a woman acolyte and her young son in the first floor apartment. He spoke of Nirvana and the spiritual path.

I signed into courses in "19th-century American Literature," "17th-Century English Prose," and "Sidney and the Sonnet Tradition." During lunch each day I reread *Anna Karenina* for relief, feeling that this was my best substitute for life, while the rigors of scholarship otherwise kept me hunched over books in my room and away from people or relationships. Graduate students at Harvard had no contact with each other, were treated coldly, and were expected to find their way around as readily as former Harvard undergraduates. I understood too well, I felt, when a fellow first-year grad student in English, the son of the Chairman of English at University of Florida, committed suicide in Inman Square by throwing himself between the wheels of a tractor trailer, bouncing off, then trying twice again. The pressure was that depersonalizing and extreme, and within two years would lead, more generally, to a social crisis: what was it to achieve? What marked you as important, valid, promising or, where women were concerned, desirable? The folk revolution was still to come, and when it did I understood it at first as a protest against excessive rigor; a collective cry (whine, I thought) of "this is too hard. No fun. No life."

In late October I drove back to Amherst to visit and to hear John F. Kennedy dedicate the newly completed Robert Frost Library—an appearance, it turned out, just weeks before his assassination in Dallas. His speech there impressed me (probably Archibald McLeish had a hand in it) because it spoke of writing as a national resource. "The nation that disdains the mission of art," he said, "invites the fate of Robert Frost's hired man, who had nothing to look backward to with pride and nothing to look forward to with hope." In Amherst terms, he sounded like an English major, the first president I knew of to voice any real appreciation of poetry or literature.

Back in my second-floor room in Cambridge—where I was, in fact, when someone outside shouted that Kennedy had been shot—I stole hours from reading and from writing papers for my literature classes in order to write stories that emerged as overly influenced now by the Transcendentalists. Finally, come spring, I was convinced that my only way to write without being drafted— at 23, I was being closely monitored by my draft board—was to apply to the Writers' Workshop at Iowa. When Iowa accepted me, I took a leave from Harvard and was granted continued deferment for graduate study at Iowa. In an attempt at a story then, I tried to project myself as a character whose promising future would soon be cut short by a physical accident: "I had paid my dues to the establishment and to my parents. Now I had at least a year free and the first chance to give my whole self to writing; I was defying the usual thing, following my own talent, out to prove myself."

The excitement of this departure was tempered by having four impacted wisdom teeth removed that summer, but at last, with the blessing and backing of my doubtful parents, I drove to visit for a few weeks in Charlottesville with Judy, Hans and the children. Having newly read Steinbeck's *Grapes of Wrath*, I started writing a story based on several employees at my family's candy factory. This I took with me as I drove on to Iowa City.

I continued to live in furnished rooms—this time in an attic, in a single family house, with the owners, a young couple living downstairs with a three year old and a wailing infant. Two other roomers shared the attic, both Taiwanese, as were three roomers in the basement, where we all shared a bathroom and a kitchen. When the roomers' phone rang, someone would call out "Yang-a-wa!" Downstairs, also, they would eat together and talk around me in Cantonese. One night, late, however, the phone turned out to be for me, Richard Yates calling.

I had read and admired Yates's 1962 novel, *Revolutionary Road*, at Amherst, and had eagerly signed up for his section. Later, we had met in office hours to discuss my novella and he persuaded me to get on with new work. Now, having just gone over the opening pages of my factory story, he was calling to congratulate me on this as "the real thing" and to find out more about me. This had to be a novel, he told me.

With his encouragement, for the next year I lost myself in creative fervor. I was celibate, anti-social, living, dreaming and waking fiction, while also teaching freshman rhetoric at 7 a.m., and taking advanced Latin and Medieval literature to continue progress on my Harvard degree. I even stayed in Iowa that hot summer, and was dismayed to learn that Yates had taken a leave to write a film in Hollywood, and that come fall, when I had been given a research fellowship, I would switch to his replacement, Nelson Algren. It turned out, in fact, that Algren disdained my work, saw me as an over-educated snob, and advised me to drop out and join the Peace Corps, see the world, serve in Africa. My progress on the novel stopped. I switched to Vance Bourjaily, but still couldn't write.

Viet Nam dawned for me during the fall of 1965, as an issue. Iowa students held draft card burnings. Marijuana and other drugs started appearing as commonplace. Hair styles went to no styles. The birth-control pill was made available to the public, chemically sanctioning the sexual revolution. My first year at Iowa I had no real contact with anybody but Yates. The second, I sought out social life from the undergraduates, not from workshop writers. Blocked or not, I still felt that I was genuine where they were mostly pretenders. In the town, I felt that "being a writer" was tolerated as being town idiot would be otherwise. No one expected accomplishment, only dreams. I met a girl, finally, by taking undergraduate French.

Back home my parents had moved from St. Davids, our family house, to a new house in nearby Villanova. If I couldn't write, if I were only wasting precious time—career time—then I'd better go back East. At least the scholarly work was something I knew I could do. The girl and I were breaking up.

To a college friend, I wrote: "I am still haughty enough to consider myself a diamond in the weeds, such as Iowa leftists who have been taking Trotsky seriously and dating Blacks for the fashion of it and handing out pamphlets for initialed organizations. I never had anything to do with the likes of these before and see them as the same animal that if they were rich would stink with Kulture and respectability. I need to be with people who have distances and vistas in them, instead of dead ends."

I was readmitted to Harvard for fall, 1966, with a scholarship, and started back east. I wrote Bob Randolph in Cambridge and got the best room in his rooming house, the third floor, front, with a balcony. With my savings from Iowa I bought a new Chevy II at home.

From our Villanova home, where I found that my belongings had been boxed and moved into "Dee's room," that my furniture remained, and that Mom had put up book shelves with my library, albeit out of order, I set out for Cambridge, stopping first in Manhattan, where I visted David Lahm, my jazzman friend from college, who was studying at Indiana but home, briefly, at his mother's Central Park West apartment.

I told him I was woman-starved, and asked about his girl, Marge Sloan, whom he'd come to visit in Boston during my Harvard year, and whom I remembered as sexy and dazzling. He spoke of her now as finished, laughing and pulling a silk nightgown from a drawer. "Here," he said, "Marge! Take it back to her in Boston." He told me about her recent visit to New York. Their main attraction had been piano, starting from his senior year at Amherst, her junior at Mt. Holyoke, when they'd worked together on a college production of "Good News"; she played classical music, while David was making jazz his life. This last visit had been awful, culminating with their sleeping in separate beds, then making love, which had been awful. I couldn't understand how making love to a beautiful girl could be "awful." He wouldn't say, but pondered the slip: "Should I burn this? Should I? I can't get rid of it. Don't know what to do with it. Shall I throw it out the window? Yes? No? Yes!" We looked out the window, down a long courtyard airshaft. Finally, he threw it out, and we leaned to watch it balloon and float in the wind, then catch in a whirlwind at the bottom with leaves several floors below on a roof-sundeck with ventilator mushrooms, on one of which it snagged (there, David informed me the next Christmas, it remained; no one wanted to touch it). We went out to a jazz bar later, and talking about girls again, I admitted that I was a sucker for glamour. He laughed sarcastically and said, "Okay, you should call Marge. You'll have a good time.

You'll get laid—or maybe you won't." And gave me her Cambridge number.

In Cambridge, I settled in my room, and concentrated on my second year of courses at Harvard. Reuben Brower, who had taught at Amherst before my time, took an interest in me in his Shakespeare course; later, he would be my thesis director. I took a seminar in Keats and one in Renaissance Humanism. I felt challenged and impassioned, though friendless, and increasingly left behind socially by my peers and my juniors.

Dance was changing from Chuck Berry and Chubby Checker's twist to the Beatles' frug to the free-for-alls of Soul. I had been in awkward transition in college from jitterbug to twist, now this. As Norman Mailer wrote in his essay, "The White Negro," white kids were learning to shake their asses.

Early on my return, I had called Marge Sloan. We were both 25. Women's Liberation was not yet fashionable, and our gender mores were closer to those of Sylvia Plath's 1950's than Gloria Steinem's 1970's. Marge was an intelligent, strong-spirited blond, privileged by background and by looks, and as confused in her way as I was in mine in fitting her felt self into available social roles. She was giving music lessons for sporadic income, working odd jobs, and presumably had some money from home, which was Long Island. She told me that she and Lahm would have been married, except that her parents had objected to his being Jewish. Her mother was a society virago: nouveau riche, a buyer for Bloomingdale's. Her father was a lawyer. She had a younger sister and brother. Not unlike the way I saw myself, she had asserted herself against her parents' expectations.

We had our collision, spiritual and physical, beginning in mutual attraction, progressing to a contest of selves, climaxing in violence, and finishing in mutual aversion and some enduring, wary regard. I kept a journal, moment by moment, charting and trying to develop the relationship in time, to understand "personality," and to understand the issues underlying our conflicts—both within each of us and between us.

When I first called I told her I was a friend of David's. She should remember me from college. He had given me her number and had said to say hello. We made a date for the next night. "Getting to know her," I wrote, "I found her lovely and wanted to touch, but felt fearful too because I felt our touching would be strong, not dalliance." Then, abruptly, parking on another date, there was lust between us and we hungrily made out. I decided that "she is the most fully attractive and suitable girl I've met." But then she let me know she didn't want me "doting." I wanted "an acknowledged preoccupation." She would invite, then dismiss me.

I set out harder to understand her, assuming this to be the cost of a special woman. "About the passion, she doesn't want to satisfy a love, just keep it chafing and tingling, which signifies that she hasn't the confidence that after sex or satisfaction that anyone would give her the attention they do when she is playing Circe with them. Beneath the femme fatale: pure cowardice." In questioning her, she led me to question myself: "Perhaps I have only despised girls; despised their presumption to any value beyond that of physical touch and beauty, or beyond their power to arbitrarily assuage my moral loneliness. I've never loved another person, whole, or completely admired and revered another spirit."

We worked to know each other, discussed books, people, ideas, needs. I read her parts of my journal. I tried to see a parallel between my preoccupation with Art (writing) and her compulsion to love something that compelling to her whole nature—Personality? Soul? People Power? Piano? Relations between us became uglier, approaching and avoiding, always. I felt I had the "right to hurt her, to slap her down. There is her responsibility for my passion, and her way of abusing it. You don't play with desire." We did end up one day, having parked and wandered in a woods in Concord, wrestling in anger; I was on top strangling her and she was reaching for a rock to club me with, but the whole thing was fantasy, an acting out of some scene in D.H. Lawrence and still at some remove, some choice from the real, and I quit in disgust and went off alone. Then we came together again, made out without having sex, and drove home.

She told me at different times about a man who had stopped her in Grand Central Station while she was in college and offered to pay her to come with him to his hotel room and to trample, in high heels, on his bare chest—which she had. She told me that when she was a baby her father, when she was crying, used to lock her in the cellar, so he could sleep—the psychological implication being that she had been compelled ever since to break in on the indifference of as many men as she could: to force them to care about her distress and make herself felt with a vengeance. Another time she told me that when she was home with her parents, her mother, "whom she loved more than anyone else," had flown out passionately and disowned her—partly over her telling them about the masochist episode; partly over their not approving of David Lahm. Her mother had said: "Marge, you're going to make a mess of yourself! You're ruining yourself. You're making it impossible for me to love you. I want to love you. I've tried as hard as I can, but you simply make it impossible!" Then she had left home to spend that summer with David, and with his jazz friends in Aspen, Colorado, where she saw "the seamy side, loneliness, and everyone tried to bed her,"; that life there completely contradicted home values and Mt. Holyoke values, and so she had swerved from the old moral code to a new one. Also that she had been bruised in Aspen when David's friends jeered at her for being a phony when she tried to express her "soul" in music. She told me too about being an epileptic. That her past fits and her family's response to them and the precariousness about any decorum is maybe the deepest clue to her self-distrust. She described her memory of certain fits, at home, on a train, in Carnegie Hall—the uneasiness, the premonitions, then the inhuman cry and bursting insight through pain, and loss of consciousness, then waking up exhausted and depressed—literally, as in Dostoyevski's *The Idiot*. She told me that she had had an older brother who had died, that his death had affected the whole family, and then when they had taken her to the hospital after the first signs of epilepsy, she had been sure that she was being taken there to die too, and that when her mother had been explaining epilepsy to her, that she had expected to be told that she only had a little while left to live because of all the weeping and sorrow of her parents. Epilepsy had seemed an open horror and tragedy to them, as if she were no good anymore, or a disgrace.

She told me too about Richard, who was married unhappily and with children, but who she had seen recently and fully realized was the man she loved, no matter the consequences. That everything was so simple with them. That he wouldn't ever have tolerated any nonsense from her, the way I did, so she wouldn't dare give him any. She orbited around him. He had taken her soul with her virginity years ago. Now he was talking about moving to Boston after her. He'd had to get married—that was what had broken them up. And then in addition to Richard, she told me about a second man she loves, Barney. That you have to take responsibility for what you tame. That she hadn't ever given me a serious love-thought. That I could never control her, never compel her as a lover does. I replied that I wouldn't want to be loved the way she described; didn't want to be orbited around or responsible for a grand and simple passion.

We both recoiled from these confidences, dizzy in spirit. She said she didn't want to see me again; saw no point in it; I was presumptuous. I said I didn't believe her.

She developed an interest in photography, taking classes and buying equipment. I insisted that since what she could do was piano, she ought to settle down and study it, get an MFA. That the fact was, instead, she made half-starts and false starts at any and everything. I decided (projecting my own frustrations) that her genius so far was only for arousing men she didn't fulfill—

cock teasing. That music was the love for her to face, foremost, before marriage; that she was afraid to pursue music because it meant work and probably never being great, but only competent, and meant being criticized. I reasoned that "being Great" was in itself too important for her; that with her pride, and the fear and defiance of her mother behind it, she felt she must be Great in order to be Independent, and that she could not bear to admit that her mother was a "greater" or "different" woman than she. More deeply than anything else this tying of pride to her mother, and the urgency of rivalry with her mother, were her sources of confusion.

We had a final phone conversation, where I said: "If you can't help yourself, and if none of your friends are good enough to help—."

"Maybe I should see a shrink, is that what you're trying to say?"

Gently, I said, yes. She said they didn't have much to say. She'd known some good ones, professionally and socially, but they all talked nonsense.

As far as our relationship was concerned, I said that being challenged to answer for yourself was the point, if there had to be a point, and she insisted that she didn't want to be challenged. "Listen, I just don't respect you, DeWitt. I don't want to see you anymore." And with that, she hung up.

From that point, I set out to outdo her social, moral, and psychological adventuring. I drove off alone to the Combat Zone in Boston, discovering a club called the Golden Nugget, filled with whores, pimps, queens and rock and roll blare—Nelson Algren territory. I started to look for other girls to prove to her my independence and desirability.

While we had been dating earlier, Marge had introduced me to a French teacher, Beatrice Gilson, also from Mt. Holyoke; and now on my rebound from Marge, at one of Bea's Harvard Square salons, I met Brigitte Cassan, from Paris, and was smitten, as if all the needs and issues that Marge had opened up in me had only been preparation for this even blinder obsession.

I had been courting Bea herself, actually, as well as involved with another Mt. Holyoke alumna in Manhattan, whom I knew from my *Redbook* summers, MJ; and the two of them, along with Marge, were part of my thinking about women my age, from my approximate background.

Bea was a social butterfly from a moderately wealthy Philadelphia family; she was intent on a fashionable marriage, and within two or three years she would, in fact, meet and marry a Punjab prince in North Africa. At this point, however, she was making do with Michele, a handsome but jobless young Parisian, who was solicitous, and willing to be trained and pruned up for her, like a pet.

MJ, on the other hand, who had chosen a singles life in Manhattan, seemed to me spiritually desperate, saying that she worked to stupefy herself and because it was better than drink (she worked at the Dreyfus Fund), that she had sex without cynicism, that she did not want motherhood and felt no maternal restlessness, only aversion. Just before I met Brigitte, I had had a surprise call from MJ, one moment sounding upbeat career girl, the next sexy siren, the next self-melodramatizing, the next self-satisfied, but all along sounding hollow, the voice of loneliness, searching not for me, so much, as for the human race. I visited New York that Saturday, took her out for dinner, and then she invited me back, matter-of-factly, for sex in her apartment—a life-giving lay for me, breaking a year's respite; though for her an act of despair. When we'd finished, she'd turned away and doubled up, whimpering: "Help me; help me. Help me!" And I'd said, confused, afraid that she was somehow damaged inside: "How can I help you? What do you mean? MJ?" And she'd lain there, clenched; then suddenly had jumped up, wrapping her nightdress close around her, and strode to her dresser, where I saw she was getting a cigarette. Then she lay back, like Marlene Dietrich, in her wrap, with her cigarette, languidly indifferent, but with the thin, vibrating nerve of pain under her pose. "And now you know," she said, exhaling. And me: "Know what?" Though I supposed she meant the hard-boiled fact that she had only used me for distraction, a quick lay. She wouldn't let me stay, even in the other single bed—"I just couldn't wake up and find you here in the morning"—and turned me out to drive all night back to Boston.

Spring, 1967. Brigitte was living au pair in a minister's house on Mt. Auburn Street. She had a Panamaian friend, Elena, whom she'd known at Swarthmore College and who now was living at Harvard's International House finishing an M.A. in Comparative Literature. The basis of their friendship was a sisterhood of misery, as I understood it; both were spirited, ambitious, imaginative, and haunted by a sense of guilt and failure. Both also were beautiful; and both had made bad marriages. Elena had been divorced recently and had a two-year old boy in her custody, kept by her parents in New York now, while she finished her degree. Brigitte had simply run away from her husband in Paris to New York and now to Cambridge. She spoke English with a thick accent. Her hair was jet black, with upward licks in front of the ears, and worn down in bangs across her forehead which gave her a funny peering look. She was a big girl, full of her own energy, with a tall girl's swagger. Big breasts, thin figure, always stylish. She would wear clacking heels, carry a little pink purse on a gold chain, and wear white net stockings, a pink skirt and white blouse. She would wave "Hello Dee!" with a mock flapper's Charleston wave, a circular gesture, palm towards me.

We started dating, dinner out, movies, drinks, parties, long walks, dinner in my room (frozen mixed vegetables and hamburger, as always, my modest fare). When we were happy, we were confederates, recognizing and believing in each other as special people in ways the world refused to recognize. I felt that what separated Marge and Brigitte from other women, like Bea, was that they got the joke. They lived within the absurd, the way George Orwell described Henry Miller. Brigitte laughed at Cambridge's "No Trespassing" signs because "trespasser" meant "to die" in French. We visited Andre Dubus, another writer friend and ex-student of Yates's from the Iowa Workshop, who had just published his first novel, *The Lieutenant*, and moved with his family to teach at Bradford Junior College, north of Boston. He was house sitting in Plaistow, N.H., on a lake. He took me on faith as an artist and a person and I saw him as an accomplished, accomplishing artist and person, as well: the kind whose society was us, and by whom we should measure others. (Andre was taken by Brigitte and later fictionalized our visit in a story called "Adultery": "Edith [that is, Andre] talked with the law student [that is, me] long enough . . . to know he wasn't Jeanne's [that is, Brigitte's] lover and couldn't be; his confidence was still young, wistful, and vulnerable; and there was an impatience, a demand, about the amatory currents she felt flowing from Jeanne . . . she [that is, Andre] watched Jeanne's eyes, which appeared vacant until you looked closely at them and saw that they were selfish: Jeanne was watching herself.")

I had a poet-friend, too, a fellow graduate student from Philadelphia, to whom I introduced Elena and with whom we'd double date.

I'll never know how much our happiness was my fantasy, but the trouble began as our desire grew. One afternoon Brigitte simply said, "Okay, I'll be over tonight, maybe." Unlike Marge, she kept her word, appearing late, to my surprise, at my room's door with a jug of wine. We made nervous love, then slept in each other's arms in my saggy bed. Next morning, she sat with her head in her hands, hung over. She had to get back to her house; I could come over later—which I did, that afternoon, still dazzled and elated, when, as she bustled around in the kitchen, making me coffee, she muttered something in her accent—What? "Je suis mal. I have VD, Dee. You should see a doctor."

I did, at the Harvard Health service, where I was treated with a civilized hilarity. The doctor got on his knees, with a culture slide, waiting for me to "milk" my penis and nothing happened. He was like a mechanic peering up underneath a car. He gave me antibiotics, and apparently I was clear of infection.

Brigitte explained that Ron, her man in New York, had given it to her. She had been waiting for it to clear up, thought it had, and then I'd kept pressing her. Part of our existential condition, I felt, was for me to respect her silence and not pry about biography— we were what we did. I forgave and laughed along with the problem, which would still force us sadly to refrain from sex and wait. This Ron had been a jerk, obviously; she'd had the brains to leave. But then she told me nonchalantly that her au pair position was ending, and her parents wanted to see her back in New York. She was thinking of going there to stay, and planned to leave that Sunday. We argued. I told her we could live together here; I'd find us an apartment. "So you want to be my man, eh, Dee?" she teased. "You're going to have to give me clothes and shoes and spending money." More seriously, she missed New York; she just needed to go and then she'd be back. I should go ahead and find a place. I accepted all this after a day or so alone of fretting, and actually drove her to the bus, keeping two suitcases she couldn't take, to send or bring down later, once she was settled.

Weeks passed. My school year ended. I waited, having found a converted garage for low rent off of Oxford Street; it stood alone like a little cottage, and she would love it. Cambridge felt changed and I felt changed and poised, but no Brigitte. I read, listened to music, sunbathed, worked on my novel, but always in reserve. At last she called: she had decided on a New York life, a job, and the Village. I gathered that whatever we had meant was now only an irritation as she sought to move on. I felt grief, as if a close friend had been killed.

Elena talked to me, then, straight talk. About how much Brigitte had held back and wouldn't share with me. How much of Brigitte's business Brigitte didn't think was my business. That her lover, Ron, had been the main contention between Brigitte and her parents. That Ron had gotten a new job and asked her to live with him in an apartment in the Village. And so she had run to Cambridge. And she had planned to summer here and visit him weekends. Also that, yes, she had had the clap from him, but that she had been cured of it during the time she was holding me off. So she had decided between him and me and that was that.

I decided that I could never accept Brigitte as some sort of platonic sister, who also had a lover. I felt that I knew her better than she knew herself, or than Elena, or than anyone else knew her. I had to see her face to face. So I made a reckless trip to Manhattan on my way home to Philadelphia, armed with her suitcases and a phone number. Elena had said to play it cool. As I dialed now from a drugstore on the upper East Side, she answered, surprised. I delivered the suitcases to their apartment nearby, hers and Ron's, just as Ron came in, playing host. He was 22, and looked like Tony Perkins. Worked as a bank teller. Was finishing an NYU degree with night courses. Wasn't happy with the city, walked the streets and noticed the dirt. They smoked pot, as no one I knew yet in Cambridge did openly. But most importantly he called himself a Communist, a revolutionary, which annoyed me, since this was his main claim to purpose in her eyes, and since he dwelt on material values, money and possessions, rather than on spirit.

I tried for two days to prove to her my resourcefulness in New York—impromptu, I had old friends here to call and stay with, parties to go to, special bars to meet friends in. I wanted to reestablish our rapport alone in this different world. However, Brigitte and I would never have a private time together again. My visits to New York, or hers to Cambridge over the coming months, were always somehow compromised, if not by Ron, then by Elena.

I did, in trying to understand Ron as my rival, later write Brigitte that I saw his politics as café posturing. I went on: she and I had shared a standard, I thought. We believed in imagination, in the capacity for experience and for transforming things to life. Guts, I wrote her. Give me a woman with guts to stand up to herself and her man, and to combine their strengths to build something more important than them both.

My feelings about my parents' marriage fed my vehemence. "Maybe it is the plight of superior women to purposely create their 'men.' But it's all such a waste—such a kind of egotism turned in on itself. Ron can't grow anymore; but you can, and maybe you think you can force him to somehow. But it is his nature to be what he is and he's going to hate you for trying. Particulars: you laugh at things that aren't funny. You act easily impressed. You don't discriminate about intelligence or humor or originality: all for his sake. Yet when you were with me, you would sneer if I said something stupid or if I made a bad attempt at being funny. And now Ron has you suspending that. He is like a narcotic, which keeps you from being yourself."

Within two months, on into the fall, having traded several receptionist and stenographer jobs, fought with her parents, and moved with Ron to a Village apartment, Brigitte did break up with him and started dating someone else. New York was making her miserable. My own fall had been a disaster. I'd been forced to take my Ph.D. orals on schedule and, stammering, red-faced, and unprepared, I had failed before an eminent tribunal, partly because of personal problems, partly because my training had been as a "new critic," and I had never studied literary history—if I hoped to pass, I was then told, I must spend another year doing precisely that.

Brigitte's friend, Elena, had recently married and moved to New York, reuniting with her son. Her new husband was a Swiss aristocrat, who had finished Harvard law and gotten a job at the United Nations, and they had a large apartment, where Brigitte now stayed. I visited there briefly, and in this theater of our friends, Brigitte refused to speak, stiffly avoiding me.

I asked her, finally, to get divorced and to marry me. I was willing to drop out of Harvard and go with her to Paris, or thought I was. She knew better. I was only fantasizing. If I had thrown over Harvard, defied my family, and tumbled forward into my draft-free late twenties, then what? I can't imagine now.

We argued. We had nothing left to say: just my choked insistence that I was lonely, and her confession, exasperated and final, that she could do nothing for me.

She went back to Paris and to her husband, I assumed; though Elena was dismayed that as a friend or lover I had let Brigitte go. Not all people learn from experiences, she lectured me; some experiences can be degrading, can destroy people. No one who understood and loved Brigitte, she said, could have let her go like that, with nobody there, no job, no prospects.

Again, I recoiled, embittered. I vowed never again—in David Lahm's words—to lose my head over a piece of tail.

At home, Chuck was Dad's pride, the model son now, having graduated from his residency and settled as a surgeon in New Jersey, about an hour's drive from Villanova. Chuck, Nancy, and their three boys had just moved from their starter house into the 20-room Victorian, with a barn out back and perhaps a two-acre yard. They were becoming prominent members of their community. I felt the pressure of Chuck's social rectitude, his marriage, and his fathering, while Dad kept worrying how much longer I would keep sowing wild oats and living only for myself.

My anxiety over the draft had eased with my twenty-sixth birthday in 1967. I could still be called, but given the military's preference for younger men, the possibility was remote. Where Nixon proposed Vietnamization—the training of Vietnamese troops to replace American troops overseas—still more and more young men were called, and a new kind of resistance was mounting. Young men of intelligence and principle, though branded by the government as cowards and outlaws and more often condemned than supported by their parents, went from destroying their draft cards, pleading conscientious objector status, contriving medical evidence of mental or physical disability, or proclaiming their homosexuality, to exiling themselves as fugitives in Canada or

Sweden. Isolated from parents and the law, they were supported, on the contrary, by the anti-war movement and by the growing counter-culture of their own generation.

I would like to say that at the time I was an informed, alert, and conscientious citizen of my times, that in principle, if not in fact, I was with the Yippies beaten by Mayor Daley's police in Chicago, that I marched with Norman Mailer's Armies of the Night and tried to levitate the Pentagon, that I supported student takeovers and sit-ins over campus governance and the university's investments not only in the war effort, but in other areas of social injustice. Following the lead of Berkeley in 1964 and Columbia in 1968, Harvard's turn at campus unrest would come in April, 1970, with the takeover of University Hall. There were also rallies, demonstrations, and at least one riot in Cambridge in spring, 1970, following on Nixon's invasion of Cambodia and the Kent State shootings in May, with students killed by National Guardsmen.

But I was more a baffled witness to the public events of these years than I was a participant. Intellectually, I was progressing slowly on my factory novel. Having taught freshman composition in the fall of 1967, I was teaching my first fiction writing class to Harvard upperclassmen in fall, 1968. I was reading books about books to prepare for my orals, which I passed in November, 1968, and then for two more years, while also teaching, I was researching and writing my thesis on *Romeo and Juliet*.

Almost immediately after Brigitte's departure from Cambridge for New York, that same summer, 1967, a twenty-two year old secretary named Vicki had moved into my Cambridge rooming house. She was pretty enough, blond, demure, though skinny. We met in the common kitchenette. She asked to use my telephone and came up to my room on that pretext. Two nights after we met, we went out drinking and dancing, got drunk, and slept together.

She was French-Canadian, from Nashua, New Hampshire, where her father owned a department store; had been to junior college and was going to night school for a B.A., which her father scorned. Played the piano. Had been to Paris, where an artist had picked her up and gotten her pregnant. Had come back home for an eight hundred dollar abortion from an elderly doctor, who later had slipped her a Mickey Finn and seduced her. Had a married man, a chemistry professor at Harvard, whom she had seduced. Worked for him as a typist late at night and made love in the coffee lounge. Had been doing this several times a week for over a year. Her parents, meanwhile, were verging on divorce, with her as their arbitrator. Father had been running with bad company from the golf club; father and mother had vicious fights; recently father had cursed mother and left, only to return to her after, her, Vicki's efforts. Also she had her best friend, Shelly, her ex-roommate, with whom she had had an affair a year or so before, and whom I'd like, and had to meet.

Vicki and I didn't last long—sex between us quickly grew apathetic, then mean—but before we lost interest, she did introduce me to Shelly, who had just moved into a new singles apartment building nearby. By contrast to Vicki, Shelly was all heart, energy, and gusto. Polish, also from New Hampshire, platinum blond, mesomorph, had had a year or two of college, age 24. By day a secretary at Polaroid, by night and weekends, the unabashed Doll Tearsheet, making the most of what she had. Smart, if not intelligent, with a prodigious memory, which she would show off at the mention of topics such as stalactites, Afghanistan, asps, urban sanitation, mysticism, or current events. She was too plump and coarse for my taste, romantically, but otherwise we took to each other and shared some taste for escapades and characters.

Pete the Undertaker was one of her dates. Big spender, he took us all out in his Cadillac for drinks. He owned a chain of funeral homes and prided himself on practical jokes, such as pulling up in his hearse next to a housewife stopped at a light and going "Boo!"

at her through a Dracula mask. He did have professional dignity, however, and when I asked him about Jessica Mitford's expose, *The American Way of Death*, said it was all lies and that he'd been on talk shows to offer the industry's response. "Listen," he confided, "it's no fun touching dead people, understand?"

Max, the Haitian Revolutionary, in exile from Papa Doc's police and dedicated to financing and supplying a rebel force, while clerking at IBM, was another friend and sometimes lover of Shelly's. He had also dated Vicki, and he would later become my friend and introduce me to the Harvard Square café pick-up scene.

But Shelly's real love was Paul Santos, a black insurance salesman, who was married with three children. Their affair had reached an impasse where they loved each other too much for half measures, yet Paul was unprepared to go public and leave his family, whom he also loved and had struggled and provided for and just recently had moved, as he put it, from the ghetto to a dream house in the suburbs. So he and Shelly were backing off from the affair, or trying to, still seeing each other, but openly seeing others, too.

When Paul and I met at Shelly's, Paul sized me up, partly thanks to Shelly's introduction, as WASP, single, son and heir of a candy factory owner in Philadelphia, aspiring writer and graduate student, and to my credit as neither tight-assed nor a snob. He himself was light-skinned (part Portuguese, from Chelsea), age 32, big-boned, round-faced with horn-rimmed glasses, and heavyset, taller than I. He was playing chess with Shelly, presumably to show that he was a thinking man, with a new B.B. King record he'd brought playing in the background.

The chessmen were black and white, like life, he said. Though he was conventionally groomed and dressed—cravat, slacks, and new loafers, rather than say, Afro haircut, mojo beads and dashiki—he had Black Power slogans at the ready. Reparations were owed. If you weren't part of the solution, you were part of the problem. Black was beautiful. It was all good, so let it all hang out.

Got to get it together. Say what you mean or mean what you say or don't say it at all. Gotta have soul. As we discussed sports stars and jazz and rhythm-and-blues musicians, I understood "soul" to be a spiritual quality involving, first, the capacity and nerve to love life; second, wisdom about suffering and loneliness, and the need for human compassion and solidarity; and third, a oneness of the spirit with the body, and the body's needs and mortality. Chuck Berry, Otis Redding, Nina Simone and Janis Joplin had "soul," for instance, where Elvis or the Beatles did not. Shelly had it, where Vicki had not; and later Paul would flatter me: "You've got soul. Henry's a soul brother."

"You know my main men; know who I dig?" Paul announced. "Jack Kennedy and Martin Luther King. Kennedy was honest except he went for power at the end, and King because he said we got to live with the white brother, we got to live in the system. I'm a militant, don't misunderstand, but I work within the system."

From the start, Paul quizzed me about "broads"; confidentially, man to man, what about all those fine-looking women I knew, and how about turning him on to a few? When I answered vaguely about my not having much luck, just teasers and heart-breakers, he said these sounded like some sick women and he was going to have to show me some real women for a change. "Sounds like we could help each other out, Henry."

We became cruising and partying buddies, setting out at first with Shelly and her roommates, or sometimes with Max and others along to O'Dee's, a soul music club in Cambridge, or similar places, where Paul would pick up the tab. He drove a four-door, red GTO, which seated eight. Next, he started calling me at all hours: "Hey, Henry, what's happening?" Did I know any broads to party with? More often than not, I'd be studying, correcting papers or working on my novel or my thesis, but he would lure me out. We'd meet at one of the Cambridge cafés, or the Boston pick-up scene, new singles clubs like the Point After. As an odd couple, we combined black and white, fat and thin, flashily dressed big spender and economizing hippie, businessman and student, his ice-breaking, my apologetic sensitivity. Openers usually led to something like, "So how did two guys like you meet?" I don't recall our ever getting past the phone number phase with strangers; usually we'd end up, the two of us alone, drinking back at my Oxford Street apartment (into which I had recently moved from my rented room). He would lecture me. "Lookit, Henry, you got the crib, you got wheels, you're a good looking cat; you got to loosen up is all."

From, in living memory, being a lynching offense, interracial dating was just becoming fashionable, at least in Cambridge, combining the glamour of social guilt, protest, and experimentation with the lure of sexual adventure. The dynamics were charged. Though some people were romantically in earnest, many were reverse racists, on both sides, attracted more for the sake of the race than the person. For many black men, as for Eldridge Cleaver, whose *Soul on Ice* was just being published, white women (especially well-educated, middle-class white women) were viewed as prized possessions; to be openly preferred by such women, as men, as intelligent, competitive adults, was to defeat the "castrating" myths of the past. More than the so-called last frontier of sex; more than drug-induced new states of consciousness; miscegenation was the greatest unknown. For many white women, the attraction involved social idealism, some moral obligation to prove equality of race and to make a social statement. Other white women felt overtly freed from questions of marriage or social identity—still considering as axiomatic that interracial marriage and mixed race children were out of the question. Many white women also shared my own attraction to a familiar, yet different culture that corrected what they felt to be inhibiting and deficient in their own backgrounds. Officially, black women condemned the fashion of interracial romance among black men as one of self-hatred and racial desertion, though I never found that attitude among the black women that I knew.

I confess that at the time I was looking for white women who were bold and sexy enough to seek interracial sex—as if, as Paul had promised, they would be an antidote to the hung-up intellectuals I usually dated—and I may also have harbored some fantasy of attracting them to my hip whiteness. I enjoyed many black women as cohorts and friends, but I myself was not looking for interracial sex.

Starting with secretaries at his insurance company, expanding through networks with downtown cronies and dating bars, as well as maintaining regular contacts in the black community, Paul knew—or set out insatiably to know—women from all over working Boston.

Somehow he had met a triad of roommates in Cambridge, with whom he fantasized staging an "or-gee." Clara was the fine, tall black woman who interested him; Brenda, also black, he was fixing up with his cousin Hector; and Beth, who was white and a high school French teacher (he promised) would go for me. So first, the girls were having a party in their Linnaean Street basement apartment. We all chipped in for fondue and Liebfraumilch (exotica to me).

In the spirit of hearty, ribald fun, with Paul's social cheerleading seconded by Clara's, we did all get along, gathered cross-legged on the floor around the fondue pot, lancing cauliflower, cubes of ham, tomatoes, and slices of garlic bread with fondue sticks, then dipping our sticks into the cauldron of white wine and Swiss cheese, stuffing ourselves, drinking, dancing, and keeping up a loud, joking banter throughout, like a jam session.

Clara was a good match for Paul, bright, assertive, and sexually sly; Brenda, who was stocky and pigeon-breasted, got into an intense political discussion with Hector. Hector was thinner and handsomer than Paul; had been draft-dodging for two futile years, attempted suicide, and was now a militant, working as a supervisor of a Roxbury social services organization. Clara and Brenda were friends from Columbus, Ohio; Brenda and Beth had met at the high school where Brenda was staff assistant and Beth a teacher. Beth was droll, tall, big-assed, a worldly single from a big family in Mattapan, who was comfortable with herself, had her degree from University of Massachusetts, Boston, had her job, and liked, as she put it, to let down her hair.

We started dancing. Dance was in freewheeling transition, so nobody really knew what was the latest, or what moves were genuine. I had evolved some crazy motion of my own, a hybrid, whereby I swiveled my hips round and round, and then snapped my fingers and did sidesteps from there, improvising; and pretty much, it sold. Some of my party-mates, in this case Clara and Brenda, would try to imitate and get it right: "Oh, teach me that! Hey, look at this!"

Following on that party, Beth and I dated alone, dinner at my apartment; we danced to Chuck Berry and to Janis Joplin, had lots of drinks, started undressing as we slow-danced, and then fell into bed. On separate, private dates, Paul and Clara had been getting it on, as had, presumably Hector and Brenda, or maybe not. Paul called me, then, wanting details, chuckle, chuckle. Said Beth had told Clara that I knew how to please a woman. Went on to propose a complicated trip, which he would pay for. He had a big insurance prospect to meet, a family friend of Clara's, back in Columbus, and Brenda wanted to fly home to pick up her car; so why not all of us go for a partying weekend? We'd fly out, stay overnight at Brenda's, drive back in her car. Don't worry about money. We'll have us that or-gee.

Though I was already tiring of Beth and had to teach Monday morning, and though Beth and I would be the only white people, I trusted Paul and went. Our jet climbed steeply from Boston—Paul loud, drinking and running his mouth at the stewardesses—then tilted down, descending, a two-hour trip.

Our objective was a settlement of ranch-style homes twenty miles outside Columbus. Clara's friend and Paul's prospective client, Charles Denton, met us at the airport, and drove us in his new

Lincoln to Brenda's, where we were staying; later we would visit his home a street over for dinner. "We're just *plain* folks," he kept explaining. In his mid-thirties, he had fine-boned features, oriental or Indian, and smooth brown skin; he wore a black mustache and his hair was meticulously groomed; his long hands gestured languidly. He wore a white turtleneck and dark silk suit.

We were welcomed as a party with high courtesy and downhome warmth. "Clara's my girl," Charles told Paul. "You be good to her, hear? Rachel's my wife, but Clara's my girl." His home resembled my own family's in Villanova.

After dinner, Charles, Beth and I sat around the kitchen table, smoking and drinking Black Bull, a 150-proof Scotch; Charles's Uncle Bill had joined us, a tall, gaunt man with a lined face, white hair, and a mouth with a few scattered teeth. Uncle Bill was shaking his head and saying, "I just don't understand, I just want to sit and listen. I'm seventy-two years old."

"You served your purpose," Charles told him, "now I'm serving mine." And turned to Beth and me. (Later I watched the old man, smiling toothily, reach out a gnarled hand to brush some spot of dirt off the shoulder of Charles's jacket.)

"Let me tell you something happened today," Charles continued, speaking to Beth and me. "These people called, these poor white trash. Guy works for me, wants to see me, a personal matter. You dig that?" His eyes held mine. "Okay, I said, come on by this afternoon. So guy drives out with his wife. They're all dressed up. Poor white trash. They see my house—they can't get over it, see?" He looked at Beth. "This was good enough for a rich white man's house; they'd never set foot inside a place this nice. So I showed them around, put on some tapes, offered them a drink. They meet my wife, my kids. They're looking all around; they're embarrassed, won't take a drink. Guy needs a loan of thirty bucks; baby's sick, kid needs clothes, rent's due. Well, now, this is the kind of guy—you're digging me—who's going to call me dirty nigger the minute he walks out. Well, I give a check says fifty dollars, not thirty. And you know what he says? He says, 'Mr. Denton, I want you to know I worked for a lotta different men in my time but you're the best boss I ever had.'" He waited for the meaning to register. "I told Paul tonight and Paul says, 'Whatta give that trash anything for? They'd kick you out on your nigger ass, they got a chance. You'll never see that fifty bucks again.' But I don't care if I don't see it again. See, that's what Paul can't understand. I'll get something out of it. One of these nights, some weekend, I'll be broken down and need a pull out, or I'll need a man, and I know now that man'll do me a favor." He winked and nodded slyly.

Later, when we were all drunker, he told us that he had come from a poverty background, a mining town in South Carolina called "Town Number Seven." Had used to run around on the streets in Columbus, and had only straightened out a couple years ago. His wife, Rachel, had straightened him out. "I used to work for the Man, you dig? There's this white cleaning outfit. They fire me. But we got a contract says they got to pay me a year's salary first; and I can't work, see, or set up any competition while they do. So I just sat around for a year. Then I set up a business, just a little business, actually, six hundred a month, and I was down there on my hands and knees scrubbing. They bought me out three months ago for $5,000. I set up again with my brothers and now we're grossing eight thousand, man! In three months! We used to clean little offices. You get one account, do a good job, word goes out, you get two, three, four places, just me and my brothers, mainly. Now we've got three cleaning crews and we're doing all corporations and expanding to Dayton. These older folks, scc, don't dig this; they've been working all their lives, and now I have it and I'm only 32. But I'm an old man. I'm not a brother, I'm a father." He wanted to dye his hair white around the edges, he said, to lend himself dignity and austerity; he looked too young for his responsibilities.

I saw him as someone waking into a dream, uncertain of his limits, and as baffled by his actions as those around him were. He was the "new man," a function of the times, ambition, industry (as Horatio Alger might put it), and luck. Partly, I felt, he was dramatizing himself for Beth's benefit, and coming on to her; partly he was admiring himself in Uncle Bill's wonder; but in large part, too, he was performing for my approval and esteem.

We drove the grueling 700 miles back to Boston next day, and wearied by the chatter and hilarity of six friends in the car, I pretended to sleep, needing to be alone. Yes, Charles, I thought, I dig; we're all petitioners.

Paul himself had achieved some affluence—he was in fact the "success" in his clan—starting with a degree from Boston University, which had been supported by his parents' lifetime of working at menial jobs. His mother had been a domestic, his father a laborer; he gave them money now. Affirmative action under Kennedy had helped him find his place as an insurance agent for New England Life, and as other government programs, such as OEO and Model Cities, encouraged black capitalism, he found his insurance clients among the new flow of blacks into the business-owning and managerial classes, many of whom were previously uninsured and most of whom, like Charles, were readier to trust a "brother" than a white salesman. He sought clients on the grapevine and also was assigned targets by the company as their racial specialist. His roistering social life was also his business life, in that sense, a way of keeping clients happy and of cultivating prospects.

He'd been a fat teenager, homely and unpopular; had had to struggle to make friends. Had gotten his first girlfriend pregnant and had had to get married too young to ever fool around. But now the lid was off. "I want bucks, booze, and broads," he would tell me, "though not necessarily in that order."

Within several months, Paul and I had become real friends, where I had had no close male friends since college. "If you were a broad, Henry," he said, "I'd be in love with you, but I ain't no queer." He went on to dramatize himself to my interest and appreciation, confiding in me as a confederate. I did serve, in fact, as an alibi for him with his wife. Once or twice he asked me to answer, if she called me, that, yes, he had been out drinking with me on such and such a night. After one party at my apartment, he stayed overnight, GTO in the driveway, and begged me to come home with him next morning as his cover. He'd tell his wife that he'd had a flat tire and that he hadn't been able to fix it until morning.

I reluctantly gave in to his pleading, as a friend, and followed him in my car out the turnpike to Ashland, and through local streets, past open spaces, a driving range, older houses, into a new tract with streets of its own, to his big new house, a two-story Georgian with attic dormer windows, two-car garage, flagstone path in front.

His wife, Peggy, opened the door, imminent with outrage, then saw me. She was attractive in a matronly way, light-skinned, careworn. Paul brusquely introduced us. And she restrained whatever fury she had ready, and struggled to put on her public best behavior and manners for my sake. Paul showed me in, invoking his pride and hers, their pride together in seeing themselves through my eyes. His kids—a girl 11, boys 9 and 6—hung back with a queer, nervous fear.

"We moved in last October," he told me, "isn't that right, Peggy?" Five rooms upstairs, study, boys' (Paul and Earl), bath, master bedroom, girl's (Nicole). Stairs. Raised living room with picture window and stereo and railing. Then foyer, dining room. Kitchen ("Want a beer? How about a beer, Henry?"—as he foraged for himself in the fridge). Den, with leather couches and a heavy corner table with an oversized Kon-Tiki lamp. And stereo speakers and walnut telephone, glass doors to patio, off kitchen then, laundry and bath.

He insisted I stay for lunch, settle down for beers and socialize, as if I had all Sunday. Peggy disappeared. With the kids, he barked orders: clean up this and this, turn off that music, get out and turn the sprinklers on, wash the car. All of which struck me as a sad, neurotic bullying, mental and physical, fueled by his guilt. "I teach my kids Black Pride," he proudly told me.

I got impromptu calls, 7 p.m., say: "Henry, my battery's dead, and I'm at Government Center, can you give me a boost?" And I would stop whatever I was doing, and drive in, hood to hood, revving my six-cylinder compact enough to start his eight-cylinder behemoth. He offered to loan me money if I needed any, though I never asked.

He told me another time that he'd just returned from a hard partying weekend in Montreal and was lying in bed with his wife when the phone rang and it was his mother, who started in about the ugly situation his sister was in with his no-good bum of a brother-in-law (she had gotten pregnant with a coil in and they had rushed her to the hospital, but no one could find the husband, and she might have been dying) and then started on about some one of her other children who had been running around with some white whore named Shelly, who used to live in Cambridge and now lived in Arlington, and he asked: who is that? who can that be? And she said, well, I thought it was probably you. And he: No. Are you off you head? All of this with his Peggy, whom he insists knows nothing about it because if she did that would be all, beside him. And now he had the question, how did this get to his mother? Did somebody look up Santos in the directory and know he came from Chelsea? Or did somebody Hector knows run her mouth and the grapevine carries?

He had other near-disasters at home: scratches on his back; lipstick on his underwear; names mumbled in his sleep.

He was like a secret agent, always at risk, always raising the stakes of deception: perhaps, I theorized, to defy his ordinary life— as employee, as husband, as father, son, as citizen—and to prove and celebrate a self freer and larger than his settled life allowed; perhaps, also, in some odd way, to revitalize and re-appreciate his ordinary life by turning its simplest gestures into heart-pounding, death-defying acts.

His reputation grew. He introduced me to other, older and more successful black businessmen friends, who were into partying at a safe distance from home, free spenders, and interested in meeting white girls. Among these cronies was a vice president of Gillette, who was a prominent Black Power speaker. Another was a local politician, who earnestly demanded: how could I be wasting my time reading Shakespeare, when there was a revolution going on? Later, another white man, Geoffrey Hughes, would join the circle; he was a public relations professional from England, divorced, and in his forties.

In his boistrous, eager way, Paul urged me to throw big parties, and before long I was serving as a broker for such men, with my Oxford Street apartment a safe house, and they were paying me for it in terms of booze and party costs. They enjoyed my poverty. Who was it called me up—a corporate somebody—quite seriously, and offered me money to follow his white wife and report back to him? He knew she was screwing a white guy and he couldn't follow himself without being spotted, but no one would recognize me. I said no thanks, it wasn't my kind of thing.

I started reading to better inform my imagination: Richard Wright, James Baldwin, Eldridge Cleaver, Ralph Ellison, Malcolm X. Meanwhile, Geoffrey Hughes was trying to start a company called "Uniloyal, Inc.," to offer "consultant services specializing in interracial affairs," and wanted me to run a seminar in black literature for upper level white executives, men like my father, for which he would charge a hefty fee in various cities. The idea was to help raise the consciousness of such executives and to better their understanding of their black employees. I already had more than I could handle, thanks. And the concept of the company itself soon proved short lived.

Time passed, and life went on for me in other ways, with other friends, while Paul would drift off for periods, too. I picked up girls now and then in the cafés with Max. November, 1968, I passed my Ph.D. orals. I began researching my dissertation. Instead of teaching freshman composition, I was now teaching fiction writing to Harvard upperclassmen.

I met a woman in the Idler with Max. She was sexy, streetwise and had grown up in Cambridge and Belmont, graduated from B.U., worked in an office for Eastern Airlines. Had traveled a lot. We dated steadily all spring. I met her parents, who were old enough otherwise to be her grandparents. I met her Cambridge friends, single and married. She did not like Paul, but did take the cause of race seriously and had gone South on civil rights sit-ins. She had friends at William and Mary, in Williamsburg, and once my teaching ended in June, we drove off to visit them and to have a lovers' weekend in Williamsburg, stopping off first to visit my parents in Villanova on the way. I had never brought a girl home before. Dad performed at his most charming. Mom attempted heart-to-hearts. They would tell me later, long after she and I had broken up, that they had known she wasn't "right"; that, in fact, they had detected that she drank secretly and too much, since the Beefeaters in our kitchen cabinet had mysteriously gone empty. Soon after she and I returned to Cambridge, she left for a summer in Spain, off her airline employee benefits; we would miss each other and promised to write.

Meanwhile, Paul called. Charles was driving to Boston with his mistress, Carmen, and wanted to throw a party in his suite in the Sheraton. Paul was closing with him on a big policy. So we all—Paul, Clara, Brenda, Beth, Hector, Shelly, and Max—gathered to welcome him. Charles looked older, having in fact frosted his hair with white. Carmen, dressed in silk tights, resembled Ruby Dee: "She still excites me after all this time," he said, "just by coming into the room." To be honest, not much happened. Some dancing, some drinks. We'd all been summoned as window dressing, as Paul offered his rich client the keys to the city. Before long, Charles and Carmen left the room for privacy, and Paul told us to leave. My own impression was wry, wondering at Charles, the family man's hypocrisy, and the corruption that went with dreams of success.

That August, Edward Kennedy, partying after his own fashion, encountered Chappaquiddick with Mary Jo Kopechne, and went on television to assure Massachusetts voters of his innocence. There was the moon landing. The Manson murders. I thought I saw an elision from moral-psycho explorations in fiction to life. People fantasized, made metaphors, read them, took drugs, then did them. The Vietnam war kept worsening.

After some silence, I received a letter from my airline agent friend dated weeks before saying that she had had a car accident and been hospitalized. She was healing but missed me. During her absence, at some chance Cambridge party, I met another woman, and as if in imitation of Paul, I started leading a double sex life. When my friend came back, she found out and we were finished. I saw her in a local bar a few weeks later and she wouldn't talk to me.

Ed Williams, one of the few black students in my class from Amherst College, had shown up at one of my parties and we'd kept in touch; he was an architect and had a big pad now on Huntington Avenue, where he was throwing an or-gee, according to Paul, and to which we were all invited. That night Paul was at the top of his form, raging and outraging to the point of collapse, smacking his lips and clutching at his crotch, gyrating, bouncing and bopping his weight around as he danced, first with this "broad," then that, like a kid on Christmas morning.

He convinced several of us to promise to meet him for his parents' moving day tomorrow. Tomorrow dawned and he called at ten and told me to meet him at the Chelsea ramp off the Mystic Bridge at noon. I was waiting there, hung over and bleary myself, wondering whether he would come, when a horn blared and down the ramp, blaring, came the GTO, with, as they sailed by: Paul, with a checkered hat on, cigar in his mouth, his malamute dog with its head out the back window, and his wife in front beside him and three kids crowded in back with the dog. I pulled out to follow; then followed down unfamiliar streets, when Santos blared again and there was an answering blare across the square from Hughes in his Dodge as he pulled into line. Up hills, down, then Paul stopped to pick up a man he introduced as his father on another corner, and we finally pulled up in front of a tenement apartment house, got out, said hello, and Paul led the way up three flights to his parents' apartment.

He was trying, impossibly, to pull his life together; to have his extremes meet, as if somehow essences could agree where social realities forbid. "Henry, my mother." I have no clear memory other than that she was proud of Paul, hardy, gracious, and good humored. We had lunch, chops and jag (a Portuguese pilaf kind of stuff). Lots of beer. We struggled with dressers, refrigerator, beds, boxes of dishes. Hector was helping. Lowering the packed up and bundled dressers and desks down over the back porch with a rope. The move was only three blocks away, but to a first floor, smaller and more to their needs with the children grown.

That same summer, Geoffrey Hughes told me that Paul was on the edge of doom. Behavior that before could be forgiven as hilarious had become increasingly reckless and sordid. Word was out, according to Hughes, that Paul had been screwing the Ashland wives, out in Ashland, which meant that word was getting to Peggy and her friends. Peggy had seen an attorney. "He's lynching himself. They're going to run him out of town on a rail. He's also in financial straits. He hasn't sold any insurance for three months. He's in hard debt. Hector has been given his IOUs to collect on. They're wondering about his usefulness at New England Life." Hughes went on to say that when he tried to tell Paul any of this, that Paul demanded names, dates, places. And if anybody told Paul about Peggy and the attorney, that Paul would go home and beat her up.

I felt naive that I hadn't sensed more hysteria beneath Paul's recent escapades. I had, in fact, met one of the Ashland wives,

Lucy, whom Paul had brought one afternoon to my apartment and then to a nearby motel. On my 29th birthday, he then had surprised me by bringing the woman's husband with him to my party as his cruising crony. Then Paul called Lucy, the wife, to tell her that her husband would be late. I marveled at the psychology of Paul's seducing both wife and husband at once. Then he told the husband about Clara's tits standing up, when he knew (and had told me) that Lucy's, the wife's, were fallen.

When Paul told me that he and Hughes were no longer talking, I decided, as Paul's friend, that I must trust him as he wished to be trusted. In all his womanizing, I had only seen good humor and consent, never anything bitter, cruel, or coercive. If he ever did harm, it would be out of clumsiness.

He stopped by towards midnight one night, after dinner with clients, and started going through his numbers, calling up girls, and running his mouth. He was talking to some girl he'd partied with from his office: "never been to Detroit. Did'ja tell her 'bout Paul Santos? Whatta mean she too old for me? Is she lookin' good? Aw, shit, I'll take some of that. Aw, she dusn' mind black cat? Whatta you mean, probably not, what I ask. You mean you know I been tryin' to tell you t'take care of Paul Santos an' fix em up, and you didn't tell her that you had the swingin'est motherlovin' cat in town? Sharon, you piss me off. You have consistently got me aggravated, got me wid some goddam hot pants. You promised to take me to the Bahamas, you didn't take me there—n'wait minute—you got my dick hard, 'bout talkin' 'bout other doggone broads, and you're screwin' all over me. Don't tell me one time that y'er gonna straighten me out and then all of a sudden decide you want it all for yourself, 'cause I already told you, you couldn't handle me all by yourself Well, you can't! It's got nothing to do with you as an individual, it's got to do with there is no one chick that can just handle Paul Santos, that's all. That's the way my temperament is. All right, just don't tell me when nobody comes in; you know, like do what you want, call Geoffrey Hughes. Oh, well, I injected him in the conversation. Because I decided to. All right, right. Why don't you just go out with Geoffrey Hughes, or uh, Bob Russell, and your other folks and just forget Paul Santos. That's all! Sharon, good night!" He hung up.

I'd been laughing and shaking my head at his performance, but then he turned and said: "Henry, who are you to talk? You don't let these bitches fool you either. You can be cold when need to be. So don't think you are so different from me. You tell them where it's at. You do it in a different way, but it's still the same thing."

Shelly was attacked that Saturday night. She had gone out to get milk at 9:30 and on her way back had passed and eyed a bearded man who then turned and seized her and gave her a beating, then fled when she fought free. He had torn her breasts out of her dress and crushed them. He didn't go for her purse or have time or place to rape her, so he must have just had psychotic anger and wanted to hurt whatever she represented. If she'd called to tell Paul first, looking for some comfort and assurance, he must have disappointed her; and as she told me now the flatness of her voice felt like an accusation. I failed as well. I was sorry, but from so many removes. I even thought, somehow too readily, I recognized her attacker's rage.

A few weeks later I went alone to see Janis Joplin in Harvard Stadium, August 15, 1970. One of a crowd of 40,000, I sat at the fifty yard line and the speaker system was on the fritz. Janis came out in dungarees and a pull-over, just another scrubby little girl, and she was impotent without amplification. All that crowd eager to marvel at her, and here she was nothing, nobody, only some chick doing her gyrations way off out there, in silence. The three-quarter moon, bright, high over the other side of the stadium passed lower and lower towards the rim of the end zone seats before the speakers crackled on and we could really hear, just in time for her last few songs.

That Labor Day I went out to Paul's with a woman I liked as a friend and a fellow writer, whom I'd met in a local writer's group.

Paul was in a new domestic mood, everybody happy and relaxed, barbecue sizzling. He took me aside at some point for cigars and J&B on the rocks, and said: "You know, Henry, I used to think I envied you, single, Harvard and all, but then one day I realized that you were hurting for what I got, the marriage and kids and house and family and the job with decent bucks; and that helped me to wake up to being who I am, you know."

I conceded that, yes, I envied him, offering up the words I thought he needed to hear.

We pretty much stopped running around together after that, as my own serial relationships seemed to me more painful and nightmarish; I struggled to finish my thesis; and inside, I was looking for permanence. Paul was right about that much.

Promises to Keep

My POET FRIEND, Bruce Bennett, had gotten his first job at Oberlin College, where he shared in founding a poetry magazine, *Field*. Now, from the summer of 1969, he'd quit teaching and moved back to Cambridge, to concentrate on his poetry. He organized a writers group, which met in members' apartments; I was invited, and later I invited my star student from Harvard, Kip Crosby, and Crosby, in turn, introduced me to a woman from Madrid, my age or older, Leonore Aparicio Hushfar. Leonore had befriended Kip's girl, Hilary, in a class at B.U. and thought her remarkable, and was aspiring to lead a literary salon herself; she also wanted to write poetry, had been a disciple of Jorge Luis Borges during his residence at Harvard, and had read Robert Frost out loud to him every morning. She, too, joined Bruce's group, and later she had parties.

My student/folk revolution/commune circle now overlapped with the Harvard grad student and local writer circles. I saw this as a wayfaring from knowing no one to having choices.

Kip and Hilary passed on Hilary's Central Square apartment to me, while the two of them moved into a commune together. A woman I met at a Harvard party and dated led me to Peter O'Malley and the Plough and the Stars pub, which had been recently rehabbed from a seamy taproom, where postal workers would drink, to a stylish recreation of an Irish literary pub, or to something like Dylan Thomas's White Horse Bar in New York. The Plough was on a corner just down the block from me. O'Malley, a tall, black-haired, hearty Irishman from Dublin, was the bartender. The woman and he had dated, and now he was planning an expedition to sail a trimaran to Rio de Janeiro, and she was tempted to join in, along with her four-year-old son. In addition to sailing, O'Malley's passion was music, in which he was taking a degree, and he would play the classical music station in the pub and give a pint to anybody who could name that tune. He seemed to share my curiosity about people and my pleasure in commotion as forms of relief from serious, creative ambitions underneath.

Teaching had started for me again, meanwhile, and my thesis work had grown difficult. The woman and I soon stopped dating.

I was smitten, pretty much at first sight, by Connie Sherbill, whom I met at Leonore's in the fall of 1970. In addition to befriending Hilary, Leonore had also befriended an even younger B.U. student, who was Connie's roommate in a Brookline apartment.

Kip, Hilary, and I were at Leonore's for brunch. Leonore hung crisscrossed chains on the window in place of curtains, had painted a slashing black and silver diagonal across the walls, had a tapestry hanging, and floors bare except for straw mats; also she had an expensive stereo system, exotic cappuccino to serve us, and a piano in one corner. At the time, a rock band was playing in Harvard Square, on the common nearby, its noise echoing in the street so loudly that we had to shout to understand each other.

The doorbell rang, then a knock at the door, Leonore went to answer, gave some excited greeting, and in came a short, plump girl, whom Hilary knew, hello, hello, and this other really beautiful girl, Connie. They had come over for the rock concert and then decided to drop by. They liked that kind of music, yes, of course! Didn't I? Connie was shy, but attentive and witty. Neither girl said much. Connie wore tight jeans and boots, and a vest; she was fresh and young, with full breasts, nice hips, shoulder-length brown hair, and eyes that sloped down, suggesting melancholy. I didn't ask her out, but I was driving back to my Central Square apartment and offered her and the plump girl a lift, dropping them off on the Cambridge side of the B.U. Bridge—stalwart, self-reliant, no-nonsense girls, I thought. I did ask Leonore about Connie later, suggesting interest. But I was involved with another girl, whom I'd met in one of Cambridge's continental cafés.

Then Leonore had a party, supposedly a birthday party for herself; lots of new people, lots to drink, dancing. And Connie Sherbill was there because Leonore had remembered that I'd liked her before. Connie and I started dancing. A boy her age was trying to interest her, but I kept dancing with her, and when we sat down, I put my hand on a bare part of her back, and she didn't flinch. She was flushed and into the party. And in the salacious spirit of the night, I said: "How about going to another party in town? One special guy, Max, I want you to meet, is supposed to meet me there. How about it?" She said sure.

So feeling physical—did I kiss her in the car?—we found our way in town. When we got to the party it had wound down; people were stoned and dancing, but Max had been there and left, and I knew no one else. So we danced a while—I was trying to impress her with the dangerous, streetwise world I inhabited—and then I asked her back to my place, and kissing me now, flushed and excited in the car, she said yes.

Perhaps on our third, or fourth date, at my apartment, Connie got a phone call from her sister in Waltham that their father had just died.

Nearly every girl I had been serious about, from my first love in high school on, had lost her father; I seemed to respond to that, and they seemed to respond to my responding. Certainly I had the conviction that family tragedy made people more real.

Now I felt Connie's loss and wasn't afraid of it. With other women, people I really didn't love, anything this serious would be something to avoid. I also liked the sense of family in Connie's Jewishness, that family for her was at the heart of what mattered, which, in different ways, was my parents' creed, too.

Now, here, unexpectedly, after only two or three dates, I was facing her family grief and driving her out Mt. Auburn towards

Waltham, where I had never been, out a winding, complicated main street I had never followed before, counting, and wincing as I counted, one funeral home after another, some seventeen in all (since then, I've realized that these were ethnic neighborhoods, Irish, Italian, Armenian, each with their own burial traditions, parishes, churches). Following her tearful directions, we found Brandeis, and across the street, the modern apartment complex where her older sister, Lonne, and brother-in-law, Larry, lived with their new baby. Connie ran sobbing into her sister's arms. Connie's date, a stranger to them, I was greeted with embarrassed politeness.

Next evening I went back with her, as the whole family gathered to sit shiva. Her mother, Hazel, and youngest brother, Ray, had flown up from Miami; her oldest brother, Danny, a rabbinical student, had come from New York. Her sister's in-laws, Mr. and Mrs. Weinstein, arrived from Newton, along with their grown children. We went outside later, at Danny's urging, to stand in the chill fall night and view the northern lights, which dimly shimmered, thanks to a trick in the atmosphere.

Connie had been born and raised in Miami. Her parents had been divorced only a year before, she said, "after twenty-four years and many attempts to patch things up." Her father, Joe, had been a truck farmer at one point, growing vegetables. Another time, which had involved their living in Panama, he had dealt in used cars. "He intimidated us," she told me, "but loved us dearly." They had had money at some point, but then had lost it. Generally, I gathered that he'd been luckless and intent on get-rich-quick deals. After the divorce, he had been alone, drinking, and financially destitute. Given that Connie loved him and was his favorite, she would torment herself now for not being there for him at the end. Deep in her own mind, he had needed her, and she had refused to see him when she could have; and she was to blame for deserting him and for his dying alone in a hotel room.

Hazel had had to rally first as a single parent after the divorce, and now as a widow. Having worked for her husband and having had to juggle an unpredictable income for years, she now made her living as a certified public accountant, while harboring passions for art, music, writing, and literature. She had put Lonne through college and seen her married to Larry in Boston. She had seen Danny, who had been a state debating champion in high school, through B.U. Then Connie; then Ray still to follow. Connie's education had been financed partly by a student loan, which Connie would be paying off for years to come.

Connie, I felt, knew life in her guts. She believed in my ambition to write, and was ready to share in sacrificing for that ambition. She had majored in art history at B.U., and her own ambition was to develop as a visual artist, and to teach young children.

By January 1971, she had moved in with me, and I would from our first sleeping together date no one else.

I need to credit now, as I did not then, the effort for her I must have posed, given my age, background, and the momentum of my life. The space we shared was mine: my furniture, my address, my phone, my record player, my records, my décor, my habits; my desk and typewriter dominating the living room, where as I worked, she would read in the bedroom. My father might call, one of his random maintenance calls, and Connie would answer, and we'd say that she was over visiting, or over for dinner. We were always lying for appearances to the official world, which included Mom and Dad, and the landlord, at least.

By then my Shakespeare thesis had been accepted, and I would have my Ph.D., officially, come June; meanwhile I still taught fiction writing and freshman composition at Harvard and worked on the novel. Having spent a total of eight years rather than the usual four completing my degree, instead of having my pick of assistant professor jobs from a bulging placement file in the English department, I found the file nearly empty. My application letters for the few jobs that seemed appropriate failed to generate an interview. Even my most influential professors had no advice or leads. An oversupply of baby-boomers receiving Ph.D.'s and declining undergraduate enrollments had combined to bring on the unforeseen: an academic depression in the Humanities, which would last, in effect, for the next ten years.

Kip and Hilary were married that Memorial Day.

When I turned thirty in June, I commented in my notebook: "I can't get a job. I can't have the things that normal people my age enjoy. I can't afford a family. When I was twenty-five, that was clearly a matter of choice. I was trying to be an artist, and I could always give up that ambition and still succeed by worldly standards. But here I am skilled, educated, and living alone on $4,000 where any stiff can make $10,000."

Connie graduated from B.U. and began working at a Head Start classroom in the basement of an Allston-Brighton church. Her BU roommates were breaking up. She took a room in Cambridge for appearances, but hardly ever slept there. Then in August, Mom and Dad visited Cambridge, and Dad assured me gruffly: "Don't worry about jobs. Persevere. You'll make it." For this visit, incidentally, Connie had had to hide her things and move back to her room, where we'd pick her up to take her for dinner or an outing, then drop her back off.

The bar down the street from my apartment, the Plough and the Stars, had put a sign in the window in the spring of 1970 asking for poems and stories for a broadsheet, and I had left a chapter from my novel there, shortly after I'd met the bartender, Peter O'Malley (whose sailing expedition to Rio had fallen through). As I stopped back months later, early in 1971, O'Malley told me that he liked the chapter and wanted to use it for the broadsheet, but the actual printing of the broadsheet had been stalled, because once they'd seen how much good work they'd gotten, they'd wondered whether they shouldn't be starting a magazine. Would I be interested in working on something like that? he asked. I answered sure, having edited the *Amherst Literary Magazine* for three years; we shook on it, and arranged to meet in the pub later with the owner, some poets, and other literary "blokes" to talk about it more.

Through the spring, in the midst of everything else, we met at the Plough, in my apartment, or in O'Malley's apartment on Green Street. The founding group included my own friends, Bruce Bennett and Kip Crosby, myself, O'Malley, and O'Malley's friends or regulars from the Plough, Aram Saroyan (son of William, who claimed that his father had already done everything worth doing with fiction), George Kimball (a Hunter Thompson fan, who had studied at Iowa, run unsuccessfully for Sheriff of Kansas City, lived on the Bowery, then come to Cambridge to write for Cambridge's underground weekly, the *Phoenix*), Bill Corbett (a poet with ties to the Temple Bar and Grolier bookstores and locally prominent writers who gathered around them, as similarly tribal writers gathered around City Lights in San Francisco or the 8th Street Bookstore in Manhattan), David Gullette (an actor and poet who taught at Simmons College), and Norman Klein (a poet who had also studied at Iowa, knew Andre Dubus, and taught at Simmons). We settled on the name *Ploughshares*. We agreed on having a different member of the editorial board serve as "coordinating editor" for each issue, with me being the first. As our streetwise entrepreneur—and partner of the six or so Irish-American investors who owned the bar— O'Malley would take care of the business matters, printing, the paying of bills, distribution, and advertising.

Some of us—not me, thank you—were dedicated subterraneans, cultural mutineers (as Ronald Sukenick would later write) who had friends, counterparts, and heroes in the Bowery, in the Village, and in Berkeley. O'Malley boasted that the Plough was a place to meet others "whose failures are more glamorous than your own." Our motives were mixed, but none, give or take some notion of O'Malley's concerning publicity for the bar, were materialistic. I saw us as primarily refugees from other places where writing had mattered: in my case, Amherst and the Iowa Workshop. I had kept alive my own sense of vocation, somewhat, despite the rigor of Ph.D. work, in Bruce's writing group and in my teaching, and for me editing and producing a literary magazine was a still wider exercise of that vocation. Another excerpt from my novel had been chosen for the issue, and this would be my first publication since college; I was eager to share my best work, especially among other writers. I also felt the need to network and to publish as part of searching for a teaching job—and this was the motive I emphasized in long-distance calls with Dad at the time (he was skeptical, and made me vow never to put money of my own into such a venture; fine, so long as it doesn't cost you anything).

Over the summer of 1971, Peter and I met with Joe Wilmott, a friend and former student of Bill Corbett's at Emerson College. After dropping out of Emerson, Wilmott had gone to work for a South Boston printer, and having been granted after-hours run of the shop, had joined with poet Thomas Lux in starting The Barn Dream Press, a small press devoted to poetry. Barn Dream (named for what cows might think at day's end), in turn, had been inspired by a professor at Emerson, Jim Randall, who had been Lux's mentor, and who was bringing out Lux's first collection of poems from his own well-established small press, Pym-Randall. Lux was a serious poet that Bruce Bennett had come to admire while cofounding and editing *Field* at Oberlin. O'Malley and I, in any case, concluded that Wilmott was sensitive to poetry, altruistic, and otherwise sympathetic to our publishing goals, and would work with us in trying to keep down costs. Part of our deal involved Wilmott's contracting the typesetting, but then using my volunteer labor in the production process: proofreading, pasting up phototype for camera-ready single pages, and, later, opaquing and stripping the negatives for offset plates. We used an old issue of *Transatlantic Review* for our first dummy, imitating its format and pasting proofs over actual pages in the issue. All of this, of course, appealed to my teenaged hobby of letterpress printing, and, as I commuted by subway to and from the print shop that humid summer, and worked whole days in the shop's airless and un-air-conditioned darkroom, the old romance of craft engaged me, as well as the chance to learn offset printing, which seemed to demand more knowledge of darkroom photography than of operating presses.

I threw myself into all of this, in the face of ignominy, my struggle with my novel, and joblessness; I thought of my effort as one of personal rehabilitation, a way to use and prove my worth, regardless of whether established "society" wanted and was willing to pay for me. Connie, meanwhile, trusted and admired my commitment and supported its supporting dreams, as well as the long-term rationale with which I tried to explain it to my father.

In September, 1971, the first issue of *Ploughshares* appeared, one thousand copies costing $2,000, a bill that O'Malley somehow settled with Wilmott's boss. Other than giving away copies to family and friends, we hadn't considered publicizing or distributing the magazine yet, but we printed a cover price both in dollars and pounds, to allow for O'Malley taking copies to Ireland. Kimball drove to Manhattan with a box and left some on consignment at the 8th Street and Gotham Bookmart. O'Malley and I left five copies here, ten there, at the various bookstores around Harvard Square. We tried selling a stack in the bar. Corbett knew a friendly bookstore in San Francisco and got them to order. We had a publication party in the bar, where a public broadcaster friend of O'Malley's interviewed us and then aired the interview on WGBH radio. Later the same friend got us to appear on a community affairs TV show, Catch 44. Thanks to Kimball and the *Phoenix* editors who drank at the Plough, a full-length review of the issue appeared in the *Phoenix*; the reviewer was the Emerson professor, Jim Randall, who quipped that "*Ploughshares* is as much a happening as a literary event," questioned the compromises of our editing by committee, regarded the fiction as competent but unoriginal, yet ended by confessing "to liking both the magazine and its promise."

From the first, *Ploughshares* lent me social identity as a writer. Through that first issue and the sample of my fiction in it—about which Dick Yates wrote me, "Perfect, don't change a word"—I was taken seriously by writers my age who had themselves managed to publish books and land teaching jobs, among them Andre Dubus, Carter Wilson, Geoffrey Clark, Sidney Goldfarb, John Bart Gerald, and Fanny Howe.

For fall, 1971, I managed to continue teaching a section of expository writing at Harvard; I also was hired to teach remedial composition as a part-timer at Simmons College. The following academic year, however, I was unemployed, though I did keep applying for jobs, and in spring, 1972, had turned down one offer to teach composition at Roger Williams College, in Rhode Island, where another student of Dick Yates's, Geoffrey Clark, had found full-time work fresh out of Iowa; and another at Wichita State in Kansas. Both schools seemed academically dismal; neither seemed worth relocating and giving up the promise of Boston for. Out in the cold—no income, no health benefits—I continued my volunteer work on *Ploughshares* and worked on my book, while I lived off of savings and Connie's meager salary from her daycare job. *Ploughshares* and its mission became so consuming that after forcing myself to canvass Harvard Square typewriter shops, bookstores, restaurants, bars, and clothiers in search of advertising, I would walk past new cars like an anarchist, angry at the unnecessary and indifferent wealth everywhere around me. *Ploughshares* became my social focus, extending to my conviction that there should be some average bracket of material need for each citizen, no more, no less, my version of socialism.

I had gone into partnership with Peter O'Malley in publishing *Ploughshares*, offering as capital my time and brains. In some way, too, I saw O'Malley and myself as an odd couple, complementing each other's strengths. Where business was concerned, O'Malley was the icebreaker, the commotion-maker, the fast-talker; then I was to do the follow-up and make the blarney real, as it were. O'Malley supposedly knew the ways of the world; I knew writing, editing, and scholarship.

From the first, however, I was committed to the magazine and its cause for keeps. And that would mean, before long—in addition to editing, pasting up in the print shop, distributing to bookstores, and selling and designing ads—having to take over most of the so-called business and legal details as well.

We opened a bank account under the name of *Ploughshares*, with O'Malley and me co-signers on all checks. We discovered grants. Bill Corbett knew Russell Banks, editor of *Lillabulero*, who was serving on the board of the Coordinating Council of Literary Magazines in New York, which sub-granted funds from the National Endowment for the Arts. O'Malley put in an application, friends lobbied friends, and we came up with our first two thousand dollar grant, which paid for Kimball's issue, but then, surprise, we had to show proof that we had matched this amount or pay it all back. At this point, I put in eight hundred dollars of savings (despite my promise to Dad), and together with a supposed list of donors from the bar and our meager revenues, O'Malley managed to raise the rest.

Next, Connie heard about the Massachusetts Council on the Arts in connection with some Head Start project and urged us to look into it; O'Malley asked around and played his Irish political card—the Plough partners knew some powers at the State House—and we went into Beacon Hill and met with a very supportive Irish-American administrator at the Council, applied for and got another two thousand dollars. Suddenly, between annual CCLM and Massachusetts Council grants, *Ploughshares* seemed possible after all, though we were now required to incorporate as not-for-profit and to apply for tax-exempt status from the IRS. O'Malley and a lawyer friend finally did the state incorporation, copying passages from a law book for our bylaws, which O'Malley regarded mainly as paper; properly bold and authentic spirits went ahead and parked in no-parking zones or lived on barter-and-cash rather than taxable income: up the system. The idea was to make the legal gestures and then do pretty much what you liked. He continued to view the magazine as a partnership between we two "directors," only instead of owning stock, we would accrue salaries on our financial statements, towards some eventual sale. The pro-bono accountant who recommended this was also accountant to the bar. From this point on, however, the future of the magazine would depend on "getting civilized." I insisted on taking over the checkbook. I did the grant writing and reporting. I dealt with the accountant. I learned nonprofit law.

In my singles life, before Connie, I had taken pride in making one small room an everywhere. In clothes, in food, in furniture, in cars, apartments, in everything but books, I lived proudly at the poverty line—proudly because this was my choice, it had its ideology, and because like a mendicant monk, my eyes were not fixed on worldly matters. But as life went on, and as that became a life that I was asking Connie to share, my confidence in two sources of my eventual rescue from genteel poverty, in tickets back, as it were, namely a full-time teaching job and family money, wore thin, if not out. And outside of "the system," I was learning, you lived one day at a time, trading on your youth and chance.

Throughout this time I was, or felt myself to be to Connie, what I dreamed myself to be: the writer about to be recognized; the spiritual and sexual seeker settled down; the schooled scholar, critic, teacher, and editor, also about to be recognized and given cultural stability with a livelihood and a good job; the provider, family man, and father of children yet unborn, which had been put off only briefly until my promise was achieved; the branch of good WASP stock, socially entrenched and better off than her own family, hence an upward opportunity in assimilated America.

We didn't rush into marriage. We talked about love, but never marriage. We were always mutually elective, a balance of powers; neither of us was without choices. Marriage was only necessary for children, and children were only possible with a Real Job and income, and a Real Job could only be had, seemingly, either by compromising my dreams and accepting an offer like Roger Williams's, or by finishing and publishing my book.

Together with dreams, however, for Connie, there was always the uncertainty. "Do you love me?" she would ask over and over, never satisfied with the answer; if you had to choose between your writing and me, would you choose me? Unfair question, I would answer. If she had to choose between having children and me, or between her religion and me, what would she choose? It was the same kind of unnecessary, extreme question that you couldn't answer until you were faced with it as a real choice and either did or did not. She must have lived with the double prospects of my success and failure, even as she got up at dawn every day and took the bus to her Head Start job, which was bringing in our only income for the time being. What if some publisher, as Dick Yates expected, on the basis of the half of my novel that was finished, believed in its prospect of being finished, and offered a contract? What if the book was published, as my students' books—Nick Gargarin's and Kip Crosby's—had been, as Andre Dubus's, as Bart Gerald's, as Fanny Howe's, as Russell Banks's? If the dreams were achieved, then what would the next dreams be? Would I still love her, would I ever commit myself to the part of me that craved the completion of children and family, or would I only give parts of myself, like a tribute or toll, that I could afford to give? Would I, once I had some public recognition, look again to glamorous, pleasure-seeking women, women who had no imagination or desire to live risks with or about me, but only to enjoy the apparent benefits?

On the other hand, what if the book was never finished, what if even I had to admit its flaws? Or what if it kept taking years and years, and then when it was finished, it wasn't published? What if all the doubters and nay-sayers were right? (And who, she must also have asked herself, who was she to question, given the years alone of this man, the complexities and experiences untold, the years of graduate school and teaching? And yet she was offering her life, and questioning was her right.) What if, indeed, realism was dead and even Dick Yates had no audience? What if there was some streak of self-defeat in Dee, afraid of real success or adulthood? What if time or love ran out?

George Kimball was supposed to have been coordinating editor of the second *Ploughshares* issue, which we only managed to publish after delays and mishaps in June, 1972; in fact, after the initial editorial meetings, George had vanished—rumor had it he was being sought for questioning by the FBI or CIA—leaving it to me to finish editing in his persona.

If the rotating editorship was going to work, we needed outside help—Kip Crosby, having married Hilary, had published his novel, and started acting as if his career had moved beyond the likes of us. O'Malley and I asked Jim Randall, since he'd reviewed us, if he would edit the third issue. Agreed. I also applied to Randall for a job teaching writing at Emerson, but he turned me down, in favor of Fanny Howe, "who had books." We started having editorial meetings in Randall's Harvard Street apartment, out of which he and his wife, Joanne, operated the Pym-Randall Press. Corbett and Gullette continued from the earlier group, joined now by the Poet-in-Residence at Emerson, Paul Hannigan, and a friend and former student of Bruce's, Katha Pollitt. Randall remained skeptical about my allegiance to realist fiction and my Harvard background, and

I often felt the outsider among his circle. He had guest-edited an issue of *Sumac* and his Pym-Randall list was impressive, including Kenneth Rexroth, Robert Kelly, Allen Grossman, Basil Bunting, and Ford Madox Ford ("our only dead poet, because he is a personal favorite and his poetry has been neglected," he wrote), and he appeared to have made numerous literary acquaintances and friends over his past twenty years in the area. Given his creative writing program at Emerson and his literary convictions and friendships, he was the unofficial pope of Cambridge literary life, excluding Harvard; he himself had graduated from B.U. His literary court, other than his apartment, was the Toga Lounge across from Harvard Yard, and his way station was the Grolier Book Shop. He brought a new level of credibility and of contacts to the magazine.

We agreed that I would do an interview with Richard Yates for his issue. Geoffrey Clark, who had had a story in the Kimball issue, had invited Yates for a reading at Roger Williams College in April, at which time I drove down, and Clark and I questioned him together. I later transcribed the tape and patched together a draft, sent it to Yates in Wichita, where he was teaching; Yates rewrote, cut, and added; I then offered extra questions by mail as well as a draft of a concluding statement about neglect and fame that I thought he should make—in all of this I was inspired by a cover interview that James Alan McPherson had recently published in the *Atlantic* with Ralph Ellison. Randall was happy with the result.

About this same time, O'Malley asked me if I knew anything about Richard Wilbur, and I said sure, that together with Robert Lowell, I thought he was the best poet since Frost. Peter took that in, then explained that he'd been seeing Wilbur's daughter, Ellen, here in Cambridge, that she was a writer, and would I mind looking at some of her stories and poems sometime. Before long they were engaged. Connie and I were invited to meet Charlee and Richard Wilbur in Ellen's apartment in one of the Harvard houses, where we stayed up most of the night drinking, telling stories, and singing along to her brother's guitar. I was dazzled. O'Malley as a quantity seemed to challenge them much as he challenged me; Ellen, with all her natural elegance, heart, and intellect, had somehow set out to redeem and direct O'Malley's raw energy (his "daemonism," as I described it to Yates), and to help him foster his talent as a composer. As a gifted writer from a writer's family, she also believed in the magazine and added to Peter's commitment to it. They were married that summer, and Connie and I stopped by their big wedding in the Berkshires, then drove on down to Philadelphia to visit my parents, where Connie argued heatedly with my father about McGovern and ending the war, and we visited my grandmother in her nursing home, as well as Chuck and his family in New Jersey, and went through all our family photographs.

Nixon was reelected. A cease-fire was called in Vietnam with the New Year. The early Watergate hearings began. By March 1973, the draft had ended and U.S. forces were leaving Vietnam. Spring, I worked with Thomas Lux in editing the fourth Ploughshares. Also my writing was getting attention.

Finally, Randall hired me as Emerson's Prose-Writer-in-Residence from July 1973 to 1974. The pay was four thousand dollars to teach two workshops, and at the time it seemed like a rescue and an affirmation. A job in the world lent force to my faith, not only to continue with *Ploughshares*, but to marry Connie.

Given Connie's and my love, and given this slim, temporary opportunity now at last, the pressures we'd been feeling both from the official world and from home to get married seemed foolish to resist. Dad bribed us with promise of a ten thousand dollar advance on my inheritance once I got married.

One Sunday morning we'd had breakfast in the corner diner, joked about marriage, then come home and embraced in our hallway, rocking back and forth and listening to the floor creak and there was nothing else to say: "How about it, want to?" I asked, as if from someplace behind my mind, someplace I trusted, where all was risk, free-fall, and life. She said yes.

We were married in her mother's new condo in Miami, August 25, 1973. My sister couldn't come. But Jack flew in with a taciturn June and served as best man. Chuck came with Nancy. I flew down with Mom and Dad. I had not been allowed to see Connie for a week, and now in her mother's house, to the harmonies of Mozart's "Jupiter Symphony," she came down from the second floor, as I waited for her at the end of the white carpet with Judge Sweet, Justice of the Peace. I was positive and confident underneath, in my troth, in my fathering to come, and in my novel still, which I never doubted would be published, never. In our wedding pictures, both at our healthiest, in the blessings and best wishes of our combined families, our faces shine with all our dreams and expectations, commitments made.

Departures

I HAD THE PERCEPTION that what Dad wanted most for each of us was something he could tell his locker partners at the golf club—facts of our lives that would do him credit in the hard, ungenerous minds of respectable, successful men, men of the world. There was no explaining Jack to such men, until, perhaps the excavating company took hold in Colorado—Jack had started a business in Ft. Collins. Judy had married a Swarthmore graduate, an engineer, a teacher. DeWitt, well, DeWitt got into Amherst College and was doing well. Before long, Jack had gotten married. Charles was going to medical school. Charles was interning at Bryn Mawr. Charles had married. DeWitt was going to Harvard for his Ph.D. Lives had to sound sound, solid. No flaws, no weaknesses, no indecisiveness, please; no one wanted to confess such things.

"We had good parents," Chuck insists now.

I had to guard against loving Mom too much, so I could go on; I had to work, on the other hand, to love Dad enough, or felt I had to. I never deserted him, but labored to communicate, labored for his approval and understanding.

The most positive things I remember about him as a father, as a person, mainly date from my college years, on. I think life eased for him emotionally, then, with all of us gone, so that he was on more equal terms with Mom, one to one, and, in fact, had her to himself again.

Again, the change in their relationship was symbolized by the move to a new house.

Before I left for Iowa in the fall of 1964, they had house-hunted and decided to move; they had found a house in Villanova, which would be their "retirement home." They bought it, and I was home in time from Harvard to see it shortly after. Ranch design. On an exposed corner property, but with a larger private backyard. Some new furniture was bought at the time of moving, and they had to do some redecorating. The former owners had been partial to gaudy valances, for instance. The inside was repainted, new carpeting put in. I was away when they actually moved, and had no say in the packing up of my own room at St. Davids, or unpacking in what would be my room here.

They would live together here until my father's death in fall, 1976, and my mother would continue in the house alone thereafter until her death in the fall of 1985.

My mother often wondered over the fact that she would live in this house more years than in any of the five or six she had managed in her life. It was not the house of her dreams so much as of Dad's. Her dream, like that of the convertible in automobiles, or a tour around the world in travel, had been for a small farm, a place with land. But the Villanova house—"the dump," as Dad proudly called it—was full of conveniences, safe, roomy, and easy to maintain and care for. Also Dad liked the location, close to the Gulph Mills entrance to the Expressway, which shortened his commute to the factory, and in amongst extant mansions and estates. One mansion, across the street, was set back on land larger than a park or golf course and was supposed to have full-sized bowling alleys in the basement. George Brown, the V.P. of Penn Bank with whom Dad played golf on Saturdays, lived down the street. (In later years, Dad would take perverse pride when the 76ers star, Julius Erving, moved in as a neighbor a few streets over.)

Dad wrote to me in Iowa, in the fall of 1964, "We are well settled now, and enjoying the new home. Quite different from previous experiences. Much simpler without sacrificing comforts and activities. Certainly less work and worry for Mother. Curtains are all fixed, pictures hung and rehung, books in place and replaced, etc. Looks as if Mother is out of business and will just have to settle for her hospital work and relax in between." (Dr. Appel recently had gotten her work as a volunteer para-therapist, helping with patients at the Philadelphia Institute, and reassuring her that her "life wisdom" and natural instincts were as valuable as a psychologist's degree.)

Giving up St. Davids was a grief for Mom; unlike Bloomingdale, which had been a hand-me-down from the Henrys, St. Davids had been her own house; it had also been a full, bustling house, until child by child we had outgrown and deserted it, and her; but even so, it still held memories. She loved the yard and gardens. Dad joked, self-disparaging, that by habit he still drove home to St. Davids after work.

But soon after they moved—I was in Iowa City—Grandpop Thralls died. Her father's illness had drained Mom in her last years at St. Davids; she travelled by car or train to her parents' Brooklyn apartment at least once each week. He died just as Mom was looking forward to the third portion of her life—"for self," as she put it—and she had to bring her mother, Ottalie, to live with her and Dad at Villanova. No one else would or could help, namely her younger sister, Aunt Janice. The Brooklyn apartment had been emptied on a certain day, and Chuck had gone with Mom and spoke afterwards with distaste of Aunt Janice and Uncle Lloyd, who had been there too and looking for valuables to seize, as petty vultures. At first, Ottalie lived in my room, then coincident with my first return, she was moved into the guest room next door.

I recall one Thanksgiving visit when Nanas Henry and Thralls were both present at Villanova, as well as Chuck and Nancy and their babies, so we had age brackets from eighties to sixties to forties to thirties to three to three months, or something like that. A time machine, clan-wise. The grandmothers would make Mom and Dad, who otherwise seemed old to me, seem young.

Finally, Ottalie's health persuaded Mom to heed Dad's advice and put her in Wynnewood, a nearby nursing home. This preceded Nana Henry needing a home, though before long Nana Henry moved there too, only to insist on another nursing home of her own style and taste in Devon. I would dutifully visit them both, every visit home. Nana Henry died first, in 1969; Ottalie not until 1978, two years after Dad himself.

The mid-sixties were also the time of my most excruciating badgering of Mom to be as honest about her feelings as I thought I was being about mine. She saved my letters, and I wince now at my impertinence and my overheated prose. "What is the basest thing you've every done in your life?" I wrote her on Valentine's Day, 1964 (I was thinking of Thoreau). "When I think of baseness and think of myself it is sinning against dignity, the worth and value of being, the dearness of life or living things or beauty. What was your most unforgivable sin? I think it is very important for me to have an idea—not necessarily for my psychological health, but for my writing. I know I am asking a lot, but you must sense the possibility of breaking through, for all of us, into a knowing of each other and ourselves."

She had always tried to keep up with my writing and reading, so we wouldn't draw apart. She read and quoted D.H. Lawrence and Tolstoy back to me. She'd even found a Lawrence quote suggesting that some things are better kept private between parents and children.

I prodded her again: "I'm not asking questions I haven't asked myself. These are things I want to know about everybody, especially those I love. I want to understand you as human beings."

Finally, she wrote back the following: "I tried. I filled a few pages and got sick when I saw what I'd written. Tore up into tiny pieces the venting of my nastiness. It is one thing to gripe and be irked in speech. The mere saying out loud what my feelings are is a catharsis. But the sound is dissipated and disappears. But when I wrote it I felt so guilty with those words on paper, in my writing,

I just had to destroy them. I said my mother is unwittingly and innocently controlling my great adventure, my life, and I'm letting her do it! Instead of putting her where she really ought to be, I'm letting her take over my energy, my time, my home—why? Your Mother is a fool, a milquetoast to her own detriment? No—You see I keep blaming her, or at least I pick on her habits and her presence to get angry at when I'm really angry at myself for 'taking her on' and angry at my sister because she has sense enough to say she doesn't want any of the responsibility and can't take any because it would interfere with her family life! But it interferes with mine. And I let it. With Daddy here 'til noon each day and Mother too, ugh, they are jealous of each other. If I talk or am in a room alone with either of them, the other one pouts! And I'd prefer neither of them for I want to do something on my own, but can only do things after they are both asleep. My enthusiasm for 'home' is at low ebb. It is not my home any more. Some days I scream inside and my food stays on my plate as I sit at the table and listen to the eating (the slurping, sucking, spitting, gulping); the breathing (so effortful, half panting—extra labor to enable Mother to slurp and gulp) and see the rapidity with which the fork or spoon gets back and forth to the mouth, as if someone were going to steal away the food if it weren't eaten in three minutes. The incessant clock watching, and habitual patterns of trips down the hall and all are petty annoyances. She's only refueling and eliminating and refueling ad infinitum. My mind and body had had enough of New York and its responsibility for the care of my parents there, so when my father died, I brought Mother here. I did not want to have her here. I knew what would happen and how I'd respond to it. But I didn't want to have her in N.Y. and still have to continue trips over there till she died.

"I'm not good for her because I never was. As a child I ignored her and became independent early, because she never could answer my questions and never had time to listen or pay any attention. She was either sick or busy with my brothers. So early in life I used to tell her I must have been adopted, because she never could be a mother to me. It must have hurt her, but I from then on used teachers and books as my 'mother.' I did not like her. I was ashamed of her grammar and her lack of knowledge and etiquette (though I knew she had had a hard early life and only to 5th grade in school). I felt sorry for her 'inadequacies' and sorry for my father because he kept on studying and learning and developing and she didn't make any effort at all to grow with him. I was proud of his achievements, but ashamed of her lack of interest in anything beyond her boys and her naps and shopping. When I was in high school, and later from college I always met my friends in New York, never had them home with me. Isn't that awful? But it was true. I was always embarrassed about my parents' home. So was my father. He used to meet others and me in N.Y., not at home. Then when he got to be a real lush, with liquor (all that was after I was married), I felt sorry for Mother, but oh, what's the use? It's all over now.

"But I inherited the responsibility of caring for his widow, whom I never loved, but for whom I have compassion, complicated by my resentment at her lack of understanding, her greediness.

"She told Anna I was married to a typewriter (I was doing two speeches for Appel last month, one before and one after Xmas. I had to work all one day and was only off the typewriter preparing her meals, putting drops in her eyes. It was not an Institute Day so she had privately planned a shopping spree and was frustrated.) Said I shouldn't work for Appel or for anyone. The home should be enough without all the other things. Anyway I just would rather not have her around dependent on me for anything, either here or in a nursing home. I guess I'd just rather the Good Lord would call an end to her life before I turn into a nasty old woman myself. Nana Henry bothers me too. I guess I'm intolerant of old people, unless they are intelligent and interested in living and life and meaning and contributing something to life. If not, they ought to be together with groups of old people and not be sapping the patience of younger ones who still have something to work toward."

Her confession oddly gratified me, even though it caused her pain. "I don't want to hurt you," I replied. "But then I think that this is my honesty to you and that honesty itself is worth pain or anger, worth no less than everything."

During my visits, after the preliminary encounters of how my life was going, graduate school, teaching, writing, my car, my health, my bank account and taxes, Dad at Villanova would retire to his chair in the corner of the living room. Reminiscent of "his chair" at St. Davids, this was his place of state, where he retired after meals or golf or after boredom with the TV. Often he fell asleep here, snoring, sitting up. He worked here too at business letters, and all financial problems, filling page after page of yellow tablets (kept in Mom's adjacent desk drawer) with scrawled numbers and columns.

A time of peak pressure on him was the selling of the factory, which went through several phases. The anxiety and negotiation, co-distribution agreements, and so forth with E.J. Brock first; then the production and supply deal with Whitman; then the negotiated sale of Henry's to PET Milk, which owned Whitman, which led to Dad's salaried semi- and then full retirement.

He was responsible to all Henrys owning stock in the company (Nana, Peggy, Kitty), as well as to eighty or so Henry employees. He wrote to me in Iowa that since none of his sons intended to succeed him and since this was a decision he was happy to support, his objectives were to ensure a running company with as many of the Henry employees continuing as possible as well as a retirement income sufficient for Mom and him to live in comfort and security.

Over and over, he considered debt, considered Mom's likely inheritance after Nana Thralls died, plus his own after his mother died, plus his net distribution from sale of the company and other settlements: all in hoping to amass some magical figure, six hundred thousand dollars perhaps, in capital that would generate forty thousand dollars annually in interest. The house was paid for. His own life insurance was paid up and would be that much more security for Mom in the event of his death. (Of course he had no way to foresee that stagflation in the 1980's would decimate the estate he actually did leave.)

Future planning of this sort became his main "job" at home after he ceased going to in to the factory, even for two or so half-days a week. He had found his successor there in Harry Strunk, a young manager from Whitman's.

His favorite exercise, however, was to rehearse the situation of each of his four children, and their children: their problems, and inevitably their successes, their happiness. He gloated, I think, given the family near-disaster of his alcoholism, in how well things had turned out. He had chosen family to live for and this now was his payoff. And look at other "respectable" families, those of relatives and associates, let alone of public figures, such as the Kennedys. Look at all those families that had had no visible disaster, no original sins, and yet suddenly now, in their children, were showing weakness, squalor, and waste.

At the time I wrote to Mom from graduate school, I wrote to him as well: "What is the dearest thing you've ever done; when have you felt cleanest, most important? When did you feel your living was the most exemplary, enthusiastic, worthwhile? Dad, was it being a father, like Chuck? Was it not drinking? Getting power back? Was it passing a good business deal? Making a bird on hole number five? What good, clean feeling did, do you, enjoy? Supporting us? Keeping us free, helping us, advising us?"

He answered me in a letter: "All of those things. You know me to a 'T.'"

I was, at the time, struggling my hardest to make them understand my passion to think and to write, to take my passion seriously. Dad, of course (Mom told me later), worried that I was going crazy, headed for my own ruin.

There were hundreds of leaving-takings over the years, with different destinations on my part, alone, married, with my daughter; all of us at all ages; in different cars from St. Davids and from Villanova, the final house. A picture never taken, really, but one that remains more fixed and vivid in my mind than any other, has Mom standing small, right arm in air, waving, trying to be brave; smiling, yet helplessly wet-eyed, and tearing our hearts, my heart. There is my car horn's toot, my wave, my glancing back, then resolutely facing forward, knowing she will watch me out of sight, that she would never, herself, turn back to her life without me as long as I was in sight. And each leaving felt as difficult and cruel as if I'd never see her again, and as if this was my doing, my fault, my necessary act of will.

We change in this ritual, as in the photographs we change in other ways. I leave St. Davids for Amherst junior year in my own car, a 1957 Chevy, which I bought second hand from the dealership in Wayne (earlier years Mom and Dad have driven me and picked me up). I leave for my summer work at *Redbook* magazine and a sublet in Manhattan. I leave, after Amherst, for Cambridge, Mass., and Harvard, still in the 1957 Chevy, with rounded back mudguards. I leave after the year of Harvard for Iowa City, 1964, by way of my summer trip to Charlottesville to visit with Judy and Hans. I leave for my second year in Iowa, 1965. I leave for my return to Harvard, this time from Villanova in a new 1966 Chevy II, which I will drive for the next sixteen years, and in the spirit of 60's nuttiness (I have just seen Antonioni's *Blow-up*), with a leopard-skin seat cover. I leave from many visits, Thanksgiving, Christmas, Easter, timed to various school vacations, back to Harvard or to my part-time jobs at Simmons or Northeastern or Emerson College, to a rented room, to my first apartment.

Before I was married, in 1973, these departures were like re-turns to combat, to fronting life alone, my own life. From a world of being cared for, as a creature, loved, and of minimal anxiety, a childhood's world; from a spacious, orderly, formally beautiful and well-kept house, from a refrigerator stocked with my "favor-ites" (hard salami, Swiss cheese, boiled ham, dried beef), from a color TV, from painfully restrained silences on Mom's part, es-pecially, so as not to disturb the genius, as I grimly withdrew to my room to write. Of course, Mom would have to interrupt— "I'll just be a minute, darling, don't mind me. You making prog-ress?"—in order to get something, some bill, some note from my desk, which was her desk when I wasn't there. Dad on the other hand would harumph! in on his own terms—"You busy?"—pretty much whenever he wished. It was also a world of frustration, a world without girls to call or to date, and my need for a girl, or the possibility of one—that call of the wild—would soon have me suf-focating, until I couldn't wait to leave.

I wrote in my notebooks, then, January, 1965, shortly after their move to Villanova: "This trip home, to a new house, I still feel pressed and cancelled even here. I remember how uneasy and restless Jack would be coming home from his life and things he couldn't talk about: longings and confidences and fears he couldn't surrender to such an audience. The expectation for you to say who and what you are; otherwise, a creeping offensive to tell you you are the same, still their little boy, limited and framed by their per-sonalities, and sensibilities, and lives. The house itself stands for that, cuts off all your pride: somehow returning to the old context, no matter what your experiences, your extensions, your vigor. Everything gets surrendered and threatened, the dead things em-phasized, the living things scorned, misunderstood, or hidden. Their minds are closed and narrow about me. Also I am only in-terested in them in terms of myself. I am impatient when Mom tries to tell me she is restless and I hate listening to her experiences at the Institute: part of the trouble is the way she tells, with wrinkled nose or an inexact enthusiasms, but also ashamed of herself. She never talks as a person about what matters to her in a way that I can listen to. Never a strong hearted, honest, sincere confidence. Never, 'Hey, listen to this.' But rather nervousness, wet-eyed, cigarette-flicking haziness."

Dad was haunted by the guilt that he had damaged Jack, that Jack's hardships were the result of Dad's own alcoholic years, and Dad both had to endure that guilt and keep trying to make up for it: so the offer to underwrite a line of credit with the bank for Jack's excavating business, the offer of business advice, and so forth, were offers of vulnerable love, which Jack did accept and reciprocate.

I think Dad felt that about all of us, the need to see that we had made it into life with strength, that none of us would go the way he had gone, or otherwise feel maimed, be unable to find respectable happiness.

Every three to four weeks Dad, sitting home, would get the impulse to phone each of us, long distance, one at a time.

Depending on time zones and who was home, I might be first or last. But he would sound pleased, as if he had tricked, surprised, or otherwise pulled a feat in getting me, talk a minute, then call Mom without telling her who it was. The calls, it seemed, were never her idea, and always seemed an extravagant surprise, "Oh, he didn't say it was you!" Other times, when I was visiting, he would call me to the phone myself to talk to Jack, Chuck, or Judy suddenly.

Returning home from Cambridge in the summer of 1967, I found Dad more and more reflective and cranky, looking out on the contemporary world, especially as it came to him through Life, TV, the Philadelphia Inquirer, Newsweek, and gossip with his business and golf club associates. The issue when I came home now was hair. I remember his urgent and embarrassed cry, "Oh, no, son, you've done a wonderful job in everything. All but this one little detail. You're doing a wonderful job, I just can't stand to see you mess it up!" And he then told Mom, apart: "I was going to take him to play golf. I stayed home for it. But I'll be damned if I'll take him anywhere looking like a damn beatnik!"

He made Villanova "unimpregnable," with his locked house and security. He was obsessed with security, being secure from chance, involvement, or change, as much as from theft; with closing himself against the possibility of intrusion. Chuck was his particular joy. Nevertheless he loved to travel, to follow us out of his own sanctuary into the alien worlds we each inhabited.

Away from home was my world of loneliness and ambition, of struggling under the idea that I could only be gifted, could only tolerate myself as an artist, and of a world of experience I thought of as beyond them, not only in my work, but in people and places and relationships, Manhattan, Cambridge, Iowa City. There was a time in Iowa City, when I was so lonely that I stared and stared into the mirror and had the impulse to put a pin in my eye, "to hurt myself inexplicably," I wrote, "and make my people at home start awake and care about me and worry about themselves: what drove me to do it?" Other moments, in Cambridge, I doubted my own existence, and sat inert, suddenly to be reassured by and grateful for my shadow on the wall. They were times of spiritual paralysis for me, and depression. Times when a call from home or to home—weekly, usually—would bring me sentimental relief.

I recall one nightmare Cambridge moment, stoned on black hash, when the girl I was with turned, in my hallucination, into all the girls I had ever been with, one after another. I would weep as I made my bed, as if in covering up the pillows, I was burying babies. Meanwhile Dad would lecture me abstractly, more and more, about being selfish, about living only for myself; about the dead end that that was in life. My time had come "to get serious about marriage."

I had learned to recognize and to value Connie as a person by the time we met, and also, I thought, to recognize my own strengths and weaknesses. While we cohabited, secretly, in my apartment from 1971, Connie kept a room across Cambridge, where when Mom and Dad came up to visit, she had us all to dinner. Later after she and I moved together into a new apartment, which she helped me to find, Dad would call our apartment, which he thought was my apartment. He would be surprised that Connie was visiting so often, if she answered the phone. We told Mom we were living together, but Mom said never to tell Dad, that he'd never understand; that he thought that was "skunky."

After our marriage, when Connie and I would visit Villanova, Dad baited Connie with his pet political or social opinions, and she would take the bait (which I had long since learned to avoid), and launch into impassioned arguments that lasted for hours. He greatly enjoyed this.

Then we would head back to Boston to tackle life together, a life of genteel poverty and of childlessness by my choice—I feared any responsibility that would force me to give up writing. Connie, in her generosity, and in her shyness in our love, deferred to my fears for as long as she could. She both sacrificed her deep need to mother and supported our lives with her job teaching in Headstart.

Dad would be with Mom in our leave-takings. He wouldn't linger, however. He would shake my hand, maybe give us hugs, run through any practical worries, oil for the car, money, give us a call when you get there, then turn and walk back inside the house. Mom would be the one who watched us out of sight.

In 1968, Judy and Hans had moved from Charlottesville to Palos Verdes Estates, outside Los Angeles, when Hans took a job at Garrett Air Research. Judy wrote to Mom and Dad that May: "The community is a nice and friendly one, through somewhat middle class and materialistic. I am resigned to the fact that wherever we live we are going to find the dominant element to be the phony 'social climbing' set. So we have every right to muddy up the place and enjoy the lovely area as much as the snobs and gimmes. I am merely mentioning them because I am so amazed at the preponderance of these people everywhere, Holland, Midwest, south, east, and here." She wrote about the children, who were doing "beautifully" in school. Johnny had tested for reading and scored equivalent to a high school senior. Bonnie tested off the measurable range, according to the school principal. Lucia's teacher said she was beyond her class in maturity, comprehension and ability. All three would be able to take free summer courses. "Hans too," Judy wrote, "is busy and well. He still loves his work, and more important, his associates. He finds them, again, more intelligent, open and communicable. This is very necessary, as its lack led to the frustrations of Charlottesville. I have the feeling that we are never going to want to move back East again, so that's a good sign of adjustment."

Despite Judy's letters and snapshots to our parents, and despite Mom and Dad's own accounts as they flew out at least once a year to visit, I could not imagine Judy's life there, not the physical place, not the children growing. I was disappointed when Judy and Hans could not make the trip to my wedding in Miami. I can't remember when Judy first met Connie—it had to be before Dad's funeral in 1976—but they already shared rapport from many long distance calls from Villanova.

I felt jealous of my nephew John for becoming the prodigy that we had each attempted to be. Troubled by his early childhood in Champaign, where he was difficult and inward, Judy had called a clinic and taken him in for psychological tests. They told her that no child in Illinois had ever tested so high.

John had begun painting at the age of five alongside Judy, who imitated Mom in working with oils. The head of the Art Department at the university was so impressed by John's drawing and painting that he allowed him to attend sketching sessions while he was still in elementary school. He sold his first painting at age nine.

After they moved to California, Judy wrote Mom about John's progress. He had graduated from Palos Verdes High School with honors in 1973, continuing his education in Fine Arts back at the University of Virginia, where he earned an A.A. in 1975. She sent us press clippings of his shows.

During the early seventies Jack and June, on the other hand, were having problems. June's children had, one by one, married and had children. June herself had a hysterectomy. Her daughter Terry, after an attempt at suicide as a teenager, proved to be a stable, loving adult, a wife and mother, and felt particularly close to Jack and to Mom. Terry and her husband, John Drage, had an army tour in Turkey, where June went to visit. The boys, however, despite Jack's best efforts at fathering, and despite the security the excavating business potentially offered (each tried working several years with Jack, at full wages) sank into the ways of local squalor, including drunkenness, child-abuse, and divorce.

Jack acquired a Beechcraft Staggerwing plane, and rebuilt and restored it, as he had rebuilt and restored antique cars before, and used it officially for business—he would fly with Dale, the youngest boy, now as the photographer, doing aerial surveys of potential contracting jobs; also Jack could place crews on jobs at greater distances, commuting with them by plane.

Unofficially, however, Jack used the plane for pleasure, with June as his co-pilot. He and June worked, hunted, and traveled together, including the flight to my wedding in Miami, where June was taciturn and subdued.

June had begun painting with a passion; at least in her own mind, she was rivaling Mom and Judy in her art. Jack made her five easels and June bought a wide selection of oil paints. The paintings themselves were primitive, yet showed her love and knowledge of nature. Mom must have written her a letter in the summer of 1974 with some gentle criticism of the painting, some confession about troubles over Nana Thralls, some advice about Terry, and some appeal to her, June, to be more supportive of and patient with Jack.

June replied: "My money went into this place, my time, 18 hrs per day work to keep a business going. So I do not have time to read your letters. Do not write any of your funny items to my children and grand children. I have thought of you as my folks. Forgave any catty remarks. Listened to all your phrases about Judy. Mother, you told me about Judy winning in a huge juried show in Virginia. I was so happy I wrote Judy a letter. But then Jack went to visit and it seems that the judges only rejected Judy's work. We all have rejects, don't we? Mother, go to church, pray. Give your own daughter attention. Poor Judy. She related unhappy memories to her brothers. Judy needs more attention than us little people in Colorado. Judy will not correspond with me, poor dear. Now your strange letter arrives. What do I chalk it off to, your old age. I phone you, then I receive strange letters. Now, I have had grounds for divorce for several years. But I am still here. Working, trying to help in the office, trying to be patient with my temperamental husband. Where did you get the idea my darling Jack was without faults? I try to ignore his faults. Dad, give mother plenty t.l.c. and she will be fine. My, she has so many worries. Grandma Thralls, children, grandchildren. I truly did not mean to add to them. Such a turmoil over my worried for my precious Terry. Really, your letter will make me be more patient with my poor Jack. How he must have suffered as a child. I see now why he comes 'Like a helpless child,' to me. 'Begging for praise' and I will donate more time to him and limit myself to only cards to you. Grow closer to God."

Terry wrote to my parents too: "Dad wanted me to write because it's kind of hard for him to write you a letter. I know you have probably noticed how unusual Mom acts. These last few months Mom has gotten worse. It's hard to admit to oneself that somebody you love could be sick. Dad has been pretty understanding although I know he has some faults to work on too."

Following Dad's sudden death, Jack spoke of taking the plane up alone over the mountains, just to get off the ground and forget his troubles.

Later Jack told me about the years that followed: that he suffered with June's moods for as long as he could, and considered, on doctor's advice, committing her to psychiatric care. She would lock him out of the house. She would run out into the yard, naked, waving a loaded gun.

Besides the death of her mother in 1965—the clan matriarch on whom June had depended all along—what seemed to trigger June's worst was Jack's prospect of financial success. After all his years of digging ditches and laying varieties of sewer and water pipe, he was working in the shop on an invention, a pipe-laying machine that would lay and grade pipe and fill the ditch with gravel, speeding up the process, taking other machines out of it, and using fewer men. The machine was taking shape out of parts of bulldozers and a hydraulic crane, and Jack was researching patents to protect his concept and design with the idea of selling it to one of several heavy equipment manufacturers for something in the range of two million dollars.

In 1979, June sued for divorce, backed by a woman lawyer, and Jack decided to get out. Let June have what she wanted, and let her go, with plenty of money to live, and to leave her mental problems to time and her doctors to decide. They liquidated Henry Excavating. She kept the house. He kept the Staggerwing and the pipe-laying machine and set out to start over.

The downturn of the economy then caused the manufacturers he had approached to defer investment, so Jack went into business for himself, making one or two machines a year. Luckily he met and married Janice soon after, a woman younger, more attractive, more intelligent and better educated, wiser, and more his natural complement than June; also a person comparably soul-made to

Jack by her own earlier marriage and life. Mom saw their marriage as a long deserved, overdue blessing for both.

Mom called one day in the fall of 1976. With a strained, shaken voice, and told me that Dad had gone into the hospital. He had jaundice. Chuck was over from New Jersey, our insider/doctor monitoring his care, and Mom was with him. No need to be alarmed, Mom told me long distance; no need to visit. You have your busy life, your teaching. He will be fine. And then she called again: he had to have an operation. And then, again: Jack was visiting from Colorado; and then Jack had gotten on the phone to say hello, and Dad was fine, he'd seen him and he was sallow-skinned, but in good spirits. Jack returned to Colorado. Another call, Dad had come through the operation on his liver, but was in a coma. No, don't come down. She was at his side, wanted to be there when he woke up. Some trouble now with his kidneys. The doctors said he was unconscious and couldn't feel pain, but he was crying out so loudly, the other patients were asking, "can't they give that man something?" Mom called to tell us he might not last another day or so, and then he was gone. I wasn't there; no goodbyes in the dusk.

We all came together from the corners of our distant lives for his funeral. There was no viewing. My mother said we wouldn't want to see him, the way his body was at the end. My mother wanted only us, our nuclear family, not my aunts on my father's side. A limousine picked us up, a silent, stoic company, confused in loss as we had been in life between love and guilt, each of us somehow having wished him out of our lives, and out of our mother's. She had chosen the most expensive coffin and arranged for a graveside service with the Presbyterian minister because "he would have wanted it that way." No tears, at least on the outside. What I recall is silence and inexorability.

I quipped in my own nervousness and guilt, on our way in the limo to the cemetery, "What we need are pain-o-meters, like turkey thermometers, so we can tell who is feeling the most pain." It wasn't the right thing to say and both Connie and Judy told me to be quiet.

The grave was in the family plot, purchased originally by my father's father in West Laurel Hill. We had been dragged here repeatedly as children and teenagers to put Easter flowers on my grandfather's broad stone at the head of the plot; he had died in 1946, when I was five; then in 1969 my grandmother had joined him; and most recently my uncle John Spaeth, a spouse, had been buried in 1974.

At the grave, we each put a flower on the casket, before it was lowered into the ground. The minister asked us to pray, and while he droned on, we exchanged uneasy glances, on our awkward best behavior to this outsider, as to the undertaker too. But again, Mom had said, Dad would have wanted it this way. I was conscious of not feeling anything most of the time, and feeling guilty for that; but as the casket was slowly cranked down, I remember, for all my irony, my disbelief, amounting almost to panic, that my father, so vivid to me always, was somehow in that casket. Alive, loved, troublesome, powerful, and that was him in there and being lowered into the earth. I couldn't believe that was him, even though I knew it was.

I remember our returning home and eating, eating, eating ravenously. Halloween was only a day or so away, and perhaps our most genuine gesture, as bizarre and true as we felt we were, was while on some errand, on impulse to go into the local toy store, Halligan's—a Mecca at least of my own childhood—and buy clear plastic masks, the kind that eerily distort your features into Nixon's, say. We wore them driving back to Villanova; and laughed and laughed together as we tried on different faces for each other, my mother too.

Dad had seen me married, but he had not lived to see a grandchild from us, though after a miscarriage in January, by March, 1977, Connie was pregnant and our daughter Ruth Kathryn was born that December.

Mom visited us two or three times in Boston after Ruth was born; then later, we visited her with Ruth for several Christmases. This was her life as a widow. "I know you know what loneliness is," she said to me once. She hadn't the energy to move or travel or make new friends. She did attend a Cornell class reunion and discover several classmates, with whom she corresponded. One visit with us her face suddenly swelled up. She had been to the dentist's, and an abscess had developed, which somehow, we later thought, may have spread infection down to her heart, triggering the heart failure to come.

The swimming pool was one of her biggest undertakings independent of Dad, and planning for, then overseeing its construction, occupied her and involved her with new people over two years. She spoke of it with embarrassed pride, like an extravagance.

The idea was partly for health (Dr. Appel in his twilight years had had a heated pool put in, where he swam daily), and partly to increase the value of the house, and hence the value of her estate to her children. She preferred to do this, she repeated, rather than travel the world or make a big show, like other women did. Also, she couldn't travel as much anymore to see her children and grandchildren, so the pool now would give them added reason to come to her.

There was the digging, the disruption; a Caterpillar bulldozer, worthy of Jack, came across the lawn and started snorting, squeaking, grunting, and digging a slanting hole, back and forth, with a dump truck taking away the dirt. This was the back lawn where I had practiced my chip shots for all my years of visits. Mom sent us Polaroid photos of the raw earth and cat tracks during the winter. They had the glass enclosure up, the roof. They dug ditches from the street and lay special gas and water lines. They had to get permits, have inspectors. Step by step. Then the concrete in the pool itself had to set, then be painted.

Finally, it was filled. Operational. We visited to see. Dad would have loved it, Mom said. And on our visits, I was sure I saw him smiling, poolside, at dusk, from the chaise in the corner. He would have savored the luxury.

An oval, 100 feet by 40 feet, and 8 feet deep at one end, where the drain was, the pool with its enclosure changed her house into a spa. An underwater light lit up the turquoise basin at night and cast ripples of light.

She had its care as an added responsibility, cleaning it with a long-handled aluminum broom, which you had to push down, all the way, the head down the side and around the curved bottom, then pull up, covering a swath twenty inches wide. She had to mix the chlorine, adjust the temperature, turn on and off the heater, open and close the roof.

Chuck's children would come, raucous and splashing. We would come. We'd all be baptized, swimming together, talking. Ruth learned to swim there, gradually.

In 1982, Chuck separated from Nancy, moved into a condo, and began a three-year divorce proceeding, which ended with Nancy being awarded a million dollars. He and Mom discussed the anguish of this at length, discussions that either I overheard when I visited, or that Mom later related to me. Mom was relieved and glad for Chuck that the divorce was going through, whatever it cost.

Though Chuck had kept up a brave front for years, I heard now that Nancy had been a terrible mother and wife. According to Mom, Nancy hated having children and had told her sons so. She went off on her own to socialize and to have affairs, leaving them on their own, while Chuck himself worked. The boys now at the ages of twenty, nineteen and seventeen had progressed from a league of mischief as brothers, reminiscent of Jack and Chuck at the same age, to problems with drugs and alcohol and repeated scrapes with the law, from which Chuck would have to bail them out. They had all worked as orderlies at the hospital, the world of Chuck's dedication and sacrifice, as we had once worked for Dad in Dad's world of the candy factory. His sons' futures worried Chuck, and with Chuck, Mom.

I remembered them from when they were younger, when we visited their Woodberry house with Dad. They were all three immersed in the fantasy game *Dungeons and Dragons*, or in various electronic games that preceded computers, throwing all their passion and intelligence into escapism as I saw it. No one from the outside world could participate in, let alone catch up with their expertise.

Chuck, Jr. (the "Jr." according to some therapist caused him always to feel inferior to his father) had tried different local colleges—Frostburg, Glassboro State—with the idea of being pre-med, but then had dropped out. Bob was in college in St. Petersburg, Florida; and Scott, supposedly (according to Nancy and to Mom, also) the most sensitive and academically gifted, was heading for Randolph-Macon in Virginia. They all loved Mom, Connie, and Ruth as a younger girl cousin, and I recall their later visits to Villanova without Nancy as upbeat and festive; though one of the last visits shocked me, as Bob, apparently drunk, had driven up to Villanova with his brothers to join his father and had swerved into a tree outside, smashing a new car more expensive than Connie and I could dream of affording. The boys were needy and begging for attention, according to Mom, but all their lives they had only been given money instead.

Mom died in 1985. Her first episode of heart failure had been on February 27. There had been a surprise midnight call from Chuck telling us she was okay—had gone into intensive care in the cardiac unit at Bryn Mawr. She, when we spoke to her, said she had thought she'd gone over, but she wasn't good enough. They'd thrown her back, like an undersized fish.

Her cardiologist, Dr. Robinson, wrote Chuck a doctor-to-doctor technical letter soon after, which explained his opinion that "this patient has: 1) Aortic valvular regurgitation, a.) secondary to previous endocarditis; 2) Possible cardiomyopathy, a.) possible acute myocarditis."

I need to register here the preciousness of that summer, during which, right up to the last, she continued to answer questions and supply memories that contributed to this narrative.

Connie and Ruth stayed with her for some nine weeks, while I came and went back to Boston and my job.

My sister came and left. Jack came and left. Chuck came up from Jersey as often as he could. But there were stretches, too, covered only by a live-in nurse. (Who smoked and otherwise got on Mom's nerves.)

We were present with Chuck, when he showed her Dr. Robinson's letter. We were having dinner around the formal table. She read the letter, then asked Chuck directly:

"How long do I have? Three months? Three years?"

He looked at her steadily: "Yes."

"Which?"

"Yes," he repeated.

Her regimen prescribed food without savor; she was forbidden all sodium, while forced to intake large amounts of potassium, mainly in the form of bananas, but sometimes, too, as medication, which cramped her stomach.

She was told to increase her activity, as tolerated, and given a small oxygen bottle and mask for when she felt dizzy. As the disease progressed, as there were other episodes of hospitalization, the smaller, portable bottle became a fixture, to be refilled from full-sized tanks as tall as she was, which were delivered by a medical service (all on Medicare) and which stood like sentinels in a corner by her bed. She lived now in oxygen, with plastic nose clips.

She woke one morning I was there, feeling, she said, "like a girl, ready to get up and chase and spank babies . . .

"I feel wonderful, like I could do anything. Chase a four-year-old down the hall and spank him. It's the most wonderful feeling after a good night of sleep, like I'm not even sick. But then I'll get up and go sit on that pot and take my shower and I'll be back here gasping. I never thought I would get old this fast. I have an old woman's body, overnight, it seems, just all at once. It's not fun."

Ruth, seven years old, would sit on her bedside, gently massaging her bony back.

We had squirrel wars. The corrugated sunroof of the pool slanted beneath several high, acorn-bearing oak trees, and while Mom was trying to rest in her bedroom, which had an entrance to the pool building, tribes of squirrels, in seeming outright malice, would shake acorns down, which would resound on the sunroof like echoing reports. This was a problem. I tried, on my visit, to throw nuts back into the branches to scare the squirrels away, couldn't throw hard or high enough; then made a slingshot, with the same result. Decided on a BB pistol, but when I called around learned they were outlawed for sale in all counties but in Lancaster, some twenty miles west; went there, bought a pistol, came home, and in some memory of my brothers at Bloomingdale, started potting away at and hitting squirrels, who chirred angrily, and who seemed to communicate and to rally with a vengeance, actually now hurling down nuts. This went on. Chuck visited and started trying to outshoot me, then Jack visited. Mom was amused, from her vantage. Gradually the squirrels retreated and avoided those trees.

The Appleford estate, a park open to the public down the street and around a corner, was a place she loved, over the years (and we with her), to walk to and to explore, admiring its gardens. These were the work of a resident Irish groundsman who was in his seventies and would talk to her about various plants. Alone there during this summer, I was taken by the beauty of a series of slim, flowering trees, which the gardener explained he had cultivated; they were called Lantana trees, and were works of nurturing art, taking months to breed, prune, and carefully transplant. I knew Mom had to see them, and we planned an outing in the Buick, her with her oxygen clips on. We met the gardener and she told him, as he asked about her health that she "was a goner," but she wanted to buy one of his Lantanas. Reluctant at first, he granted her wish, and gingerly transported a potted sapling home with us, taking the length of the back seat and its branches out one open window, where he would visit later to prune and water and see, as a gesture of caring, for its health. The tree, her last plant, which we kept in the swimming pool enclosure, along with her other exotic plants, gave her joy. (Uncared for after her death, it withered in the closed house, and was later thrown out.)

Several times my leaving, or Judy's, or Jack's, or Chuck's would trigger another episode of heart failure. The one time I was there with her during an attack, I had driven down in our second old car, a Plymouth Duster with a faulty cooling system, and in my attempt to drive back to Boston after dinner had gotten no farther than the tollgate to the New Jersey Turnpike, when a radiator hose burst and I had been stranded, tow truck, all-night repair shop, and so forth, and I had driven slowly back to Villanova through North Philadelphia, stopping to cool down, then starting a little more. I arrived back at Villanova unannounced, full of my own trouble—it must have been 2 a.m.—and Connie rushed me to Mom who was in the midst of an attack.

The ambulance had already been called. She lay curled up, clenched, and gasping for oxygen, and we were trying to keep her calm, when the siren pulled up out front with flashing lights. Paramedics came hustling up the lawn carrying a wheeled stretcher, came in and down the hall and into her room; were administering adrenalin, talking on a walkie-talkie to a doctor, taking readings, gently getting a blanket under Mom, then lifting, sliding her onto the stretcher, and rolling her out. They carried her down the lawn, into the back of blockish van, its lights flashing, and Connie and me got in with her, beside her, held her hand, while the medics continued to monitor and work, and we took off. With the siren at its heehaw blast, we jounced over potholes, it seemed, for a rough, rocking, and too slow ride; then we were there, and they took her into emergency intensive care, and wouldn't let us follow. But then some minutes later, we were allowed to join her at her bedside behind green curtains. As always, it seemed, at times of personal crisis, there was a raucous person through the curtain in another bed, a diabetic woman recovering from insulin shock, insisting that she wasn't diabetic. Mom rolled her eyes at us. She looked better now, and the monitor showed her heart-rate slowing; she would come through this time, again.

One of the last last times (there were five or six), I drove back to Boston on the New York parkways, 2 in the morning, filled with the sense of losing her. I had the overpowering sense of her spiritual presence, that this moment, this, as I drove, she had died; this was my time of weeping, of grief, and of farewell.

Her next episode of failure, combined with the extreme pain of eating, hospitalized her in a private room, where we all visited, and where the nurses seemed distracted and inattentive when she needed medicine. We heard reports, later, that when Chuck visited her, she was up and feeling spunky, indeed had been waltzing with Chuck, when her monitor fell off and a nurse came rushing in.

My first book in the world, an anthology of stories from twelve years of *Ploughshares* appeared, along with a full-page feature on me in the *Philadelphia Inquirer*, which she showed around the hospital.

Chuck called to tell me that she had had enough. That they could prolong her time with medicine, but that it would also prolong her agony, and that she had decided not to take it. She would probably only have a few days left. We could call; she had the phone by her bed. I made my last long distance call, and told her I loved her, that the torch was passed. "I know you do, and I love you. There's nothing more to say," she said. "Don't waste your dime." Then she hung up.

We heard at 5 a.m., first dawn, Sept. 6, 1985. Chuck called, and said that she was gone. "We are her now," I said, words I had rehearsed.

It had proven to be a summer of departures and arrivals, a sequence and an image that was culminated by her own departure, at last. She had asked to be cremated, a first in our family. Again we gathered at the West Laurel Hill plot. Judy and Hans, and the grandchildren John, Lucia, Bonnie; Jack and Janice, and the granddaughter Terry; Chuck and his sons, Chuckie, Bob, and Scott; Connie, Ruth and I; Mom's sister Janice, and Uncle Lloyd from New Hampshire. We each laid a yellow rose on the casket, which held the urn. Again, the minister, a stranger to us; and again the graveside service: words so empty that they seemed like an offense.

David Jung Min Henry, my adopted son, only an idea or hope at the time, which we had talked about with Mom, would be born some twelve thousand miles away in Korea one week later, September 15. Our decision to adopt had followed on three years of treatments for secondary infertility, and I had needed Mom's support to let go of my wish for a birth child, and to go along with Connie's readiness to adopt. We had signed with an international adoption agency, completed our home study and attended Korean culture classes, and Mom had shared in our anticipation. Of course, we wouldn't hear that an infant had been assigned to us until five months after she was gone.

She left us, at last. We were the ones left. The ones staying.

Once I had left home, categorically, to make my own life, in some deep sense, which I never truly spoke to myself (though I understood now my father's warning from years before about cutting the apron strings and never measuring a wife by her), my true love indeed was my mother, my dream to love her romantically, in spite of the impossibility, spirit to spirit, across the years; also Judy merged into this dream.

All other women failed to satisfy this deeper loneliness and hunger, and my refusal or inability to commit to them with my life, involved a continued yearning and search. I felt, from time to time, wrenchingly, that if only Mom were my age, were young, that we could command the world together. (I wonder now if that notion didn't condition other impossible loves. I know I was inordinately moved by Colette's *Cheri and The Last of Cheri*.)

The summer of Mom's dying—Mom whom I never touched unguardedly or hugged because of the strength of our feeling—my first real wholehearted giving up to Connie was a ceremonial swim, naked, in Mom's pool, while Mom slept in her distant bedroom. When Connie and I had been new to each other, when we had first met and slept together, I had brought to her all my resources of "experienced" sex; but then, once we were living together, and later, married, I began withholding part of myself, as did she. No oral sex, no innovations, just perfunctory missionary posture, and getting it over with to buy myself space, space in which I kept wildness secret, in reserve, as both beyond her and importantly private, mine.

At this moment, however, in Mom's world, and with her blessing, in the face of death, I consciously chose Connie as the only woman in my life, for my life. I felt this as a transfer from Mom, from mother, to wife.

Then David arrived. Born September 15, and assigned to us in January, arriving in March, 1986.

Also Hans departed by June, 1986, staggering Judy with his surprise determination for divorce—leaving for a younger woman, whom he had been seeing secretly—and forcing her to start over at age fifty-two. This was followed by the news, in the course of some phone conversation, when I suggested she travel east, and maybe John with her and something about his having a girl, or someday getting married, and she said, "Didn't you know? John is gay." That that was news that Hans had not been able to take.

In 1987, I saw John and his work in San Francisco and met Bruce, his friend and lover, with whom he then lived, sharing a house on Divisadero Street. Then he learned a few months later that they both had AIDS. Later, after he was ill, while John was visiting Judy in Pasadena, their home for years, Connie flew out with Ruth and David to see him. In one snapshot from that visit, John, mustached and balding, poses typically in the backyard with a suction-tipped arrow dangling from his forehead, hamming the pose of either El Greco's *Crucifixion* or the *Temptation of St. Anthony* or both, flanked by his mother in blue sunglasses and Bruce; Connie; and my children on the other side. He would in the two years to come be hospitalized repeatedly with pneumonia and be surrounded by his sisters, his mother, Bruce, and his friends, as he grew weaker. He died, age thirty-four, on July 25, 1990.

That September, our fifth year without Mom, our fifth, thanks to her legacy, in our house, David turned five.

I told Mom during her last summer, in one of my goodbyes, that I was "sound," and she said nothing could make her feel more satisfied, if that were so. Sound, healthy, self-accepting, world-wise, self-wise, self-sufficient, able to cope. Opposite to maimed, wounded, dependent, or incomplete.

I'm not sound, really, except in averages, like the accruals of a mutual fund. My life's curve, for all its losses and gains, shows its steady rise in gratitude, meaning, and pride.

I don't know how I choose or if I choose rightly, or what right is, honorably, or by nature. The examples trouble me, Mom's of self-martyrdom and frustration; Dad's of expiation for some natural monstrosity.

I abandon, rather than finish this narrative at the age of fifty-two, wondering what next. When I think of Mom's life, or Dad's, or the lives of my brothers, sister, nephews, nieces, or those of friends so far, I have no futurisms or foresights. Who could foresee the Depression? Who Grandpop Henry's heart? Who my fiftieth year? My fifty-first? The best we can hope for is some constancy, some casting forward of self, of legacies, talents, values, loyalties. But endings? Judy? She may prevail. She may kill herself. She may reconcile with Hans. She may marry someone new. Or not. Or she may reveal some other, truer meaning and resilience, relying on her talents, her love of people, and her closeness to her daughters and her grandsons. She has finished California State College. She has started teaching art in a school for the learning disabled. She is building a thriving business with Lucia, carrying on where John left off in sculpting collector dolls, which Lucia then paints, costumes, and creates as characters, and which sell in the range of six thousand dollars.

I am humbled by unknowing.

Endings are for the dying, and even for them, more wishful than certain. Let's say this story ends as it did for my father. Family transcendent. Chuck happily married, his boys prospering, good at sports, good at school, Nancy an obedient and clan-observant wife. Cooker of Thanksgiving clan reunions. Jack enduring with June. June mellowing into a menopausal fog. Dee married after all and unpublished, but succeeding in the academic world, marrying Connie. Jewish, my gosh, but times are changing.

Or. End with Mom's closure. Let's say, as she thought, Judy was happy with Hans. John would live and prosper as an artist. Jack, having put June behind him, would find a new, fulfilling life with Janice and would sell his pipe laying machine to a manufacturer, thereby becoming rich, and able to enjoy long-deserved ease and happiness. Chuck, his own divorce settled at last, would find new happiness. Connie and I would prove stable. Ruth would prove to be a vicarious prodigy. David, if he came, a genius and president of the reunited Korea. My fiction would be published. Say. End it there.

Or. End after her death. End with Hans divorcing Judy. End with Johnny dying of AIDS. End with whatever I make of life.

"I love Connie and she saved your life from the jerk you were. And you were a jerk," Chuck tells me long-distance, having read and struggled on a personal level with this book. He disagrees even with the documented aspects of the narrative. "It wasn't like that." He argues with the dates and facts. He questions the things that Mom has told me. Or that Judy or Jack have told me. I know he feels patronized. I know he has his own scars and is living to deny them. "I resent your stereotyping me as a conservative or racist or anything else. You lay all these attributes on me. But you have no idea who I really am."

He talks of retiring early from medicine, demoralized by the cost and insult of malpractice suits, malpractice insurance, and government regulations. Although he is dating different women, he lives alone and calls each of us in turn—Judy, Jack, me, his sons—for long, rambling conversations, pointedly at his own expense. Partly, like Dad, he is working to bring us together. But he is also lonely and depressed. Judy says he is drunk when he calls her, and that he passed out once on the phone; occasionally I hear ice cubes in a glass, but I don't ever find him slurring words, irrational, or incoherent. Sometimes when he calls, I am working late at night, and I have my own ice cubes rattling in vodka.

He is attempting to justify himself to me. I try to humor him and to cheer him up. But he keeps after me about *truth*. Yes, he hates the idea of socialized medicine, for instance, but that doesn't make him mean or indifferent to those who can't afford care. Do I know how often he has operated for free when patients can't pay? Do I know that he has secretly put several poor kids through college? These acts of conscience are his own business, just as it is his own business that in Seattle, say, before he shipped for Korea, he had had a prostitute. "So? Are you going to write *that*?" He comes back to his truth that Mom and Dad loved each other, only that; that this is what he saw in their visits to his home in New Jersey.

I reply, yes, but that I had also lived with their frustrations and regrets, and that life was complex that way. "Don't get into me about Dad," Chuck says. "He could have lived. He could have had another ten years." He starts to break down and weeps, choking, gasping sobs: "Jesus!" He has told me this several times before: that his own medical judgment had been against Dad's liver operation, but that he had kept silent out of deference to Dad's doctor and had let the operation go ahead. I try to comfort him, saying that he was not responsible.

He has never broken down like this with me before.

"Okay. Okay. I have to go," he says.

Epilogue

As I look through a store of snapshots, I contemplate different aspects of my father. He is in Colorado, at Jack's, being silly for the camera and for all of us, as he rides one of the children's old two wheelers, knees out, ass spilling over the seat, handlebars unsteady, big grin, farm country in the background. Another time, on a trip with Mom to visit me before my marriage, he poses self-mockingly outside a bookstore in Salem, Massachusetts, pretending to read in a folding chair, with stacks of books rising precariously on both sides. But the last is at the Philadelphia Small Press Book Fair, the summer before his death. This is an open-air "people's" event, like a literary flea market, and takes place on the esplanade that stretches into the city from the steps of the Philadelphia Museum of Art. I have rented a booth for *Ploughshares*, and Connie and I have driven down with our signs, books, collapsable camp table, table cloth, and chairs. Dad sits keeping me company at the table. Beside us is the representative for Ishmael Reed's *Yardbird Reader*, with whom Dad starts up a conversation. Dad wears his dark glasses, smokes. Connie must have taken the picture. I wear my fullest hippy hair, overgrown, thick horn-rimmed glasses, and smoke a pipe. I have no job as yet. We have no child. Dad can't know what to make of this world I have chosen, but where I am recognized and move with purpose, much as Jack does with his machines excavating, or Chuck at rounds at his hospital. Or, indeed, Dad himself did in the candy factory. He is bemused and tolerant. He may think I am crazy, but he makes the effort to share and to visit this world of my mendicant, anti-establishment publishing. He always defers the intellectual part to Mom, but still he is there, wishing me the best.

This last picture of Dad reminds me also of my struggles now with Ruth.

"I'm not living to please you!" she protests to me hotly in front of Judy, during one of Judy's rare visits, which is occasioned by a regional doll show, where Judy is representing Friedericy Dolls.

"Yes," Judy interjects, trying to moderate, "but, Ruth, isn't it good to know that people care about you?"

Ruth hovers at her own departure: from me, from her mother, from David. She is in her senior year of high school. She is academically gifted, spirited, contentious, and generous of heart. Her room resembles a set for, perhaps, Dickens' *Old Curiosity Shop*. She has practiced leave-takings with boyfriends, girlfriends, privacies, the telephone life, overnights and camp, her driver's license. She has an adult, complex inner life. She is applying to colleges. She may try volunteer work for a year, before beginning college.

Whatever her choices, they will be hers. I'm glad for this, and glad that as a young woman, she has more options in life than did my mother, Judy, or even Connie. Our part is to be here for her as needed. And if the father in me has been overly protective, possessive, and judgmental, I know deep down I trust Ruth. She is her own story now.

About the Author

DEWITT HENRY is the author of a novel, *The Marriage of Anna Maye Potts* (winner of the inaugural Peter Taylor Prize for the Novel), and a midlife memoir-in-essays, *Safe Suicide: Narratives, Essays, and Meditations.* Both are sequels to *Sweet Dreams.* The founding editor of *Ploughshares,* for which he received a 1992 Massachusetts Commonwealth Award, he is a Professor at Emerson College and lives with his family in Watertown, Massachusetts. For details, see www.dewitthenry.com.

CPSIA information can be obtained at www.ICGtesting.com
Printed in the USA
BVOW041623120911

270960BV00001B/8/P